Mastering QuickBooks 2022
Third Edition

The bestselling guide to bookkeeping and the QuickBooks Online
accounting software

Crystalynn Shelton, CPA

BIRMINGHAM—MUMBAI

Mastering QuickBooks® 2022
Third Edition

Copyright © 2022 Packt Publishing

Producer: Tushar Gupta
Acquisition Editor – Peer Reviews: Saby Dsilva
Project Editor: Namrata Katare
Content Development Editor: Lucy Wan
Copy Editor: Safis Editing
Technical Editor: Tejas Mhasvekar
Proofreader: Safis Editing
Indexer: Hemangini Bari
Presentation Designer: Ganesh Bhadwalkar

First published: December 2019
Second edition: January 2021
Third edition: January 2022

Production reference: 3010222

Published by Packt Publishing Ltd.
Livery Place
35 Livery Street
Birmingham
B3 2PB, UK.

ISBN 978-1-80324-428-0

www.packt.com

Contributors

About the author

Crystalynn Shelton, CPA is the author of two Amazon Bestsellers, *Mastering QuickBooks 2020* and *Mastering QuickBooks 2021*. She has a degree in accounting from the University of Texas, Arlington, and is a licensed CPA and Advanced Certified QuickBooks ProAdvisor. Crystalynn has managed accounting teams at Fortune 500 companies such as Texaco and Paramount Pictures. She ran her own bookkeeping practice for 3 years and worked for Intuit (QuickBooks) for 3 years as a senior learning specialist. Crystalynn provides training, consulting, and coaching services to small businesses looking to get a handle on their bookkeeping. She is also an adjunct instructor at UCLA Extension, where she teaches accounting, bookkeeping, and QuickBooks to hundreds of small business owners and accounting students each year.

When she is not working, she enjoys traveling and trying new restaurants with her husband. Visit her website at https://crystalynnshelton.com/ to sign up for her monthly blog.

To the editors, proofreaders, and technical writers at Packt, thank you for all of your hard work to help make this book possible. To the small business owners all over the world, YOU are my inspiration for writing this book. I hope it helps you to understand how important it is to stay on top of your business finances.

About the reviewer

Dominique Waits is a CPA, Chartered Global Management Accountant, and Certified Quick-Books ProAdvisor (recognized as a Top 100 ProAdvisor) with over 25 years of experience in both public accounting and private industry and an exceptional record of service. She is currently employed by Blue & Co., CPAs, a regional public accounting firm with offices in Kentucky, Indiana, and Ohio. She serves as a manager in the tax and business service departments, where she supports multiple clients with tax return preparation, financial planning, outsourced accounting, and QuickBooks services. She is also a trainer and consultant for a vast array of QuickBooks products including Desktop, Online, Enterprise, Point of Sale, and Payroll, with accounting expertise both as a CPA and a business owner.

Dominique is married and the mother of a teenage daughter, who she spends most of her free time chauffeuring and cheering on at sports events. She and her family enjoy working at their church, volunteering, and vacationing on a beach whenever possible. When Dominique has a moment to relax, she enjoys lounging with a glass of iced tea and a good book.

I would like to first thank my husband, Chris, and my daughter, Mackenzie, for allowing me to use some of my free time to review this manual. They understood that this was an important opportunity and encouraged me along the way. I would also like to thank my employer, Blue & Co., for supporting this project and sharing their enthusiasm, and particularly Director John Copeland for his encouragement.

Join our book's Discord space

Join the book's Discord workspace for a monthly *Ask me Anything* session with the author:
https://packt.link/QuickBooks

Table of Contents

Section 2: Recording Transactions in QuickBooks Online

Chapter 7: Managing Sales Tax   191

Chapter 8: Recording Sales Transactions in QuickBooks Online   201

Chapter 9: Recording Expenses in QuickBooks Online   221

Appendix

Preface

Intuit QuickBooks is an accounting software package that helps small business owners manage all their bookkeeping tasks. Its complete range of accounting capabilities, such as tracking income and expenses, managing payroll, simplifying taxes, and accepting online payments, makes QuickBooks software a must-have for business owners and aspiring bookkeepers.

The goal of this book is to teach small business owners, bookkeepers, and aspiring accountants how to properly use QuickBooks Online. Using a fictitious company, we will demonstrate how to create a QuickBooks Online account; customize key settings for a business; manage customers, vendors, and products and services; enter transactions; generate reports; and close books at the end of the period. QuickBooks records debits and credits for you so that you don't have to know accounting. However, we will show you what's happening behind the scenes in QuickBooks so that you can understand how your actions in QuickBooks impact financial statements. We will also provide you with tips, shortcuts, and best practices to help you save time and become a QuickBooks pro.

The US edition of QBO was used to create this book. If you are using a version that is outside of the United States, results may differ.

Who this book is for

If you're a small business owner, bookkeeper, or accounting student who wants to learn how to make the most of QuickBooks Online, this book is for you. Business analysts, data analysts, managers, professionals working in bookkeeping, and QuickBooks accountants will also find this guide useful. If you are planning to take the QuickBooks Certified User (QBCU) exam, this book is an excellent study guide. No experience with QuickBooks Online is required to get started; however, some bookkeeping knowledge would be helpful.

What this book covers

Section 1: Setting Up Your Company File

Chapter 1, Getting Started with QuickBooks Online, starts off with a brief description of QuickBooks Online, then it outlines the key features in all four editions of the software. We also explain how to choose the right edition for your business. There are step-by-step instructions on how to create a QBO account and how to navigate the software. Finally, we provide you with some basic book-keeping knowledge to help you understand what's going on behind the scenes in QuickBooks.

Chapter 2, QuickBooks Online Advanced, includes a deep dive into the features included in this top-tier QuickBooks Online subscription. We show you how to access the QuickBooks Online Advanced test drive account, how to add custom fields, how to manage customized user permissions, what workflow automation is and how to use it, how to import invoices and budgets, and much more.

Chapter 3, Company File Setup, shows you how to customize the QuickBooks Online account created in *Chapter 1* to meet your business needs. First, we explain the documents and key information you will need to have handy for the setup. Next, we walk you through all of the available preferences in QBO and explain the purpose and benefit of utilizing the various options available.

Chapter 4, Migrating to QuickBooks Online, gives you all the information required to migrate to QuickBooks Online from platforms such as Excel, QuickBooks Desktop, or another accounting/ bookkeeping software.

Chapter 5, Customizing QuickBooks for Your Business, introduces customization for the chart of accounts and then dives into the different ways of connecting bank accounts and credit cards to your QuickBooks Online account, followed by granting users access to your QuickBooks data.

Chapter 6, Managing Customer, Vendor, and Products and Services Lists, gives you a detailed insight into how to manage your customers, vendors, products, and services. This includes importing customer, vendor, and product and services data from an Excel spreadsheet and manually entering it into the software.

Section 2: Recording Transactions in QuickBooks Online

Chapter 7, Managing Sales Tax, covers how to set up sales tax for the various tax jurisdictions you are required to collect sales tax for, how to create an invoice with sales tax, and what reports will help you to report and pay the appropriate sales tax amount when it becomes due.

Chapter 8, Recording Sales Transactions in QuickBooks Online, starts by giving detailed information on different forms of sales, followed by information on how the customer can record payments using different methods, and finally teaches you how to initiate refunds for your customers.

Chapter 9, Recording Expenses in QuickBooks Online, teaches you how to enter and pay bills for your QuickBooks Online account. Then, we'll start exploring how to manage recurring expenses, followed by writing and printing checks.

Chapter 10, Reconciling Downloaded Bank and Credit Card Transactions, gives you a brief overview of the banking center in QuickBooks Online and gives you a deep understanding of how the bank rules work, followed by how to edit QuickBooks Online transactions, and finally how to reconcile bank accounts.

Section 3: Generating Reports in QuickBooks Online

Chapter 11, Report Center Overview, takes you through the Report Center, followed by the different reports available, how to customize and export reports, and finally how to send reports via email.

Chapter 12, Business Overview Reports, discusses the three primary reports that provide a good overview of your business: the profit and loss statement, balance sheet report, and statement of cash flows. It also covers the Cash Flow planner and the Audit Log.

Chapter 13, Customer Sales Reports in QuickBooks Online, focuses on reports that will give you insight into your customers and sales. We will discuss what information you will find on each report, how to customize the reports, and how to generate each report.

Chapter 14, Vendor and Expenses Reports, dives into what information you can expect to find in each report, how to customize the report, and how to generate it. This chapter also discusses ways that you can use the report to help you manage your expenses and cash flow.

Section 4: Managing Employees and Contractors

Chapter 15, Managing Payroll in QuickBooks Online, shows you how to set up your payroll system, how to generate payroll, and how to fill payroll tax forms and payments.

Chapter 16, Managing 1099 Contractors in QuickBooks Online, talks about how to set up 1099 contractors, tracking and paying 1099 contractors, and how to generate the 1099 year-end report.

Section 5: Closing the Books and Handling Special Transactions

Chapter 17, Closing the Books in QuickBooks Online, covers the steps needed to close your books each month or for the year; including but not limited to reconciling all bank and credit card accounts, making year-end accrual adjustments (if applicable), recording fixed asset purchases made throughout the year, recording depreciation, taking a physical inventory, adjusting retained earnings, and preparing financial statements.

Chapter 18, Handling Special Transactions in QuickBooks Online, starts by showing you how to use apps in QuickBooks Online. Apps are a great way to help you streamline day-to-day business tasks that can be time-consuming. It also covers how to record credit card payments from customers, keep track of petty cash, and record delayed charges.

Appendix

At the end of the book, there is a brief section called *Shortcuts and Test Drive*, which summarizes the keyboard shortcuts you can use in QuickBooks Online to save time, and also provides links to the QBO test drive account as well as a QBO discount code. This is followed by the *QuickBooks Certified User Exam Objectives*, where you'll find the full list of things you need to know to pass the QBCU exam, along with references to where the relevant content appears in the book – a handy reference for revision.

To get the most out of this book

This book is ideal for anyone who has accounting/bookkeeping knowledge as well as those that don't. Each chapter builds on the knowledge and information presented in the previous chapters. If you don't have any experience of using QuickBooks Online, we recommend you start with *Chapter 1, Getting Started with QuickBooks Online*, and complete each chapter in the order it is presented. If you have experience of using QuickBooks Online, feel free to advance to the chapters that cover the topics you need to brush up on.

Download the example code files

The code bundle for the book is hosted on GitHub at `https://github.com/PacktPublishing/Mastering-Quickbooks-2022-Third-Edition`. We also have other code bundles from our rich catalog of books and videos available at `https://github.com/PacktPublishing/`. Check them out!

Download the color images

We also provide a PDF file that has color images of the screenshots/diagrams used in this book. You can download it here: `https://static.packt-cdn.com/downloads/9781803244280_ColorImages.pdf`.

Conventions used

Bold: Indicates a new term, an important word, or words that you see on screen. For example, words in menus or dialog boxes appear in the text like this. Here is an example: "Click on the **Accounting** tab located in the left menu bar and select **Chart of Accounts**."

CodeInText: Indicates text that the user should type into a field or search bar. For example: "The email address in our example is George_Jetson@thejetsons.com."

QBCU-relevant headings will appear like this $\boxed{\text{QBCU } 5.4.5}$

> QBCU-relevant subsections will appear like this. $\quad$ **QBCU 5.4.5**

Warnings or important notes appear like this.

Tips and tricks appear like this.

Get in touch

Feedback from our readers is always welcome.

General feedback: Email feedback@packtpub.com, and mention the book's title in the subject of your message. If you have questions about any aspect of this book, please email us at questions@packtpub.com.

Errata: Although we have taken every care to ensure the accuracy of our content, mistakes do happen. If you have found a mistake in this book we would be grateful if you would report this to us. Please visit http://www.packtpub.com/submit-errata, selecting your book, clicking on the Errata Submission Form link, and entering the details.

Piracy: If you come across any illegal copies of our works in any form on the Internet, we would be grateful if you would provide us with the location address or website name. Please contact us at copyright@packtpub.com with a link to the material.

If you are interested in becoming an author: If there is a topic that you have expertise in and you are interested in either writing or contributing to a book, please visit http://authors.packtpub.com.

Share your thoughts

Once you've read *Mastering QuickBooks® 2022, Third Edition*, we'd love to hear your thoughts! Scan the QR code below to go straight to the Amazon review page for this book and share your feedback.

https://packt.link/r/1803244283

Your review is important to us and the tech community and will help us make sure we're delivering excellent quality content.

Section 1: Setting Up Your Company File

1

Getting Started with QuickBooks Online

QuickBooks is the most popular accounting software for small businesses. The desktop version has been around for more than 25 years and the online version more than 10 years. It is affordable, easily accessible, and ideal for non-accountants. Many competitors have great software but you need accounting or bookkeeping knowledge to use it whereas someone without this knowledge can set up and use QuickBooks. Before diving into the nuts and bolts of setting up QuickBooks for your business, you should understand what QuickBooks is, and what your options are when it comes to using it. Once you know what your options are, you will be in a better position to choose the version of QuickBooks that will best suit your business needs. We will then show you how to create a **QuickBooks Online** (**QBO**) account, and how to navigate in QBO.

If you don't have previous experience as a bookkeeper, then you will need to know a few book-keeping basics before you get started. In the *Small business bookkeeping 101* section, we cover five key areas in terms of recording transactions in your business: money coming in, money going out, inventory purchases, fixed asset purchases, and liabilities. In this section, we will also cover the importance of the chart of accounts, accounting methods, and what double-entry bookkeeping is.

We will cover the following key concepts in this chapter:

- What is QuickBooks?
- Exploring QuickBooks Online editions
- Choosing the right QuickBooks Online edition
- Creating a QuickBooks Online account

- Navigating in QuickBooks Online
- Small business bookkeeping 101

Once you've got these key concepts under your belt, you will be ready to dive into setting up your business in QBO.

 The US edition of QBO was used to create this book. If you are using a version that is outside of the United States, results may differ.

What is QuickBooks?

QuickBooks is an accounting software program that allows you to track your business' income and expenses. One of the benefits of using QuickBooks is having access to key financial reports (such as profit and loss) so that you can see the overall health of your business at any time. Having access to these reports makes filing your taxes a lot easier. QuickBooks has been around for almost three decades, and it is the accounting software used by millions of small businesses around the globe.

QuickBooks comes in two formats: software that you can install or download on a desktop computer, and a cloud-based program that is accessible from any mobile device or desktop computer with an internet connection.

The cloud-based version, **QuickBooks Online (QBO)**, is available in four editions: Simple Start, Essentials, Plus, and Advanced. The desktop version, **QuickBooks Desktop (QBD)**, also comes in four editions: QuickBooks Mac, Pro, Premier, and Enterprise. In this book, we will focus on QuickBooks Online, discussing each of its editions in detail next. However, if you need additional information regarding QuickBooks Desktop, visit https://quickbooks.intuit.com/.

Exploring QuickBooks Online editions

QuickBooks Online comes in four editions:

- Simple Start
- Essentials
- Plus
- Advanced

Each edition varies in terms of the price, the number of users to which you can give access, and the features included.

The following figure gives a summary of QBO pricing and features for each edition of QBO at the time of writing:

QBCU 1.1.1

	Simple Start	Essentials	Plus	Advanced
Cost	$25	$50	$80	$180
Maximum number of users	1	3	5	25
Track income and expenses	✓	✓	✓	✓
Invoice and payments	✓	✓	✓	✓
Tax deductions	✓	✓	✓	✓
Reports	General	Enhanced	Comprehensive	Powerful
Receipt capture	✓	✓	✓	✓
Mileage tracking	✓	✓	✓	✓
Cash flow	✓	✓	✓	✓
Track sales and sales tax	✓	✓	✓	✓
Time tracking	✓	✓	✓	✓
Estimates	✓	✓	✓	✓
Pay 1099 contractors	✓	✓	✓	✓
Bill management (accounts payable)		✓	✓	✓
Time tracking		✓	✓	✓
Inventory tracking			✓	✓
Project profitability			✓	✓
Analytics and insights				✓
Batch invoices and expenses				✓
Customized access				✓
Exclusive Premium Apps				✓
Dedicated account team				✓
On-demand training				✓
Workflow automation				✓
Data restoration				✓
Task management				✓

Table 1.1: QuickBooks Online edition comparison

As you can see from the preceding table, all four editions of QBO include the following features:

- **Maximum number of users**: Each plan includes a set number of users; Simple Start includes one user, Essentials includes three users, Plus comes with five users, and Advanced includes up to 25 maximum users. In addition, each plan includes one or more accountant users. For example, you can give a bookkeeper or your certified public accountant access to your books.

- **Track income and expenses**: Keep track of all sales to customers and expenses paid to vendors.

- **Invoice and payments**: Invoice customers, enter payments, and stay on top of unpaid invoices.

- **Tax deductions**: Keeping track of all expenses will ensure you don't miss out on any tax deductions you may qualify for.

- **Reports**: QuickBooks includes preset reports so you don't have to create them from scratch. The number of reports available is based on your subscription plan. Simple Start includes the minimum number of reports and Advanced includes the most reports.

- **Receipt capture**: Use your phone or mobile device to snap a photo of a receipt and upload it to QuickBooks. You can also link expense receipts to transactions.

- **Mileage tracking**: Automatically track miles with your phone's GPS and categorize them as business or personal trips.

- **Cash flow**: Stay on top of your cash flow by using the cash flow tools available in all QBO plans.

- **Track sales and sales tax**: Keep track of sales tax collected from customers, submit electronic payments to state and local authorities, and complete required sales tax forms and filings.

- **Time tracking**: Employees and contractors can enter time and apply it to a specific customer or project.

- **Estimates**: Create a quote or proposal and email it to prospective clients for approval.

- **Pay 1099 contractors**: You can keep track of payments made to independent contractors and generate 1099 forms at the end of the year.

The Simple Start plan is the most economical, at $25 per month, on sale currently at $12.50 per month. It includes one user and two accountant users.

The Essentials plan is the next tier and starts at $50 per month, on sale currently at $25 per month. It includes three users and two accountant users.

Unlike Simple Start, you can manage bills (also known as **accounts payable, A/P**) with the Essentials plan. The Plus plan is $80 per month, on sale currently at $40 per month. It includes five users and two accountant users. Unlike the Simple Start and Essentials plans, you can track your inventory and project profitability with the Plus plan. The Advanced plan is the top-tier QBO plan. It starts at $180 per month, on sale currently at $90 per month, and includes up to 25 users and 3 accountant users.

 Keep in mind that pricing is subject to change and that the pricing reflected in this book is based on what is reflected on the Intuit website at time of writing.

We will discuss the features of each plan in more detail, and how to choose the right QuickBooks Online version for you, in the next section.

Choosing the right QuickBooks Online edition

QuickBooks Online is ideal for solopreneurs, freelancers, and mid-to-large-sized businesses with employees and 1099 contractors. 1099 contractors are also known as independent contractors, who you may hire to provide services for your business. Since they are not employees of the business, you must provide a 1099 form at the end of the year to any contractor you have paid $600 or more to in the calendar year.

The needs of your business will determine which edition of QBO is ideal for you. The following provides some additional insight into the ideal businesses for each edition of QBO.

 When you purchase a QBO subscription, you can track business finances for *one* business. If you need to track more than one business, you will need to purchase a QBO subscription for each business entity that you have.

QBCU
1.1.2

QBO Simple Start

QBO Simple Start is ideal for a freelancer or sole proprietor that sells services only, and no products. You may have employees that you need to pay, or 1099 contractors. The majority of your expenses are paid via online banking or wire transfer, so you don't need to write or print checks to pay bills.

QBO Essentials

QBO Essentials includes all of the features found in QBO Simple Start. QBO Essentials is ideal for freelancers and sole proprietors that only sell services and no products. You have employees and/or contractors whose time you need to keep track of in order to bill back to clients. Unlike QBO Simple Start, you pay most of your bills by writing checks, and you need the ability to keep track of your unpaid bills. QBO Essentials is the next step for small businesses that may need more reporting options.

QBCU
1.1.2

QBO Plus

QBO Plus includes all of the features found in Simple Start and Essentials. Unlike QBO Simple Start and QBO Essentials, QBO Plus is ideal for small businesses that sell products, since it includes inventory tracking. Similar to QBO Simple Start and QBO Essentials, you can pay employees. If you tend to work on a project basis, QBO Plus is ideal because you can track the profitability of all of your projects.

QBO Advanced

QBO Advanced includes all of the features found in Simple Start, Essentials, and Plus. QBO Advanced is ideal for businesses that have more than five users needing access to their data. QBO Advanced is QBO Plus on steroids: it includes all of the features found in QBO Plus, along with some great bonus features, such as on-demand online training for your entire team, and Smart Reporting with Fathom.

The bonus features you will find in QBO Advanced are as follows:

- **Analytics and insights**: Track key performance indicators (KPIs) and create presentation-ready reports.

- **Batch invoices and expenses**: Allows you to enter, edit, and email hundreds of invoices, checks, expenses, and bills instead of entering them one by one.

- **Custom user access**: Provides a deeper level of user permissions that allows you to manage access to sensitive data, such as bank accounts.

- **Exclusive premium apps**: Intuit has more than 600 best-in-class apps to customize Quick-Books for your business needs. For example, Amazon Marketplace Connector is available to automatically sync eCommerce sales to QuickBooks.

- **Dedicated account team**: With a QBO Advanced subscription, you will have access to a team of experts who will learn how your business works in order to answer your questions. They will also provide additional resources that will help you to better manage your business financials.

- **On-demand training for staff**: With QBO Advanced, on-demand online training videos help you and your staff get up to speed on how to use QBO. This training has an annual value of $2,000 but is included with your subscription to QBO at no additional cost.

- **Workflow automation**: Save time and minimize risk by implementing automation for repetitive tasks.

- **Analytics and Insights**: Using an app called Smart Reporting with Fathom, you can measure profitability, cash flow, and other KPIs. You can also compare, rank, and benchmark multiple companies, clients, or franchises. This feature is not available in any other QBO edition.

- **Data restoration**: Continuously back up changes to your company file or restore a specific version.

- **Task management**: Create and assign tasks to staff as well as implementing reminders to ensure deadlines are met.

For more in-depth information about the features and benefits of QBO Advanced, head over to *Chapter 2, QuickBooks Online Advanced*. In that chapter, we take a deep dive into all of the features available in the top-tier QBO plan.

Depending on your business and individual circumstances, you should now be able to determine whether you will need QBO Simple Start, Essentials, Plus, or Advanced. It is important to pick the right version for you so that you have access to the appropriate features you will need. Now that you know about QBO, we will show you how to create a QBO account.

Creating a QuickBooks Online account

The first step to setting up your business in QBO is to create a QBO account.

In this section, we will create a QBO account for **Photos by Design**, a fictitious business we will use to demonstrate features and explain concepts taught throughout this book. Photos by Design is owned by a sole proprietor who provides photography services for special occasions such as weddings, graduations, and baby showers. Photos by Design is in its first year of business with no employees. However, the owner does hire a few contractors to help meet the demand during the peak months of the year.

To create a QBO account, you need to go to the Intuit website and select a QBO subscription plan.

Follow these steps to create a QBO account:

1. Open your web browser and go to the Intuit website: `www.intuit.com`.

2. Click on **Products** and select **QuickBooks**, as shown in *Figure 1.1*:

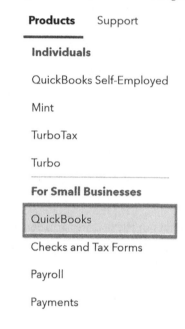

Figure 1.1: Navigating to QuickBooks

3. Click on **Plans & Pricing**, as indicated in *Figure 1.2*:

Figure 1.2: Choosing Plans & Pricing

4. Choose from one of four pricing plans: Simple Start, Essentials, Plus, and Advanced, as indicated in *Figure 1.3*:

Figure 1.3: Choosing a pricing plan

Pricing is as of the writing of this book and is subject to change. To get a discount on your QBO subscription, use my referral link: `https://quickbooks.grsm.io/crystalynnshelton4264`.

5. After selecting a plan, you will be asked if you want to continue without payroll. Select this option; in *Chapter 15, Managing Payroll in QuickBooks Online*, we will cover payroll in more detail.

 Pro Tip: Intuit has a service called QuickBooks Live that connects you with a bookkeeper, who can assist you in getting things set up properly and managing ongoing tasks.

6. Select **Off** for the Live Bookkeeping option.

7. Create an Intuit account by providing your business email address, mobile number, and password, as indicated in *Figure 1.4*:

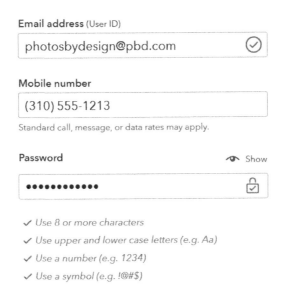

Figure 1.4: Creating an Intuit account

8. The following welcome screen will appear:

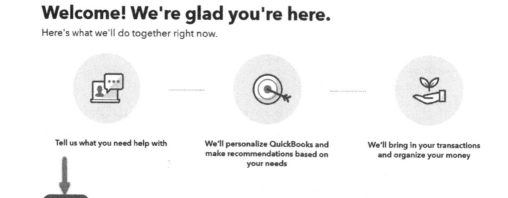

Figure 1.5: Welcome screen after account creation

Click **Next** as indicated in the screenshot above.

9. The following screen will appear:

Figure 1.6: Entering your legal business name

Type your legal business name as shown in the screenshot above and click the **Next** button.

10. The following screen will appear:

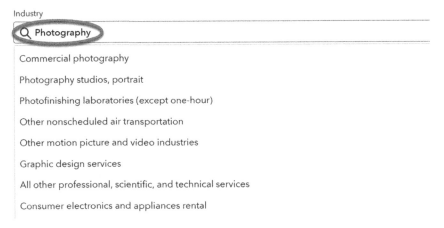

What's your industry?

Start typing and select the option that fits best. You can always change it later.

Figure 1.7: Entering your industry

In the **Industry** field, type the industry that your business falls into and you will see a variety of options that you can choose from. Photos by Design falls into the **Photography studios, portrait** industry:

What's your industry?

Start typing and select the option that fits best. You can always change it later.

Figure 1.8: Confirming your industry

 Pro Tip: QuickBooks uses the industry selection to create a chart of accounts. While you do have the option to skip this field, I *don't* recommend it. Instead, pick an industry that is the closest match to your business.

11. On the next screen, you will select your business structure, as indicated below:

What kind of business is this?

Tell us about your business structure. We use this to help categorize your transactions.

Figure 1.9: Selecting your business structure

 Pro Tip: Most small businesses start out as sole proprietors. If you're not sure what your business structure is, talk to your accountant. You can always select **I'm not sure** and answer this question in the company settings section that we will explore in *Chapter 3, Company File Setup*. However, it's important that you select a business structure in order to customize QuickBooks for your business.

Select **Sole proprietor** for Photos by Design and click **Next**.

12. On the next screen, select how you make your money: providing services, selling products, both, or something else. Photos by Design generates sales by providing services and selling products, as indicated below:

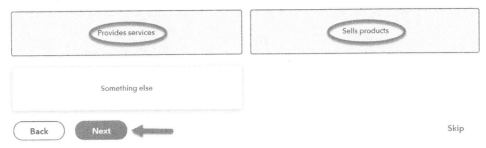

Figure 1.10: Selecting how your business makes money

Click the **Next** button.

13. On the next screen, select your role in the business so that QuickBooks can customize your user experience to meet your specific needs. Choose **Bookkeeper or Accountant** for Photos by Design and click the **Next** button as indicated below:

Figure 1.11: Selecting your role in the business

14. On the next screen, select the type of people that work at the business. Photos by Design is a sole proprietorship with one owner who occasionally uses contractors. These selections have been made as indicated in *Figure 1.12*:

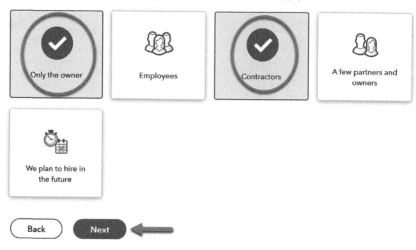

Figure 1.12: Selecting who works at the business

Click **Next**.

15. The following screen will appear:

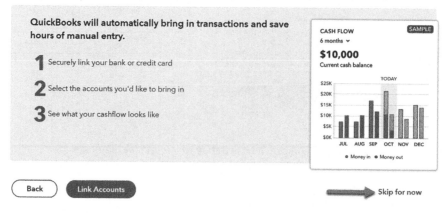

Figure 1.13: Option to link your QuickBooks accounts

QuickBooks allows you to link your bank and credit card accounts so transactions are automatically downloaded. We will cover this in *Chapter 5, Customizing QuickBooks for Your Business*, so let's **skip this step** for now.

16. On the next screen, you can choose any apps you are currently using or would like to use.

Pro Tip: One of the benefits of using QBO is the ability to connect it to more than 600 apps that are available in the Intuit App Store. The advantage of connecting apps to QBO is it allows you to share data from other programs with QBO, eliminating manual data entry altogether.

Choose **I don't use any apps** for Photos by Design, and click the **Next** button as indicated below.

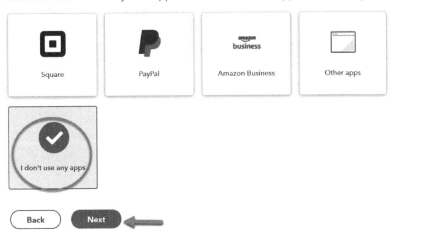

Figure 1.14: Selecting apps you already use

17. Click **Next** again.

18. On the next screen, you can select the transactions you plan to track in QuickBooks. This information will further customize your interface to meet your needs. The selections for Photos by Design are indicated in *Figure 1.15* with a checkmark:

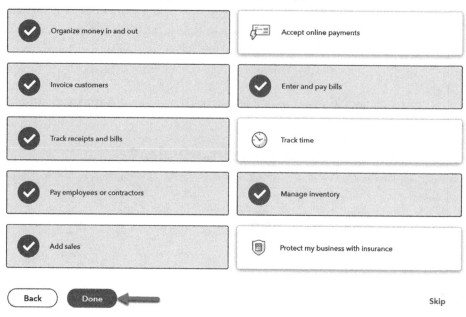

Figure 1.15: Selecting what you want to use QuickBooks for

After making your selections, click **Done**.

19. The following screen will appear:

Ready for a free trial of QuickBooks Payroll?

We make it easy to pay your employees or contractors and file payroll taxes. Plus, the first 30 days are on us.*

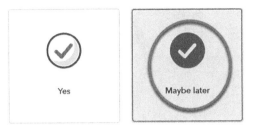

*$75/mo + $8 per employee per month after trial period ends. Terms & conditions

What you get with QuickBooks Payroll:

Automated payroll and tax filing

Same-day direct deposit[1]

Time tracking

Access to payroll experts and HR support center

[1]May be subject to eligibility criteria, not all customers will qualify

Figure 1.16: QuickBooks Payroll free trial

QuickBooks allows you to run full cycle payroll for your employees and contractors. You must sign up for a payroll subscription, which is an additional monthly fee. Photos by Design does not have employees and a payroll subscription is not required to pay contractors.

Select **Maybe later** as indicated in the screenshot above and click **Done**.

20. You will see the following message appear:

Welcome to QuickBooks!

Let's show you around so you can get down to business.

Figure 1.17: Completing the account setup

You have completed the initial QuickBooks setup. Now, you can either click on the button at the bottom to **Take a quick tour** or close out of this screen by clicking the **X** in the top-right corner.

Now that you have created your QBO account, you are one step closer to managing your books. Next, we will show you how to navigate through the program, which will help you locate what you need to get your business set up.

Navigating in QuickBooks Online

QBO is a very intuitive software. The initial home page is customizable so you can see key data such as invoices, expenses, profit and loss, bank accounts, and sales. There are a variety of ways you can navigate within the program, including via these:

- Dashboards
- Left navigation bar

- Icons

- Menus (including within the gear icon and the Quick Create menu)

Let's look at the QBO dashboard and left navigation bar first.

QuickBooks Online dashboard and left navigation bar

QBCU
5.3.2

To explore what a QuickBooks dashboard looks like, we will use our sample company, **Photos By Design**:

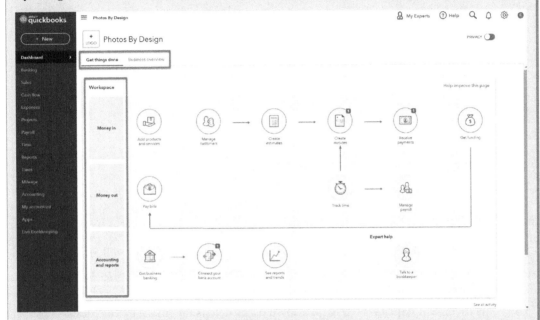

Figure 1.18: QuickBooks dashboard

The dashboard includes two views, **Get things done** and **Business overview**, as indicated by the two tabs at the top of the screen.

The **Get things done** view includes a workspace broken down into **Money in**, **Money out**, and **Accounting and reports**. Icons that represent tasks associated with a particular transaction, such as Money in, appear in the order that they should be completed, with arrows pointing to the next step in the process.

Click on the **Business overview** tab and the following screen will appear:

Figure 1.19: Business overview tab

A brief explanation of the information that appears on the QBO dashboard is as follows:

- **PROFIT AND LOSS**: A snapshot of your total income and expenses will appear in this section. You can select the time period (for example, monthly, quarterly, or annually) you would like to view from the drop-down menu in the upper right-hand corner. Click on the **Income** or **Expenses** bar to drill down to the details that make up the totals.

- **EXPENSES**: In this section, you will see a summary of expenses by type (for example, office supplies, bank fees, and so on). You can select the time period you would like to view this information for (for example, monthly, quarterly, or annually) from the drop-down in the upper-right corner of the tile.

- **INVOICES**: In this section, you will see a summary of paid and unpaid customer invoices. Plus, you will see the number of payments that have been received from customers that have been deposited or are waiting to be deposited. If you click on the tile, you can drill down to the specific invoices and deposits that make up the totals that appear there.

- **BANK ACCOUNTS**: A list of all the bank accounts you have connected to QuickBooks Online will appear in this section, along with the balance per the bank and, below that, the balance currently in QuickBooks.

You can connect bank and credit card accounts to QuickBooks so that your transactions will automatically be downloaded for you. In *Chapter 10, Reconciling Downloaded Bank and Credit Card Transactions*, we show you how to manage downloaded banking transactions.

QBCU
5.3.2

- **SALES:** This tile shows a line graph of how sales are trending for a period of time. You can select the time period from the drop-down menu in the upper right-hand corner.

The left navigation bar is another way you can maneuver around QuickBooks. In addition to the dashboard, it includes quick access to key areas such as **Banking, Sales, Cash flow, Expenses, Projects, Payroll** (if applicable), **Time** tracking, **Reports, Taxes, Mileage, Accounting**, and other areas, as shown below:

Figure 1.20: The left navigation bar

Now that you have a better understanding of the dashboard and the left navigation bar and how to customize them to fit your needs, let's look at the next navigation tool: icons.

QuickBooks Online icons

The following screenshot shows the common icons that can be found on the QBO home page:

Figure 1.21: Icons on the home page

The following are the options you can see:

- **My Experts (1)**: Access to a live bookkeeper who can help you get your books set up is available through this link. You can also upgrade your QuickBooks Online subscription or access a QuickBooks ProAdvisor through **My Experts**.

- **Help (2)**: If you have a question or need to learn how to do something in QBO, you can click on this icon to launch the help menu. You will find detailed support articles, video tutorials, and access to a sample company file in this section.

- **Search (3)**: If you need to locate an invoice, bill, or any transaction, you can do a global search of the program by typing an amount name, the name of a vendor, or any information in this field to search for it.

- **Notifications (4)**: Notifications about changes that have been made to your account or upgrades to your QBO subscription can be found here.

- **Gear (5)**: This icon will display a menu of tasks that you can perform in QBO. Tasks related to global company settings, lists, and tools such as reconciling and budgeting can be found here.

- **Account info (6)**: This button allows you to log out of QuickBooks or manage your Intuit account.

As we mentioned previously, the QBO icons allow you to navigate the program so that you can quickly get to the information you need. In addition to icons, the QBO menus allow you to access your overall company settings, lists, tools, and your company profile. We will cover QBO menus next.

QuickBooks Online menus

In addition to the left navigation bar, there are a couple more menus you can use to navigate QBO.

The first menu is accessible through the gear icon, located in the upper right-hand corner, next to the **Notifications** icon. The following screenshot shows the menu that will be displayed when you click on the gear icon:

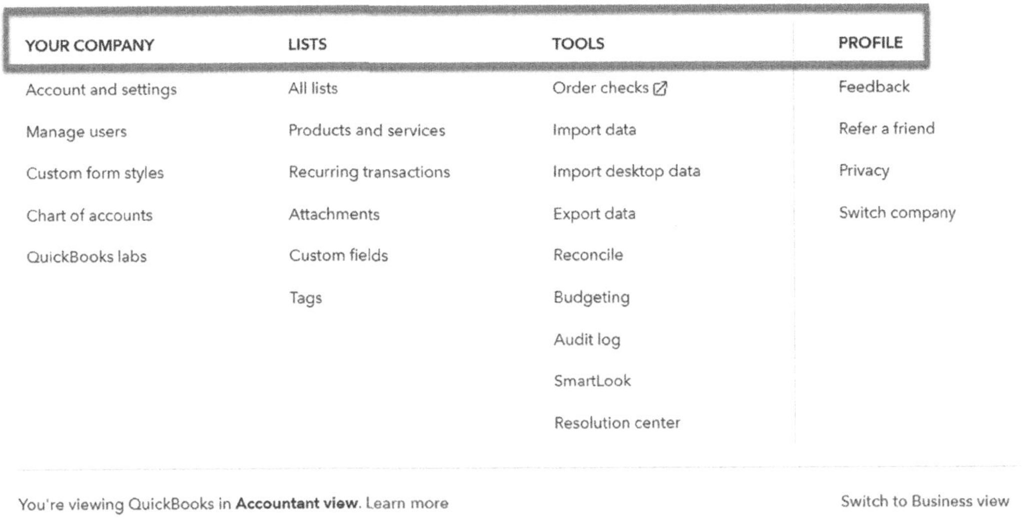

YOUR COMPANY	LISTS	TOOLS	PROFILE
Account and settings	All lists	Order checks ⬀	Feedback
Manage users	Products and services	Import data	Refer a friend
Custom form styles	Recurring transactions	Import desktop data	Privacy
Chart of accounts	Attachments	Export data	Switch company
QuickBooks labs	Custom fields	Reconcile	
	Tags	Budgeting	
		Audit log	
		SmartLook	
		Resolution center	

You're viewing QuickBooks in **Accountant view**. Learn more   Switch to Business view

Figure 1.22: Menu options after clicking the gear icon

A brief description of the areas of QBO that you can access through the gear icon is as follows:

- **YOUR COMPANY**: This section includes global company account settings, which we will explore in detail in the next section. It also allows you to access **Manage users**, which is where you can give others access to your QuickBooks data. You can launch the **Chart of accounts** from here and also **QuickBooks labs**, which is the testing area for new features that are in beta.

- **LISTS**: The **LISTS** menu includes all QuickBooks lists, such as customer listing, vendor listing, and products and services listing. Recurring transactions are available here and any files or images that you have attached to QuickBooks transactions, such as receipts or signed contracts, are accessible in the form of attachments. If you have added custom fields or tags, you can access those lists from this menu.

- **TOOLS:** The QBO subscription that you have will determine the tools that are listed in this section. We are using the QuickBooks Plus subscription, which includes budgeting and SmartLook. It also provides us with the ability to import data such as banking transactions, customer and vendor lists, a chart of accounts, and products and services.

- **PROFILE:** The profile menu includes a user profile (specific to the user that's currently logged in), a **Feedback** section where you can submit recommendations or issues to the Intuit team, the option to refer a friend, and the built-in privacy features included in QBO. If you have multiple QBO companies, you can choose **Switch company** to navigate from one company to another.

The second menu that is available in QuickBooks is the Quick Create menu. You can access this menu by clicking on the **+ New** button located at the very top of the left navigation bar. The following screenshot shows the menu that you will see when you click on the Quick Create icon:

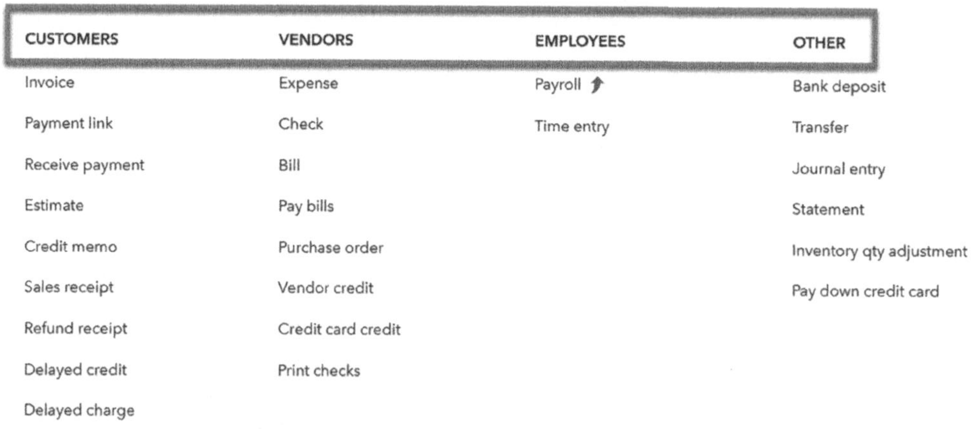

CUSTOMERS	VENDORS	EMPLOYEES	OTHER
Invoice	Expense	Payroll 🕊	Bank deposit
Payment link	Check	Time entry	Transfer
Receive payment	Bill		Journal entry
Estimate	Pay bills		Statement
Credit memo	Purchase order		Inventory qty adjustment
Sales receipt	Vendor credit		Pay down credit card
Refund receipt	Credit card credit		
Delayed credit	Print checks		
Delayed charge			

Figure 1.23: The Quick Create menu

Brief descriptions of the areas of QBO that you can access through the Quick Create menu are as follows:

- **CUSTOMERS:** Most of the transactions that pertain to customers can be found here, from creating invoices and sales receipts to accepting customer payments.

- **VENDORS:** The tasks related to vendors can be found in this section. This includes recording expenses, writing checks, tracking unpaid bills, and creating purchase orders.

- **EMPLOYEES:** If you sign up for a QuickBooks Payroll subscription, you can access all payroll-related tasks in this section. This includes adding new employees, setting up employee deductions, running payrolls, and making payroll tax payments.

- **OTHER:** This section includes making bank deposits, bank transfers, recording journal entries, generating customer statements, making inventory adjustments, and paying down credit cards.

In this section, we have learned how to access the menus of QBO, all of which give you access to your company information, lists, tools, and profile. In addition, the Quick Create menu allows you to access customers, vendors, employees, and other areas of QuickBooks. From *Chapter 3*, *Company File Setup*, onwards, we will show you how to navigate through these and customize QuickBooks for your business. To conclude this chapter, we will introduce you to a few important bookkeeping concepts you need to help you use QuickBooks.

Small business bookkeeping 101

If you are an aspiring accountant, the concepts that we will cover in this section will be familiar to you. However, if you are brand new to bookkeeping, make sure you grab a notepad to take notes, and a cup of coffee to stay alert.

One of the benefits of using QuickBooks to manage your books is that you don't need an accounting degree to learn how to use the software. However, you should have a basic understanding of how bookkeeping works and what's happening behind the scenes in QuickBooks when you record transactions.

The main areas of your business include the following:

- Money coming into your business (sales)
- Money going out of your business (expenses)
- Inventory and fixed asset purchases
- Tracking the money you owe (liabilities)
- Using the chart of accounts to properly track everything
- Accounting methods: cash versus accrual
- Double-entry bookkeeping

Let's discuss each of these areas in more detail.

Recording sales

Every business generates sales by either selling products, services, or a combination of the two. For example, a freelance photographer provides photography services for weddings, graduations, and other special events. A retailer that sells custom T-shirts in various sizes and colors provides a product to generate sales.

In general, there are two types of sales: **cash sales** and **credit sales**. The primary difference between the two is in terms of when you receive payment from your customer. Cash sales are sales that require payment at the time a product is sold or services have been provided. For example, let's say a customer walks into a T-shirt shop and buys a T-shirt. This sale would be considered a cash sale because the sale of the T-shirt and payment by the customer take place at the same time.

Credit sales are the opposite of cash sales because the sale and the payment by the customer take place at separate intervals. For example, let's say the freelance photographer spends four hours at a wedding and sends their customer a bill a few days later. This is considered a credit sale because payment will take place sometime in the future after services have been rendered.

For bookkeeping purposes, credit sales are recorded as accounts receivable. **Accounts receivable**, also referred to as **A/R**, is the money that is owed to a business by its customers. We will talk more about how to keep track of your A/R balances later on.

Recording expenses

The majority of the money that flows out of a business is used to pay for business expenses. Business expenses can be categorized as **recurring** or **non-recurring**. A recurring expense is one that repeats, such as rent, utilities, and insurance.

A non-recurring expense is one that is unexpected or takes place less frequently. For example, if a photographer's camera stops working and they need to spend money to get it repaired or buy a new one, this would be considered a non-recurring expense because it was unexpected.

QuickBooks is designed to help you easily track both recurring and non-recurring expenses. In this book, we will cover how to create recurring transactions in QuickBooks so that you don't have to manually enter them each time they occur. Plus, you will learn how to pay non-recurring transactions by writing a check, making online payments, or paying with a credit or debit card.

Recording inventory and fixed asset purchases

To keep track of all the costs and quantities for each item that you purchase, you would create a purchase order and send it to your vendor supplier to place an order. When you receive the goods, you would record them in your inventory. As you sell products to customers, you would record the sale in QuickBooks so that your inventory, cost, and quantities can be adjusted in real time.

If you purchase computers, printers, or other equipment for your business, these items are called **fixed assets**. When you record these items in QuickBooks, they will be categorized as fixed assets. Fixed assets should be **depreciated** over their useful life. Depreciation is the reduction of the value of an asset due to wear and tear.

Recording liabilities

Many people think that liabilities are expenses, but they are not. A liability can be described as money that is owed to creditors. For example, a loan you have with a financial institution or money that you owe to vendor suppliers, which is also called **accounts payable**. The primary difference between expenses and liabilities is that if you were to go out of business tomorrow, you would no longer have to pay expenses. Instead, you would stop making payments for utilities, and you would lay off employees to eliminate payroll expenses.

On the other hand, if you go out of business, you still have to pay your outstanding liabilities. They don't just disappear as expenses do. For example, if you have an outstanding loan with a bank, you still owe that money and will have to contact the financial institution to make payment arrangements. The same would apply to unpaid bills for products and/or services you received. This means you would have to contact the vendor/supplier and notify them you were going out of business in order to make payment arrangements.

Understanding the chart of accounts

The chart of accounts is a systematic way of categorizing financial business transactions. Every transaction for your business can be categorized into one of five primary categories: Assets, Liabilities, Owner's Equity, Income, and Expenses.

Here is a brief description of each category, with an example:

- **Assets**: Assets are items that your business owns. For example, the money in your business checking account is an asset, and the inventory that you have on hand is an asset until it is sold.
- **Liabilities**: As discussed, liabilities consist of money that you owe to creditors. This includes loans, lines of credit, and the money owed to vendor suppliers (for example, A/P).
- **Owner's Equity**: Equity is everything the owner has invested in the business. For example, any money that you invest in your business is equity.
- **Income**: Proceeds from the sale of products, such as T-shirts, or services such as photography or consulting.
- **Expenses**: Payments made to maintain daily business operations. This includes, but is not limited to, rent, utilities, payroll, and office supplies.

When setting up your QuickBooks company account, you don't have to worry about creating a chart of accounts from scratch. Instead, QuickBooks will create a default chart of accounts based on the industry your business falls into. However, you can add and edit accounts to fit the needs of your business.

QBCU
1.2.3

Choosing an accounting method

One of the key decisions a business will make when setting up their books is which accounting method to use. There are two accounting methods to choose from: **cash-basis accounting** and **accrual accounting**. The primary difference between the two accounting methods is the point when you record sales and purchase transactions in your books.

Cash-basis accounting involves recording sales and purchases when cash changes hands. Let's say a photographer is not paid right away for most of their jobs, but instead, they send an invoice to the customer that includes a payment due date. Until the photographer receives payment in cash, or by check or credit card, they do *not* count the photography services as income under the cash-basis accounting method.

Accrual accounting involves recording sales as soon as you have shipped the products to your customer or have provided services. Going back to our photographer example, the photographer would count the services they provided as income once they finished taking pictures, regardless of when the customer pays for the services.

In general, most small business owners will start out using the cash-basis accounting method. However, according to the Internal Revenue Service (IRS), there are certain types of businesses that are not allowed to use this method of accounting.

The following businesses should **never** use cash-basis accounting:

- **Businesses that carry an inventory**
- **C-corporations (regular corporations)**
- **Businesses with gross annual sales that exceed $5 million**

One of the benefits of using QuickBooks is, regardless of which accounting method you choose, it does not change how you record transactions. As a matter of fact, you can start recording transactions in QuickBooks and decide later on which method you will use. This is because, at any time, you can run reports for either method (cash or accrual). QuickBooks will determine which transactions belong on the report based on the accounting method chosen.

Understanding how double-entry bookkeeping works

You may have heard the term **double-entry accounting/bookkeeping**. This means that for every financial transaction you record, there are at least two entries—a debit and a credit. This ensures that both sides of the accounting equation always remain in balance.

The accounting equation is as follows:

```
Assets = Liabilities + Owner's Equity
```

Let's look at the following example. A T-shirt business owner goes out and purchases $100 of T-shirts from a supplier. They don't pay for the T-shirts right away, but the supplier will send a bill later on. For this transaction, inventory increases by $100 and liabilities increase by $100. Since both assets and liabilities increased, our books remain in balance.

The impact of this transaction on the accounting equation is as follows:

```
Assets = Liabilities + Owner's Equity
$100 = $100 + $0
```

Behind the scenes in QuickBooks, the following journal entry would be recorded for this transaction:

Financial impact	Account	Amount
Debit (Dr.)	Inventory (T-shirts)	$100
Credit (Cr.)	Accounts Payable	$100

Table 1.2: Example journal entry

We will discuss journal entries in more detail in *Chapter 17, Closing the Books in QuickBooks Online*.

In this section, we have covered the seven main areas of focus for managing the books for your business: money coming into a business in the form of sales to customers; money going out of a business for expenses such as office supplies and rent; inventory and fixed asset purchases, and how to record them on your books; money you owe to suppliers and creditors (liabilities); how to manage the chart of accounts; the two accounting methods (cash-basis versus accrual); and how double-entry bookkeeping works.

Summary

In this chapter, we explained what QuickBooks is and introduced you to the QBO product line. We covered setting up your QBO account and basic navigation using dashboards, icons, and online menus in QBO. We also provided tips on how to choose the right software for your business, and we provided you with some bookkeeping basics. Having a good understanding of the QuickBooks product line will help you to choose the best product for your business. In addition, having a basic knowledge of bookkeeping helps you understand the accounting that is taking place behind the scenes in QuickBooks when you enter an invoice or pay a bill.

In the next chapter, we will take an in-depth look at all of the features and benefits included in QuickBooks Online Advanced, including but not limited to customized fields, custom user permissions, workflow automation, importing invoices, creating budgets, batch-creating invoices, and much more.

Join our book's Discord space

Join the book's Discord workspace for a monthly *Ask me Anything* session with the author: `https://packt.link/QuickBooks`

2

QuickBooks Online Advanced

QuickBooks Online (QBO) Advanced is the top-tier QuickBooks Online subscription plan. As mentioned in the previous chapter, it includes all of the features found in QBO Simple Start, QBO Essentials, and QBO Plus, in addition to many more features. Some of the features are as follows: you can add up to 25 users; it includes 48 additional custom fields; you can create customized performance charts; it has granular user permissions similar to QuickBooks Desktop Enterprise; it has workflow automation to reduce manual tasks; it offers the ability to import invoices and budgets; and it allows you to do batch data entry. These are just a few of the many features included in QBO Advanced.

QBO Advanced is ideal for businesses that are currently using QBO Plus and have outgrown it, as well as current QuickBooks Desktop Enterprise customers looking to move to the cloud. The ideal business has more than 10 employees, sales receipts that exceed $500,000, and annualized revenue that continues to increase substantially.

We will cover the following key concepts in this chapter:

- Accessing the QuickBooks Online Advanced test drive account
- Setting up customized fields
- Managing customized user permissions
- Using workflow automation
- Importing invoices and budgets into QuickBooks Online
- Batch-creating invoices in QuickBooks Online
- Smart Invoicing
- Reclassify transactions

- Custom reminders

- DocuSign integration

- Using online backup and restore

- Utilizing the performance center and custom charts

- An overview of the Fathom reporting app

- Priority Circle membership

 The US edition of QBO was used to create this book. If you are using a version that is outside of the United States, results may differ.

Accessing the QBO Advanced test drive account

To demonstrate the key concepts outlined in the introduction to this chapter, we will use the QBO Advanced test drive account. This account includes data for Craig's Design and Landscaping Services, a fictitious business. There are a couple of ways in which you can access the test drive account. You can log in to your existing QBO account, click the **Help** icon, and type test drive in the search field. The second way to access the test drive account is to paste the URL into a new web browser page. Copy the URL in *step 4* and bookmark it for next time.

Follow these steps to access the QBO Advanced test drive account:

1. Log in to your existing QBO account.

2. Click on the **Help** icon located in the upper-right corner of the home page, as indicated here:

Figure 2.1: The Help icon

3. In the QB Assistant pane that pops up, click the **test drive** button as indicated by the first arrow in the figure below. If you don't have that option, scroll down to the search box, type test drive, and click the arrow to the right as indicated at the bottom of the figure. If you get a "gateway error", enable cookies and click the refresh button before you try to access the test drive file again.

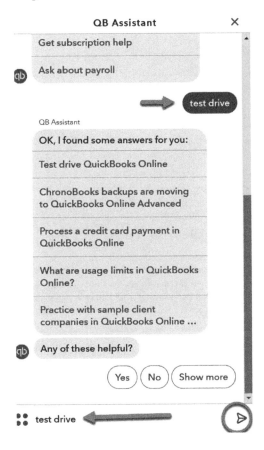

Figure 2.2: Accessing the test drive from QB Assistant

4. The following page will appear:

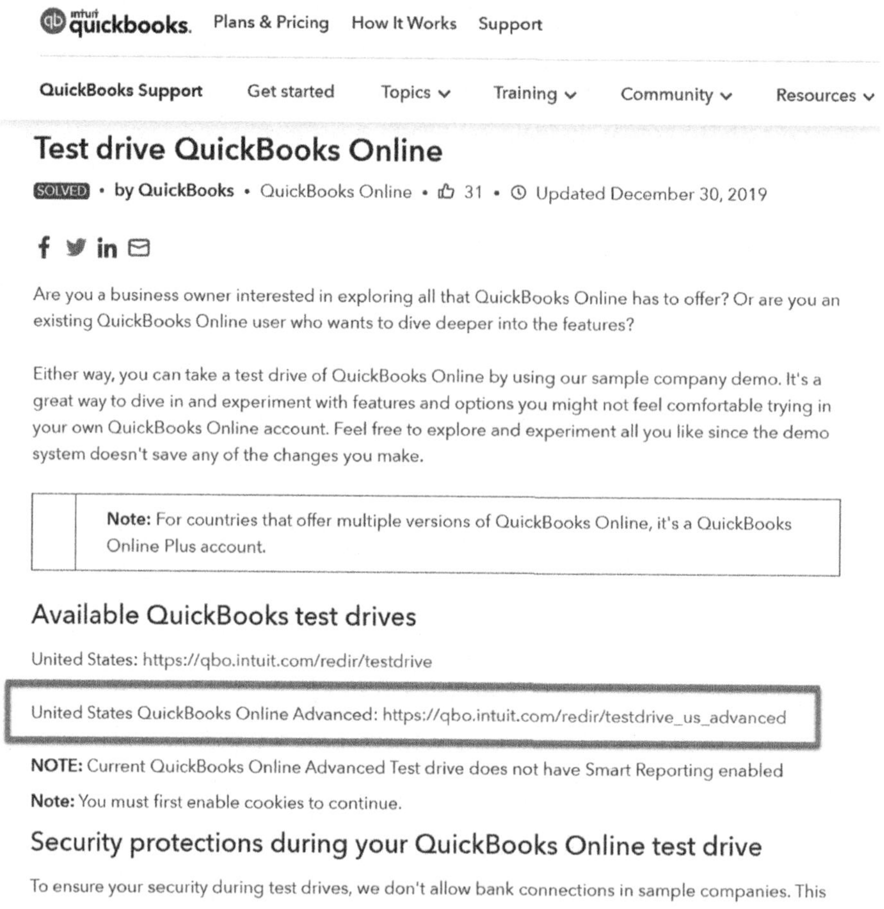

@ intuit **quickbooks.**   Plans & Pricing   How It Works   Support

QuickBooks Support   Get started   Topics ⌄   Training ⌄   Community ⌄   Resources ⌄

Test drive QuickBooks Online

SOLVED • **by QuickBooks** • QuickBooks Online • 👍 31 • ⏱ Updated December 30, 2019

f 🐦 in ✉

Are you a business owner interested in exploring all that QuickBooks Online has to offer? Or are you an existing QuickBooks Online user who wants to dive deeper into the features?

Either way, you can take a test drive of QuickBooks Online by using our sample company demo. It's a great way to dive in and experiment with features and options you might not feel comfortable trying in your own QuickBooks Online account. Feel free to explore and experiment all you like since the demo system doesn't save any of the changes you make.

> **Note:** For countries that offer multiple versions of QuickBooks Online, it's a QuickBooks Online Plus account.

Available QuickBooks test drives

United States: https://qbo.intuit.com/redir/testdrive

United States QuickBooks Online Advanced: https://qbo.intuit.com/redir/testdrive_us_advanced

NOTE: Current QuickBooks Online Advanced Test drive does not have Smart Reporting enabled

Note: You must first enable cookies to continue.

Security protections during your QuickBooks Online test drive

To ensure your security during test drives, we don't allow bank connections in sample companies. This

---

Figure 2.3: The Test drive QuickBooks Online page

Click on the link as indicated in the preceding screenshot to access the **United States QuickBooks Online Advanced** test drive. If you are currently logged in to QBO, you will be logged out of your company file.

5. The following welcome page will appear for **Craig's Design and Landscaping Services**, a fictitious company:

Figure 2.4: Craig's Design and Landscaping Services welcome page

While you will be able to complete most of the exercises in this chapter using the QBO Advanced test drive account, there are a few features that are not fully functioning. In these sections, we have provided you with step-by-step instructions and screenshots where possible. Please also note that your work in the test drive account is saved as long as you remain logged in. Once you log out of the test drive, your work will no longer be accessible.

Now that we have shown you how to access the QBO Advanced test drive account, we will take you through several exercises to demonstrate the key concepts of this chapter.

Setting up customized fields

Custom fields can be used to filter customers, sales, purchasing, expense, and vendor reports. QBO Advanced is the only QBO subscription that includes customized fields. A total of 48 custom fields can be created in QBO Advanced. Custom fields are split between customers, sales, purchase/expense, and vendor fields. A total of 12 custom fields are available for each of these 4 groups.

Follow the steps given here to add a custom field:

1. In the upper-right corner of the QBO screen, click on the **gear** icon, as indicated here:

Figure 2.5: The gear icon

2. Select **Custom fields**, as indicated in the following screenshot:

Figure 2.6: Custom fields in the LISTS menu

3. The following window will appear:

Figure 2.7: Custom fields window

Click the **Add custom field** button, as indicated in the preceding screenshot.

4. The following window will appear:

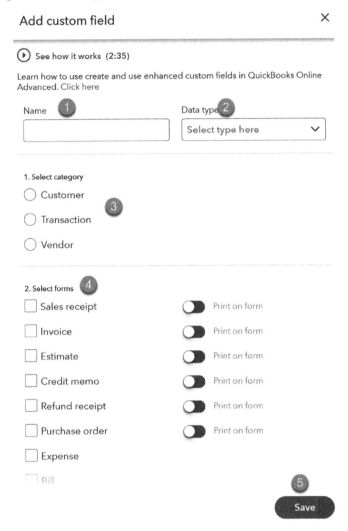

Figure 2.8: The Add custom field window

 Pro Tip: At the top of the screen, there is a **See how it works** link. This is a step-by-step video tutorial that will show you how to add a custom field.

Below is a brief description of the fields that need to be completed:

- **Name (1)**: Type the name of the custom field here (for instance, Sales Rep).
- **Data type (2)**: When it comes to the type of data entered, you have four options to choose from: text and number, number only, date, or drop-down list. Since we are creating a list of sales reps, we will select a drop-down list. When you choose **Dropdown list**, a couple of blank fields will appear. Type C. Shelton into the first field and D. Wade into the second field, as shown here:

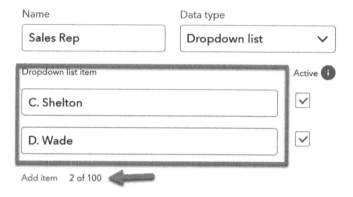

Figure 2.9: Adding drop-down list items

 Notice that directly below the drop-down list there is an option to add an item. Currently, we are only using two fields, but you can add up to 100 items in a drop-down list.

- **Select category (3)**: You can choose to create the custom field to be used for a customer, a transaction, or a vendor; choose **Customer**.
- **Select forms (4)**: You can choose to use the custom fields on a variety of forms. In addition, you can choose to have the field printed on the forms or just have it display in the software only. Choose **Sales receipt** and **Invoice**. We don't want to print these fields on forms, so leave the toggles as they are.

Click the **Save** button **(5)** to save the custom fields.

In our example, we have created a custom field called **Sales Rep** that will appear when creating sales receipts and invoices. By including the **Sales Rep** field on these key documents, it will also show up on reports.

Reports can be filtered by the **Sales Rep** field so that you can review sales for each sales rep individually or as a collective group.

Here is a table that includes examples of the types of custom fields you can create:

Field	Examples
Customer	Sales Rep, Contract Renewal, Birthday, Policy, or Contract Numbers
Sales	Sales Rep, Job Site Foreman, Contract Number, Project Supervisor, or Purchase Order (PO) number
Purchase/Expense	A/P Contact, Contract Number, PO number
Vendor	A/P Contact, Sales Rep, Contract Number, Expiration Date

Table 2.1: Custom field examples

In this section, we have shown you how to create customized fields for various stakeholders. In the next section, we will talk about how to customize user permissions.

Managing customized user permissions

QBO Advanced gives you more control over what areas of QuickBooks you can give users access to. In *Chapter 4, Migrating to QuickBooks Online*, we will discuss the five user types available in all subscriptions: standard user, company administrator, reports only, time tracking user, and accountant user. In addition to these user types, QBO Advanced also includes four additional user roles: Accounts Receivable (A/R) Manager, Sales and Inventory, Workers and Sales reports, and Custom roles.

A brief explanation of these roles follows:

- **A/R Manager:** This role allows the user to access the entire sales cycle, with the exception of sales and bank deposits. Sales and bank deposits give the user the ability to receive payments in undeposited funds and create bank deposits.

- **Sales and Inventory:** This role combines sales and inventory access into a single role so that stock levels can be updated as needed.

- **Workers and Sales reports:** This role can be used for sales managers with sales reports access. It allows them to make vendor payments, calculate commissions, and add commissions to paychecks.

- **Custom roles:** This role enables the admin to assign permissions for a broad range of roles.

Now, we will show you how to create and assign a custom user role to a user. Follow these steps to create a custom user role:

1. In the upper-right corner of the dashboard, click on the **gear** icon, as indicated below:

Figure 2.10: The gear icon

2. Select **Manage users**, as indicated here:

Figure 2.11: Manage users in the YOUR COMPANY menu

3. The **Customize user permissions** window will appear:

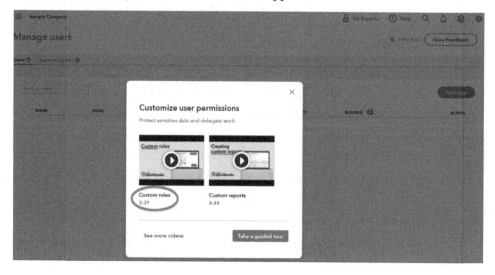

Figure 2.12: The Customize user permissions window

You can click on the **Custom roles** video for instructions on how to add a role. Click the **X** in the upper-right corner to close the pop-up window and then click the **Add user** button located on the right side of the **Manage users** screen, as indicated below:

Figure 2.13: The Add user button

4. The following screen will appear:

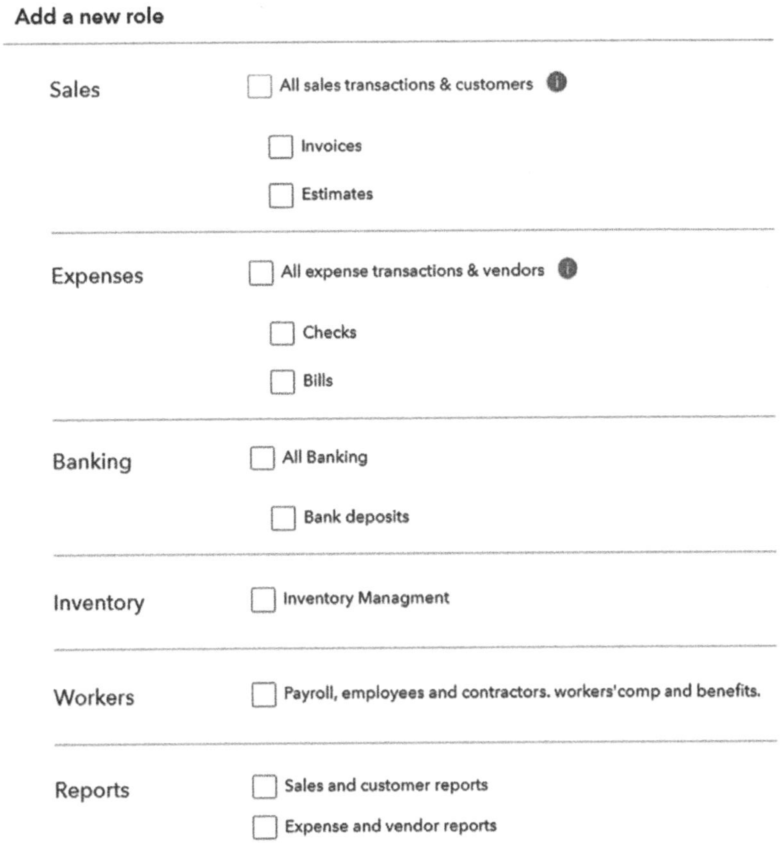

Add a new role

Sales	☐ All sales transactions & customers ⓘ
	☐ Invoices
	☐ Estimates
Expenses	☐ All expense transactions & vendors ⓘ
	☐ Checks
	☐ Bills
Banking	☐ All Banking
	☐ Bank deposits
Inventory	☐ Inventory Managment
Workers	☐ Payroll, employees and contractors. workers'comp and benefits.
Reports	☐ Sales and customer reports
	☐ Expense and vendor reports

Figure 2.14: The Add a new role screen

Put a checkmark next to the areas of QuickBooks you would like to permit this role to access.

5. Follow the onscreen prompts to save the new role.

Now that you have created a new role, you can assign it to a user. Follow these steps to assign the new role to a user:

1. From the **Manage users** screen, click on the **Users** tab and then click the **Add user** button, as indicated here:

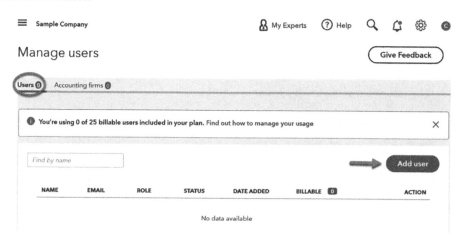

Figure 2.15: The Add User button

2. The **Add a new user** window will appear. Click the drop-down in the **Custom role** field, as indicated here:

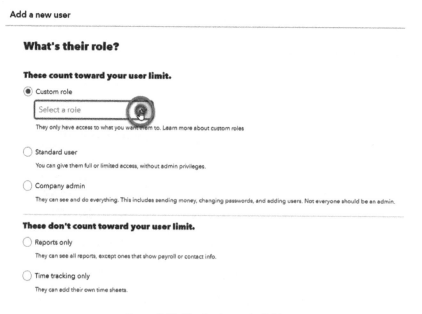

Figure 2.16: The Custom role field

Select the custom role that you created in the previous step and choose **Next**.

3. The following screen will appear:

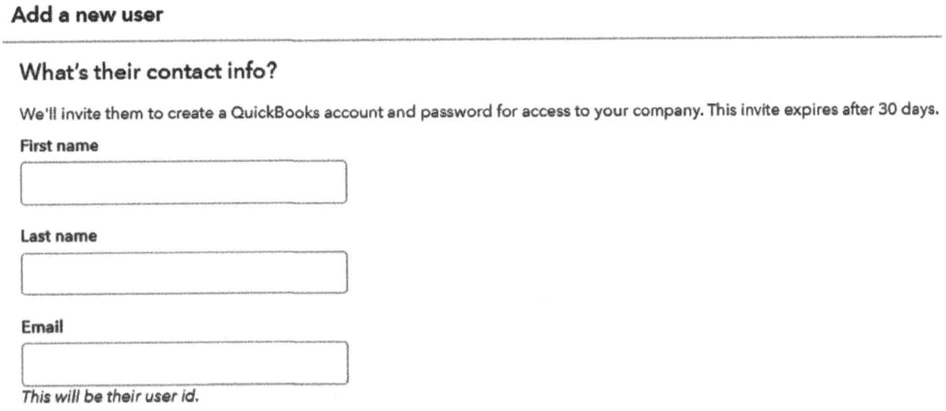

Add a new user

What's their contact info?

We'll invite them to create a QuickBooks account and password for access to your company. This invite expires after 30 days.

First name

Last name

Email

This will be their user id.

Figure 2.17: Adding contact info

Complete the fields with the user's name and email address. When you click the **Save** button, an email invitation will be sent to the user.

 If the new user does not accept the invitation within 30 days, it will expire. If this happens, you can resend the invite directly from the **Manage users** page. Just navigate to the gear icon and click **Manage users**. The status of all email invites will be listed.

An improvement made to the custom sales role is the ability to delegate sales form duties to sales reps by location, allowing them to create estimates, invoices, sales receipts, credit memos, refunds, and more for their own sales territories.

This new feature gives you the following capabilities:

- Sales users now have the ability to receive invoice approval tasks, if they are designed to approve invoices
- Sales users can be notified of past-due invoices by Admin users via Tasks
- Sales managers can be added with only the locations they are authorized to manage

Below is a snapshot of this new functionality:

Add a new role

Sales	☑ All sales transactions & customers ⓘ	All locations ⌄
	☑ Invoices	+ Add new
	☑ Estimates	☐ Select all
		☐ California
Expenses	☐ All expense transactions & vendors ⓘ	☐ NJ
	☐ Checks	☐ Texas
	☐ Bills	
Banking	☐ All Banking	
	☐ Bank deposits	
Inventory	☐ Inventory Managment	
Workers	☐ Payroll, employees and contractors, workers'comp and benefits.	

Figure 2.18: Adding a location to a sales role

You can see how you can add the specific locations to a sales role so that each salesperson can see the territory they are responsible for and no more. You can access this new feature within the **Manage users** page.

Using workflow automation

Workflow automation is used to remind those responsible for tasks that those tasks need to be completed. Reminders to pay a vendor, make a bank deposit, or approve invoices can automatically go out via email, mobile devices, or push notifications to one or more persons who are responsible for completing a given task.

Follow these steps to access workflows:

1.   Click on the **gear** icon.

2.   Select **Manage workflows** below the **TOOLS** column, as indicated here:

Figure 2.19: The Manage workflows option in the TOOLS column

3.   The following window will appear:

Figure 2.20: Workflows window

Click the **Create workflow** button.

4.   The following **Workflows** screen will appear:

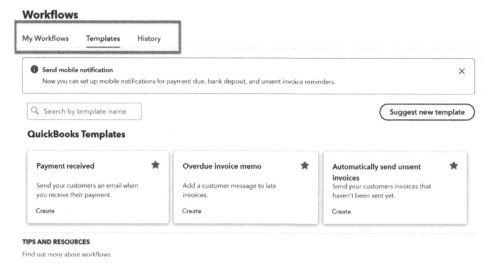

Figure 2.21: The Workflows screen

There are three primary sections to a workflow: **My Workflows**, **Templates**, and **History**. A brief explanation of each of these sections follows:

- **My Workflows:** This tab lists all the workflows that have been initiated or used.

- **Templates:** This tab lists the predesigned workflows that can be adopted or used. A list of the templates available along with a brief description is as follows:

    - **Pay vendor reminder:** Automatically reminds the party responsible to pay bills when they become due.

    - **Payment received:** Automatically notifies customers that a payment has been received on their account.

    - **Payment due reminder:** Automatically notifies customers when their invoice is overdue.

    - **Overdue invoice memo:** Automatically stamps a memo on an invoice when it becomes overdue. The overdue memo is visible on the invoice when it is printed or emailed.

    - **Bank deposit reminder:** Automatically reminds the responsible party to create bank deposits after the undeposited funds account exceeds a predetermined value. This notification is sent via email or a push notification. A link to the undeposited funds screen is included in the notification.

- **Auto send unsent invoices**: Automatically sends invoices that have been marked to send later to customers.

- **Unsent invoices reminder**: Automatically sends the responsible party a notification regarding invoices that are due and need to be sent to customers. This notification is sent via email or a push notification.

- **Invoice approval**: Automatically sends a reminder to the responsible party that invoices are awaiting approval.

- **History**: This tab keeps a record of the workflows used along with the outcome and the date.

 Invoices created by an administrative person are automatically approved. In addition, recurring invoices do not go through the approval process.

Follow these steps to initiate a workflow:

1. Click on the **Templates** tab, as indicated in the following screenshot:

Workflows

My Workflows   Templates   History

ℹ **Send mobile notification**
Now you can set up mobile notifications for payment due, bank deposit, and unsent invoice reminders.

🔍 Search by template name

QuickBooks Templates

Payment received ★	Overdue invoice memo ★	Automatically send unsent invoices ★
Send your customers an email when you receive their payment.	Add a customer message to late invoices.	Send your customers invoices that haven't been sent yet.
Create	Create	Create

Figure 2.22: The Templates tab

2. Click the **Create** link at the bottom of the template you want to use. For this example, we will use the **Payment received** template.

3. The Payment received template will appear, as indicated in the following screenshot:

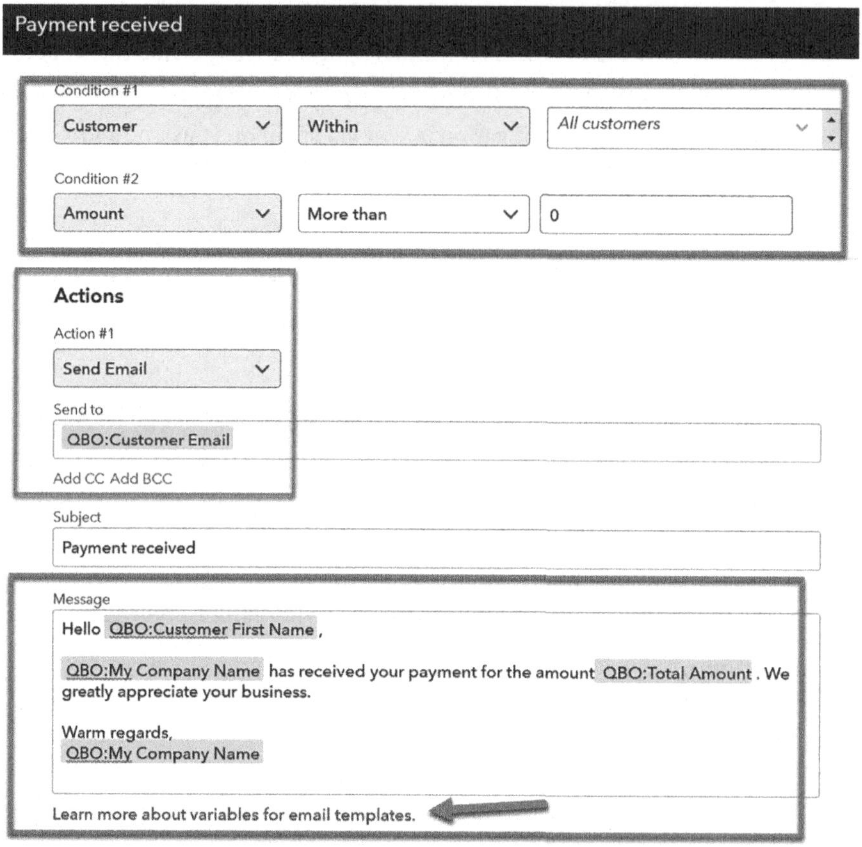

Figure 2.23: The Payment received template

Here is a brief explanation of the information in the preceding screenshot:

- **Condition 1**: This is the first condition that must be met in order to execute the workflow. The first two fields (**Customer** and **Within**) are not editable, but in the last field, you can select the customer(s) this workflow will apply to (all customers, or choose specific customers).

- **Condition 2**: If applicable, you can create a second condition that allows you to set a predetermined amount if needed. Otherwise, you can leave this condition blank.

- **Actions**: The action that needs to be taken if one or both of the conditions are met appears in this field. These fields are automatically set by QuickBooks and therefore not editable, so you will leave them as is.

- **Message**: In this field, you can create a customized message that your customers will receive. You are able to edit the information that appears here. However, you need to click the **Learn more about variables for email templates.** link to learn more about how to edit the message.

4. Click the **Save and Enable** button located at the bottom of the screen and the following screen will appear:

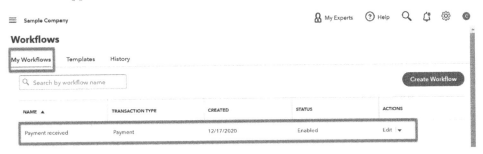

Figure 2.24: Viewing the newly created workflow

The **Payment received** workflow now appears below the **My Workflows** tab with a status of **Enabled**. To make changes, simply click the **Edit** link below the **ACTIONS** column, as indicated in the preceding screenshot.

Importing invoices and budgets into QuickBooks Online

In *Chapter 6, Managing Customer, Vendor, and Products and Services Lists*, we will cover importing customers, vendors, and products and services into QuickBooks. In this section, we will show you how to import invoices into QuickBooks. Importing your data into QuickBooks can save you a lot of time that would have been spent manually entering this information into QuickBooks. In addition to saving time, importing data will ensure more accuracy and consistency than manual data entry. If you use budgets in your business, you may want to consider importing your budget data into QuickBooks. Importing budgets is only available in QBO Advanced.

Follow these steps to import invoices into QuickBooks:

1. From the **gear** icon, select **Import data**, as indicated in the following screenshot:

Figure 2.25: The Import data option under TOOLS

2. The **Import Data** screen will appear:

Figure 2.26: The Import Data screen

Select **Invoices**.

3. The following window will appear:

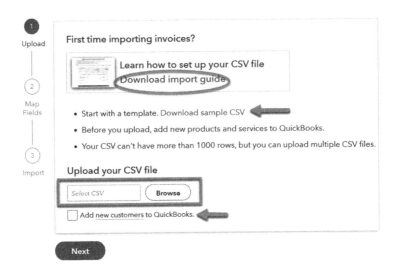

Figure 2.27: Importing invoices – the Upload step

Three steps must be completed to import invoices into QuickBooks. First, you need to upload your invoice information in CSV file format. Download the import guide to learn tips and tricks for importing. Also, download the sample CSV file so that you can see how your data should be formatted before uploading.

 For your convenience, you can also find both the import guide and the sample CSV in the GitHub repository for this book: `https://github.com/PacktPublishing/Mastering-Quickbooks-2022-Third-Edition/tree/main/Chapter02`

Second, you will map the fields in your CSV file with the fields in QuickBooks. The final step is to review the data to ensure accuracy before submitting it for import. Let's go through all these steps:

4. Click the **Browse** button and select the CSV file saved on your computer. The filename should appear in the box to the left of **Browse**, as indicated in the following screenshot:

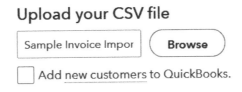

Figure 2.28: Uploading a CSV file

Pro Tip: By checking the **Add new customers to QuickBooks** checkbox, QuickBooks will add any new customers you have included in the file to your customer list.

5.   The **Map your column headings** screen will appear:

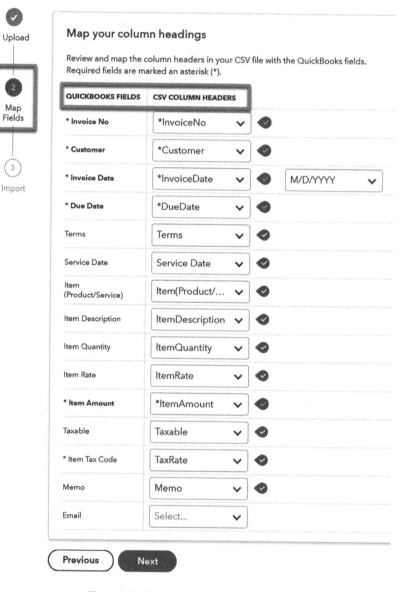

Figure 2.29: Map your column headings

In this step, you will map the columns in your CSV file with the fields in QuickBooks. Do this by clicking on the drop-down field below the CSV file column to make your selections. For example, the column that includes your invoice number should be mapped to the **Invoice No** field in QuickBooks.

 While you could ideally map all of the fields listed here, the only required fields are the ones that have an asterisk (*) next to them: **Invoice No, Customer, Invoice Date,** and **Due Date.**

6. Click **Next** and the following screen will appear:

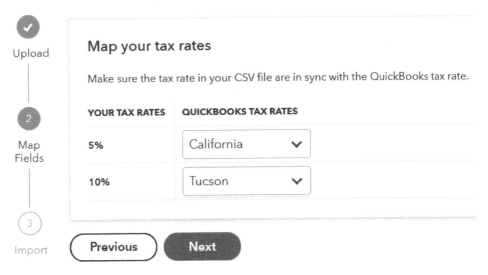

Figure 2.30: Map your tax rates

If you have sales tax rates, this screen will pop up. Select the appropriate state from the drop-down menu, as shown in the preceding screenshot.

7. Click **Next** and the following screen will appear:

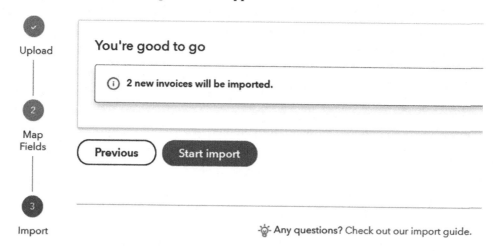

Figure 2.31: Importing invoices – the Import step

Be sure to verify that the total number of invoices that will be imported is correct before starting the import.

> Once you click the **Start import** button, there is no way to undo this action. Therefore, make sure that the number of invoices you are importing is correct.

8. Click the **Start import** button to import the invoices into QuickBooks. Once the import is complete, the following message appears:

Figure 2.32: Invoice import complete

Click **OK** and you will return to the **Import Data** screen.

One thing to keep in mind is that if an invoice has more than one line item, you must include one row for each item on the invoice. There is a maximum of 1,000 rows allowed per CSV file. Therefore, if your file exceeds 1,000 rows, you will need to create a new CSV file and upload them separately. Refer to the import guide for more details on troubleshooting errors when importing data into QBO. The invoice import guide can be found here: `https://github.com/PacktPublishing/Mastering-Quickbooks-2022-Third-Edition/blob/main/Chapter02/Invoice%20Import%20Guide.pdf`

Importing budgets into QuickBooks Online

You can save time by importing company-wide and generic budgets rather than using actual reporting. This feature is ideal for non-profit organizations that need to manage profit and loss budgets.

In *Chapter 12, Business Overview Reports*, we will cover how to create a budget from scratch. However, if you build your budget in a different program and would like to import it into QBO, you can do that with a QBO Advanced subscription. The file format must be a CSV file or it will not work.

Please note that the **Import budget** feature is disabled for the test drive account, so you will not be able to follow along if you are using it. Screenshots in this section have been taken using a non-test drive account.

Follow the steps below to import a budget:

1. To access the **Import Budget** feature, click on **Budgets** on the left navigation bar and choose **Import budget**, as shown below:

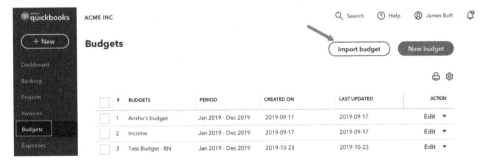

Figure 2.33: Importing a budget

2. Your data should resemble the image of the budget template below:

ACCOUNTS	JAN	FEB	MAR	APR	MAY	JUN	JUL	AUG	SEP	OCT	NOV	DEC	TOTAL
▾ INCOME													
Billable Expense Income													
Design income	0.00	0.00	0.00	0.00	0.00	0.00	0.00	0.00	0.00	975.00	1,275.00	0.00	2,250.00
Discounts given	0.00	0.00	0.00	0.00	0.00	0.00	0.00	0.00	0.00	0.00	-89.50	0.00	-89.50
Fees Billed													
▾ Landscaping Services	0.00	0.00	0.00	0.00	0.00	0.00	0.00	190.00	90.00	400.00	797.50	0.00	1,477.50
▾ Job Materials													
Decks and Patios													
Fountains and Garden Ligh…	0.00	0.00	0.00	0.00	0.00	0.00	0.00	0.00	323.00	422.00	1,501.50	0.00	2,246.50
Plants and Soil	0.00	0.00	0.00	0.00	0.00	0.00	0.00	131.25	0.00	0.00	2,220.72	0.00	2,351.97
Sprinklers and Drip Systems	0.00	0.00	0.00	0.00	0.00	0.00	0.00	0.00	108.00	0.00	30.00	0.00	138.00
Total Job Materials	0.00	0.00	0.00	0.00	0.00	0.00	0.00	131.25	431.00	422.00	3,752.22	0.00	4,736.47
▾ Labor													
Installation	0.00	0.00	0.00	0.00	0.00	0.00	0.00	0.00	0.00	0.00	250.00	0.00	250.00
Maintenance and Repair	0.00	0.00	0.00	0.00	0.00	0.00	0.00	0.00	0.00	50.00	0.00	0.00	50.00
Total Labor	0.00	0.00	0.00	0.00	0.00	0.00	0.00	0.00	0.00	50.00	250.00	0.00	300.00
Total Landscaping Services	0.00	0.00	0.00	0.00	0.00	0.00	0.00	321.25	521.00	872.00	4,799.72	0.00	6,513.97
Other Income													

Figure 2.34: Budget template

3. Review the template for accuracy and click the **Import** button located in the lower-right corner when you are ready to import the data.

After importing your budget into QuickBooks, you will be able to run a budget versus actuals report to see how well your actuals are tracking against your budget.

You can save a ton of time creating recurring invoices in QuickBooks by using the batch-create invoice feature. We will cover this topic next.

Batch-creating invoices in QuickBooks Online

Batch-creating invoices is an alternative to importing invoices into QBO. It's ideal for businesses that need to create several invoices that will include the same (or similar) services. For example, a property owner may need to bill their tenants for their monthly rent. If you have 10 tenants that pay $1,000 a month, you can quickly generate 10 invoices using batch create.

Follow these steps to generate a batch of invoices:

1. Click the **+ New** button located on the left navigation bar, as indicated below:

Figure 2.35: The New button

2. Select **Batch transactions** under the **OTHER** column, as indicated in the following screenshot:

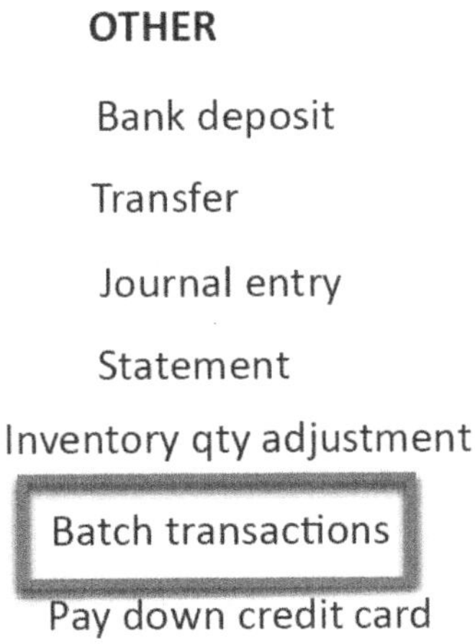

OTHER

Bank deposit

Transfer

Journal entry

Statement

Inventory qty adjustment

Batch transactions

Pay down credit card

Figure 2.36: Selecting Batch transactions

3. The **Batch Transactions** screen appears as follows:

Figure 2.37: The Batch Transactions screen

This screen resembles and works like an Excel spreadsheet. First, you will select the transaction type you are importing. There are six to choose from: **Invoices**, **Bank Deposits**, **Sales Receipts**, **Checks**, **Expenses**, and **Bills**. Next, you will select the action you wish to take: **Create**, **Modify**, or **Delete**. To complete the spreadsheet, put your cursor in each field and enter the information required, pressing *Tab* to move between fields.

For example, in the following screenshot, we have created an invoice to bill a customer for weekly gardening services at $100:

Figure 2.38: Example of a completed invoice

4. To create a duplicate invoice for other customers, click on the number to the left of the customer name and the following dialog box will appear:

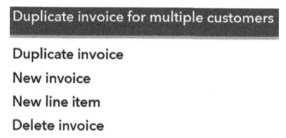

Figure 2.39: Invoice options

You can duplicate this invoice for multiple customers, duplicate this invoice, create a new invoice, add a new line item to the existing invoice, or delete the invoice.

Click the **Duplicate invoice for multiple customers** option.

5. The following window will appear:

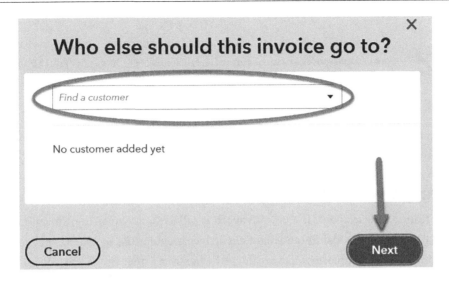

Figure 2.40: Duplicating an invoice for multiple customers

From the drop-down menu, select each customer for whom you would like to create the invoice and then click **Next** when you are done.

6. The following screen will appear:

Batch Transactions

Select transaction type	Action	TOTAL						
Invoices	Create	$500.00						

	Customer	Email	Terms	Invoice Date	Due Date	Product/Service	Description	Qty	Rate	Amount
1	Amy's Bird Sanctuary	Birds@Intuit.com	Net 30	12/18/2020	01/17/2021	Landscaping:Gardening	Weekly Gardening Service	2	50	100.00
2	Bill's Windsurf Shop	Surf@Intuit.com	Net 30	12/18/2020	01/17/2021	Landscaping:Gardening	Weekly Gardening Service	2	50	100.00
3	Diego Rodriguez	Diego@Rodriguez.com	Net 30	12/18/2020	01/17/2021	Landscaping:Gardening	Weekly Gardening Service	2	50	100.00
4	Geeta Kalapatapu	Geeta@Kalapatapu.com	Net 30	12/18/2020	01/17/2021	Landscaping:Gardening	Weekly Gardening Service	2	50	100.00
5	Kookies by Kathy	qbwebsamplecompany@yahoo.com	Net 30	12/18/2020	01/17/2021	Landscaping:Gardening	Weekly Gardening Service	2	50	100.00
6										
7										
8										
9										
10										
11										

Figure 2.41: Successfully duplicated invoices

There will be an invoice listed for each customer selected in the previous step. You can add additional customers, save your work, and come back later on to make additional changes, or you can save and send the invoices via email to your customers.

If you prefer to import invoices instead of entering them manually, the batch invoicing sample template can be found here: `https://github.com/PacktPublishing/Mastering-Quickbooks-2022-Third-Edition/blob/main/Chapter02/Batch%20Invoicing%20Template.csv`

Now that you have a better understanding of how batch-creating invoices can save you time, we will discuss Smart Invoicing next.

Smart Invoicing

A new feature now available in QBO Advanced is called Smart Invoicing. Smart Invoicing uses artificial intelligence to identify and highlight invoice irregularities so you can spot potential problems quickly. For example, invoices are flagged whenever a quantity or price detail falls outside the expected range for a given customer. The irregular values are highlighted and explained so the person creating the invoice or the approver can take a look at them.

Below is an example of an invoice with the Smart Invoicing feature turned on:

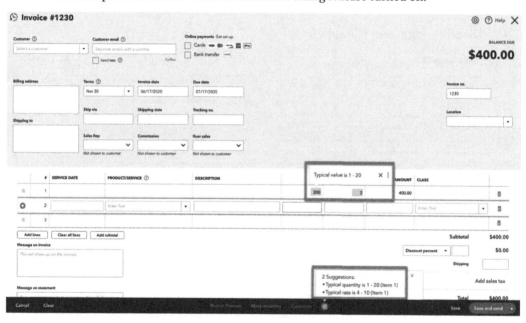

Figure 2.42: Smart Invoicing in action

Notice that both the quantity and the unit cost are highlighted with a comment right above that indicates the expected value for these fields. If you don't want to see the comments, you can turn off Smart Invoicing in company preferences (click on the **gear** icon and select **Account and settings**), or you can turn off suggestions at the user level.

Next, we will cover an existing feature in QBO that is now available to QBO Advanced subscribers – Reclassify transactions.

Reclassify transactions

The Reclassify transactions feature is not new. However, in the past, it was only available for accountant users; now it is available to Admin users who have a QBO Advanced subscription. Reclassify transactions allows you to modify a batch of transactions all at once. For example, if you find that the expense account for checks written to a vendor has been categorized incorrectly, you can use the Reclassify transactions feature to make the correction for a batch of checks at once.

Follow the steps below to access the Reclassify transactions feature:

1. Click on the **gear** icon and select **Reclassify transactions**, as shown below:

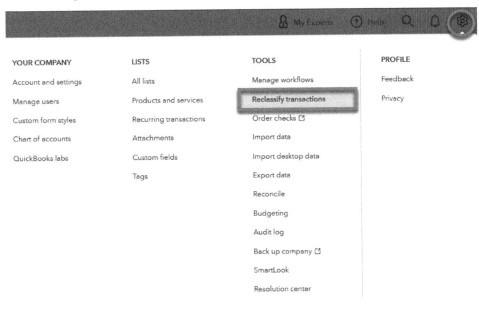

Figure 2.43: Selecting Reclassify transactions

2. The following screen will appear:

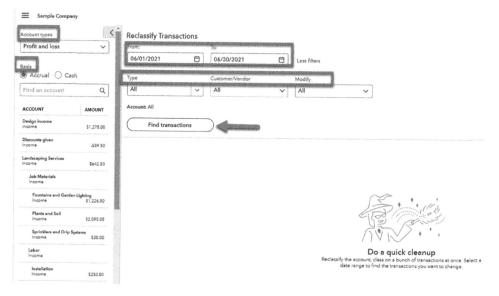

Figure 2.44: The Reclassify Transactions screen

A brief explanation of the information required in this screen is as follows:

- **Account types**: From the drop-down, you can select profit and loss accounts or balance sheet accounts. If you need to reclassify accounts that are both profit and loss and balance sheet accounts, you will need to do them separately.

- **Basis**: Select the accounting method that you use – accrual or cash. This will determine which accounts appear during the search.

- **From/To**: Select a date range to search for transactions.

- **Type**: Narrow your search by selecting the type of transactions. From the drop-down, your options are bill, check, credit card credit, credit memo, deposit, expense, invoice, journal entry, refund, sales receipt, and vendor credit.

- **Customer/Vendor**: You can filter by a specific customer/vendor or select **All** from the dropdown.

- **Modify**: From the dropdown, you can choose to modify all data or just the accounts.

3. Click the **Find transactions** button to search for any transactions that meet the criteria.

The Reclassify tool will save you time that you would have spent manually making corrections to your data. It is a great tool to use when you need to do a quick cleanup as you discover errors, or at the end of the year to ensure the accuracy of your financial statements before filing your tax return. If you don't have QBO Advanced, you can still edit the original transactions or use a journal entry to reclassify them.

Custom reminders

A major improvement to QBO workflows is allowing users to create automatic custom reminders with "if-this-then-that" logic. Reminders are triggered when user-defined conditions are met. They will come in the form of tasks in the QBO Advanced task manager, customer emails, text messages, or push notifications. Custom reminders can be found by clicking on the gear icon and selecting **Custom workflows**, located below the **TOOLS** column.

For example, a user can set custom reminder emails to both the customer and the sales rep to remind them that the due date for an invoice is coming up. The emails can also be customized to be sent a predetermined number of days prior to the due date, along with invoices over a certain amount for specific companies.

The screenshot below demonstrates an example of the conditions that can be created and the push notification that is received as a result of the custom reminder:

Figure 2.45: Specifying a custom reminder

In the preceding screenshot, the condition is when an invoice payment status is unpaid. When this condition is met, QuickBooks will send a reminder 3 days before the invoice is due. The message will be sent via email, text message, or push notification within QBO.

DocuSign integration

One of the newest features in QBO Advanced is the integration of DocuSign. You can now easily sign, send, and manage digital documents directly from your QuickBooks Online Advanced account. eSignatures allow signees to receive and sign documents from any computer or mobile device with an internet connection.

 Please note that the **DocuSign** feature is disabled for the test drive account, so you will not be able to follow along if you are using it. Screenshots in this section have been taken using a non-test drive account.

Below is a screenshot of what this feature looks like when the DocuSign app is downloaded and implemented:

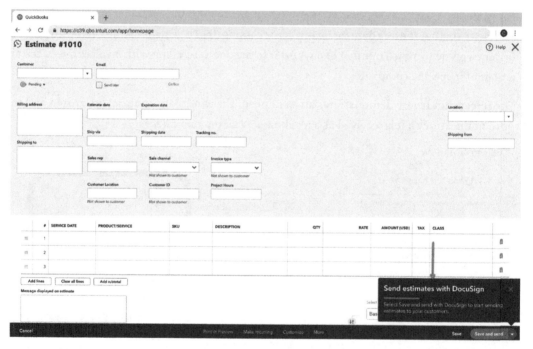

Figure 2.46: DocuSign notification

In the bottom-right corner of the preceding screenshot, there is a notification that alerts the user that they can send estimates to their customers with DocuSign.

Using online backup and restore

Similar to QuickBooks Desktop products, you can save a backup copy of your QBO data with your QBO Advanced subscription. This feature gives your accountant or administrative personnel the ability to continuously back up data and then restore it to a point in time as needed. Online backup and restore captures transaction data, list data, and other elements such as attachments, company information, exchange rates, and preferences. However, it does not record things such as custom reports, recurring transactions, and bank feeds.

You can access the backup tool from the gear icon. After clicking on the **gear** icon, select **Backup Company**, listed below the **TOOLS** column.

Here is a brief description of the three types of backups available:

- **Full backup**: This type of backup saves everything in the chart of accounts.
- **Incremental backup**: This backup only saves changes made since the last backup was made.
- **Complete backup**: This backup saves everything, including company data.

After reviewing your options for backing up and restoring your QBO data, you should be able to use this information to determine which type of backup will work best for you. While one of the benefits of using QBO is that your data is automatically stored in the cloud through Intuit, you can also keep a backup on hand if you prefer to do so.

Utilizing the performance center and custom charts

QBO Advanced offers the ability to create custom KPI dashboards and other user-defined charts. This will give you insight into those areas that might require additional oversight or management. The performance center is only available in QBO Advanced. One of the features within the performance center is custom charting. Custom charting allows you to visualize your financial data in chart format, which can be easier to understand than just plain numbers. You can create a chart that allows you to include up to 10 groups of values on a single chart. For example, revenue can be tracked by products and services, classes, locations, projects, and employees. You can also micro-filter specific customers, classes, locations, and more.

The following datasets can be used to create custom charts:

- Expenses
- Revenue

- Gross profit

- Net profit

- Accounts receivable

- Accounts payable

- Cost of Goods Sold (COGS)

- Current ratio

- Quick ratio

When you set up your QuickBooks account, you select the industry your business falls into. This allows you to compare benchmark info when running reports in the Performance center. QBO uses real-time data for custom charts, which means report visualization is 100% accurate. Currently, existing reports are updated every 4 hours.

Follow these steps to access the performance center:

1. From the left menu, click on **Reports** and select **Performance center**, as indicated in the following screenshot:

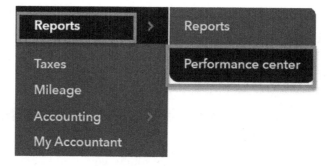

Figure 2.47: Navigating to the Performance center

2. Select the **Add New Chart** button.

3. Select from one of the following 10 datasets, as indicated in the following screenshot:

Figure 2.48: Choice of datasets for the dashboard

Click **Continue**.

4. Complete the following fields of information:

   - **Name**: Select a name for the chart, for example, Revenue by Department.

   - **Time Period**: From the dropdown, select the time period for which you wish to see data; for example, this year to date.

   - **Group by**: Select how you would like the report to be grouped. Since we want to see revenue by department, we will group by class. Each department is set up as a class in QuickBooks.

5. Click the **Add to Dashboard** button.

 While you are not able to fully access the custom chart builder with the test drive account, note that there are a number of ways to filter data with the chart builder. In addition, you can also compare data to previous periods. For example, you can compare revenue for this year with last year.

Now that we've covered the basics of how to utilize the performance center and custom charts so that you can visualize your financials, we will discuss the Fathom reporting app next.

Fathom reporting app

The Fathom reporting app takes QuickBooks reports to a whole new level. This app syncs data from QBO to enable advanced analysis and visualization. Fathom syncs data once every 24 hours, but you can instruct it to update immediately if needed. Similar to the performance center, you can access Fathom reporting from the **Reports** menu. There are three menu options available: **Analysis**, **Reports**, and **Settings**.

 Please note that the **Fathom Reporting App** feature is disabled for the test drive account, so you will not be able to follow along if you are using it.

Here you will find a brief explanation of the reporting menus available in the Fathom reporting app:

- **Settings**: In this tab, you will define the parameters for the data you want to analyze and report on. This is done within the **KPIs** (short for **Key Performance Indicators**) menu of the **Settings** tab. Consult with your accountant to determine your target for each KPI you decide to track.
- **Analysis**: In this tab, you can perform a key analysis of the KPIs selected in the **Settings** tab. This data will help to support discussions on strategy for various aspects of your business.
- **Reports**: Reports give you the ability to create report packages for a variety of audiences. For example, you can create a package for a CFO that includes granular data, whereas you can create higher-level packages for the board of directors.

With Fathom reporting, you will gain insight into how your business is performing compared to other businesses within your industry. In addition, access to key performance indicators will assist you in making better business decisions.

Priority Circle membership

Another feature that sets QBO Advanced apart from other QBO subscriptions is it includes membership in Priority Circle. Priority Circle membership gives you access to three types of services: a dedicated account team, 24/7 premium support, and QBO on-demand training.

These services are ideal if you have a medium or large team that needs to get up and running on QuickBooks quickly. Unlimited access to these services is included in the QBO Advanced subscription, so there is no additional charge.

Here is a brief description of the services included in Priority Circle membership:

- **Dedicated account team**: This includes access to a team of QBO experts who can provide answers to the most common product-related questions. These experts will be familiar with your business when you call in, which will ensure that the answers you receive are applicable to your business needs.

- **24/7 premium support**: This service includes front-of-the-queue access from the support team. This team is trained to answer all of your technical questions related to QuickBooks.

- **On-demand training**: This service includes access to a suite of self-paced training videos that will teach you the basics of QuickBooks, QuickBooks Payroll, and the QBO Advanced features. It has an annual value of $2,000 and includes the following courses:

    - Mastering Accounting Basics for QBO

    - Mastering QBO Level 1

    - Mastering QBO Level 2

    - Mastering QBO Payroll

    - QBO Advanced Features

You can access these videos from the **My Experts** icon located in the upper-right corner of the QBO home page, as indicated in the following screenshot:

Figure 2.49: The My Experts icon

 Keep in mind that the Priority Circle team is not able to answer questions related to your business strategy, tax, accounting, or which apps to choose. You will need to consult with a QuickBooks ProAdvisor or your accountant on these matters.

Summary

In this chapter, we have provided you with a detailed look at the features that are only available in the top-tier QBO plan, QBO Advanced. The topics we covered included accessing the QBO test drive, using customized fields on forms, setting custom user permissions to control what areas of QuickBooks you give other users access to, how to use workflow automation to streamline deadline-driven tasks, importing invoices and budgets to save time, utilizing batch-entry transactions to create invoices, Smart Invoicing, reclassifying transactions, custom reminders, DocuSign integration, the options you have for backing up your QBO data, how the performance center and custom charts work, an overview of the Fathom reporting app, and what's included in Priority Circle membership. Now that you have a better understanding of what's included in QBO Advanced, it will help you to determine whether it is the right subscription for your business.

In the next chapter, we will show you how to create your company file. This will include setting up company preferences and the key information you will require in order to do so.

Join our book's Discord space

Join the book's Discord workspace for a monthly *Ask me Anything* session with the author: `https://packt.link/QuickBooks`

3

Company File Setup

Picking up where we left off in *Chapter 1, Getting Started with QuickBooks Online*, we will show you how to customize your **QuickBooks Online (QBO)** account through the company preferences. Company preferences allow you to establish how sales and expenses are recorded, how payments are handled, and other advanced settings, such as selecting the start of your fiscal year and which accounting method to use.

Before we dive into company preferences, we will spend some time discussing key information and documents that you need to have handy. This will help you to include as much information as possible; otherwise, you will be missing key details that should appear on customer invoices, documents, and forms that can be produced in QuickBooks. In addition, we will show you how easy it is to edit information in this section whenever you need to.

In this chapter, we'll cover the following topics:

- Key information and documents required to complete the company file setup in Quick-Books Online
- Setting up company preferences in QuickBooks Online

 The US edition of QBO was used to create this book. If you are using a version that is outside of the United States, results may differ.

Key information and documents required to complete the company file setup in QuickBooks Online

Before we get into the mechanics of creating your company file, you will need to gather some key documents and answer a few questions first. This information is necessary so that you can customize QuickBooks for your business. Plus, having this information at your fingertips will help you to complete the company setup a lot faster.

The information you will need to know includes the following:

- **Company name:** This needs to be the legal name or the business name that should appear on all legal documents and payroll forms.

- **Company contact information:** This will include the mailing address, business telephone number, business email address, and website address of the company.

- **Industry:** In QuickBooks, you will select the industry that your business falls into. Using this information, a default chart of accounts list will be created for you.

- **Federal tax ID number:** A nine-digit number that identifies your business to the IRS. If you don't have a federal tax ID number, you can use your social security number.

- **Company organization type:** In QuickBooks, you will need to select from one of the following organization types: sole proprietor, LLC, nonprofit, C-corporation, or S-corporation.

- **Fiscal year:** In QuickBooks, you will need to enter your company's fiscal year. For example, if you are on a calendar year, it will be January 1 to December 31.

- **List of products you sell:** If you have a lot of products and services, you should create an Excel or CSV spreadsheet that includes the product name, product description, cost, price, and quantity on hand. This information can be imported into QuickBooks in just a few minutes.

- **List of services you sell:** Similar to products, you should create an Excel or CSV spreadsheet that includes the name of the service, a brief description, and the price. You can import this information into QuickBooks.

- **List of sales tax rates:** A list of each city, state, or jurisdiction for which you are required to collect sales tax, along with the name of the tax authority that you pay, is required to properly set up sales tax in QuickBooks.

- **List of customers:** Customer contact details, such as an address, email address, telephone number, Facebook address, or other information you have on file can be entered into an Excel or CSV file if you wish to import the information into QuickBooks.

- **List of vendor suppliers**: Vendor contact details, such as a remit-to address, email address, telephone number, primary contacts, and other information you have on file can be entered into an Excel or CSV file if you wish to import it into QuickBooks.

- **Chart of accounts list**: Your current list of accounts can be entered into an Excel spreadsheet if you wish to easily import it into QuickBooks.

 Pro Tip: Be sure to have a copy of your most recent bank and credit card statements, along with the last bank reconciliations completed.

By taking the time to gather these documents, you will ensure that you are not missing key information when you create forms such as customer invoices. In addition, your financial statements will be more accurate and reliable.

QuickBooks includes default settings that are called preferences. You can edit preferences to customize them to your specific business needs.

Setting up company preferences in QuickBooks Online QBCU 1.2.1

Before you start entering data into QuickBooks, you should spend some time going through the company preferences, which allow you to activate features that you would like to use and deactivate features that you don't plan on using. Click on the **gear** icon and select **Account and settings**, located below the **Your Company** column.

Company preferences are made up of seven key areas:

- Company
- Billing and subscription
- Usage
- Sales
- Expenses
- Payments
- Advanced

Let's look at each one of these in more detail.

Company settings

In your company preferences, you will provide basic information about your business, such as the contact email and telephone number, where customers can reach you, and your mailing address. The contact information that's included in this section will appear on customer invoices and emails that are sent to them so that they know how to get in contact with you. You will also provide your company name and entity type (sole proprietor, partnership, LLC, C-Corp, or S-Corp). It is also a good idea to enter your **employer identification number** (**EIN**) in this section. This information will be used to file payroll tax returns and it can also be used by your tax preparer when filing your taxes.

A brief explanation of the entity types is as follows:

- **Sole proprietor**: A business that has one owner. Sole proprietors generally file a Schedule C to report their business income and expenses, along with IRS Form 1040.

- **Partnership**: A business with two or more owners. Partnerships generally file IRS Form 1065 to report their business income and expenses to the IRS.

- **Limited Liability Company** (**LLC**): A company with one or more owners who are not personally liable for the LLC's debts or lawsuits.

- **C-Corp**: A corporation that is taxed separately from its owners. Corporations typically file IRS Form 1020 to report business income and expenses.

- **S-Corp**: A closely held corporation that elects to be taxed under IRS Subchapter S. S-Corps typically file IRS Form 1020S to report business income and expenses.

Once you have filled in the **Company** settings, this page should resemble the one for our fictitious company, Photos by Design, shown in *Figure 3.1*:

Account and Settings

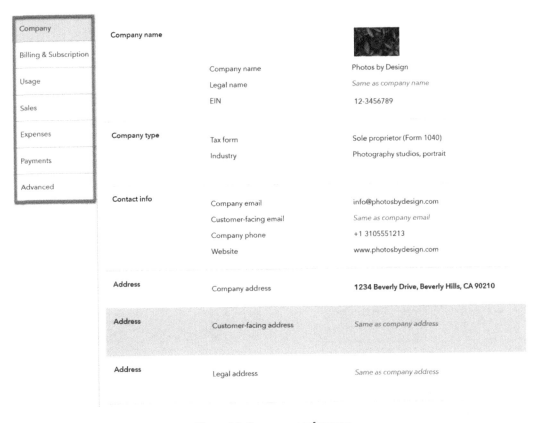

Figure 3.1: Company preferences

The information provided in the **Company** preferences can impact several areas of QuickBooks, such as customer invoices, tax forms, and documents. Therefore, it's important to complete this information in its entirety before you begin using QuickBooks to track your business activity. Next, we will explain what information you will find in the **Billing & Subscription** preferences.

Billing & Subscription settings

The **Billing & Subscription** settings provide details of the QBO plans and services you have subscribed to. Your screen should resemble the one for our fictitious company, Photos by Design, as shown here:

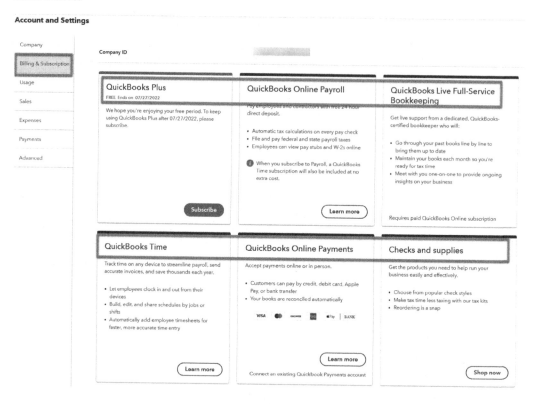

Figure 3.2: Billing & Subscription settings

A brief description of the information you will find in the billing and subscription settings is as follows:

- **QuickBooks subscription:** Your subscription status will appear in this section. In our example, we are using QBO Plus. If you are currently using a trial version, it will show you the date the trial expires. After the trial period ends, you can click the **Subscribe** button to sign up for a paid account. If you are already signed up for QBO, you will see an upgrade and downgrade button should you decide to change your subscription plan.

- **QuickBooks Online Payroll:** If you have subscribed to Payroll, the details of your payroll plan will be in this section. If you would like to sign up for a payroll subscription, click on the **Learn more** link and follow the onscreen prompts to select a payroll plan.

- **QuickBooks Live Full-Service Bookkeeping**: QuickBooks provides bookkeeping services for those small businesses that need it. You can click on this tile to learn more about the plans available.

- **QuickBooks Time**: This is a time tracking tool that integrates with QBO. If you have employees in the office or out in the field, they can clock in from any mobile device with an internet connection. Click on **Learn more** for more information.

- **QuickBooks Online Payments**: If you would like to accept online payments from customers, sign up for QuickBooks Payments services. With this service, your customers can pay their invoices online via ACH bank transfer, debit card, or credit card. Click on the **Learn more** link to sign up; note that additional fees will apply.

- **Checks and supplies**: If you write a lot of checks to pay bills, you should consider printing checks directly from QuickBooks. You can order checks from Intuit by clicking on the **Shop now** button. You can also order checks through your bank.

Now that you know how to review your subscription status and what services you are subscribed to, you need to know what your usage limits are. We will discuss what usage limits are and how they can affect your QBO subscription next.

Usage settings

A few years ago, Intuit implemented usage limits on all QBO plans. What this means is that each plan will have a maximum number of billable users, classes, locations, and accounts that you can add to the chart of accounts. The following is a brief description of these:

- **Billable users**: The total number of users you can give access to your QBO account. This includes bookkeepers, accountants, employees, and contractors.

- **Classes**: Depending on your business, a class can represent departments, office locations, or product lines. For example, our photography business could create a class for each type of event (for example, weddings, birthday parties, baby showers, and so on). One of the benefits of using classes is the ability to generate reports you can filter by class.

- **Locations**: If you have multiple locations, you can turn on location tracking in QuickBooks. One of the benefits of using locations is you can generate reports and filter by location.

- **Chart of accounts**: We discussed the chart of accounts in the *Small business bookkeeping 101* section of *Chapter 1, Getting Started with QuickBooks Online*. The chart of accounts is used to classify your day-to-day business transactions. For example, office supplies and telephone expenses are two accounts that appear on the chart of accounts.

The following is a summary table that includes the usage limits for each QBO plan:

	QBO Simple Start	QBO Essentials	QBO Plus	QBO Advanced
Classes and locations (combined)	0	0	40	Unlimited
Chart of accounts	250	250	250	Unlimited
Tag groups	10	20	40	Unlimited
Billable users	1	3	5	25

Table 3.1: QBO usage limits for each plan

Here is a brief explanation of the usage limits for each QBO plan:

- **QuickBooks Online Simple Start**: QBO Simple Start does not have the ability to track classes or locations. You can have up to 250 accounts on the chart of accounts list. One billable user and two accountant users are included in this plan.

- **QuickBooks Online Essentials**: Similar to Simple Start, QBO Essentials does not have the ability to track classes or locations. You can have up to 250 accounts on the chart of accounts list. Three billable users (that is, bookkeepers or employees) and two accountant users are included in this plan.

- **QuickBooks Online Plus**: QBO Plus allows you to track classes and locations. You can add up to a total of 40 classes and/or locations combined. Five billable users and two accountant users are included with this plan.

- **QuickBooks Online Advanced**: QBO Advanced allows you to track unlimited classes and locations. In addition, 25 billable users and three accountant users are included with this plan.

Your usage settings should resemble the ones for our fictitious company, Photos by Design, as shown in *Figure 3.3*:

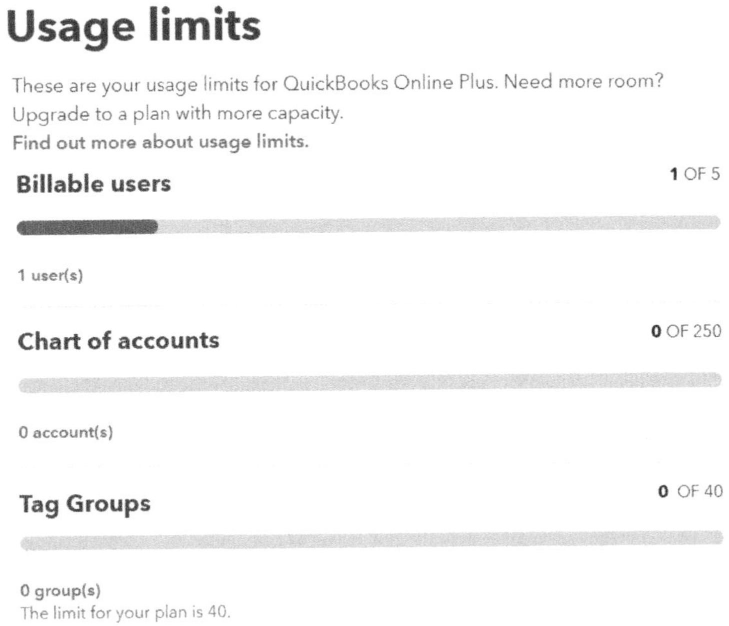

Usage limits

These are your usage limits for QuickBooks Online Plus. Need more room?
Upgrade to a plan with more capacity.
Find out more about usage limits.

Billable users

1 OF 5

1 user(s)

Chart of accounts

0 OF 250

0 account(s)

Tag Groups

0 OF 40

0 group(s)
The limit for your plan is 40.

Figure 3.3: Usage settings

As we mentioned previously, usage limits can impact the number of users you can add to QBO and the classes, locations, and accounts you add to the chart of accounts. This can have a significant effect on how much you pay for your QBO subscription if you hit the maximum usage settings and need to upgrade.

Sales settings

The **Sales** settings allow you to select and customize invoices, estimates, and sales receipt templates. In this section, payment terms are set for customers. If you have a few customers whose payment terms differ, you can customize payment terms when you add a new customer. If you offer discounts to customers or require upfront deposits, you can turn these features on here.

The following is a screenshot of the settings for **Sales**:

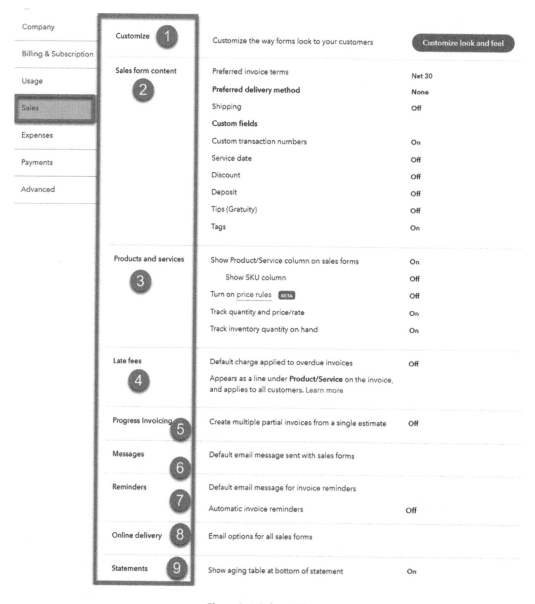

Figure 3.4: Sales settings

Here is a brief explanation of the information you can update/change in the sales settings:

- **Customize (1)**: This setting allows you to customize the look and feel of the invoices, estimates, and sales receipt forms. By clicking on the **Customize look and feel** button, you will be able to select a template design, add your company logo, colors, and font, and determine what information you would like to appear on each form.

- **Sales form content (2)**: In this section, you can select the default payment terms for most customers. For example, if the invoice due date for most customers is Net 30 days, you will make that selection in the **Preferred invoice terms** field (shown in the preceding screenshot). If you have customers that have different payment terms, you can select those terms when you add the customer to QuickBooks.

QBCU 2.3.3 If you offer customer discounts, accept deposits, or want to add custom fields, you will also turn these features on in this section. The main reason why you may want to offer customer discounts is to incentivize customers to order more, or use it as a way to reward customers who make frequent purchases. If you decide not to activate discounts now, you can always return to **Sales form content** settings and turn discounts on later on.

- **Products and services (3)**: The **Products and services** settings allow you to determine what information you would like to appear on the sales form. You can turn on **price rules**, which is a feature that allows you to set up automatic discounts for certain customers or on specific products and services. If you want to track inventory, you will need to turn on both the **Track quantity and price/rate** and **Track inventory quantity on hand** features.

- **Late fees (4)**: Create a default charge that is automatically applied to delinquent invoices.

- **Progress Invoicing (5)**: Progress invoicing allows you to bill a customer in installments. For example, imagine you have a job that is going to result in $100,000 in revenue but you are required to complete certain milestones before you can submit an invoice. Progress billing allows you to create multiple invoices for one estimate. QuickBooks allows you to run reports that will show you how much you have billed against the estimate and the remaining amount to be billed.

- **Messages (6)**: When you email invoices, sales receipts, or estimates directly from Quick-Books, you can customize the message that is included in the body of the email. You can also select whether you want the invoice to be attached to the email as a PDF document or whether you prefer the invoice details to be included in the body of the email.

QBCU 2.3.2

Below is a screenshot of the custom email message options you can choose from:

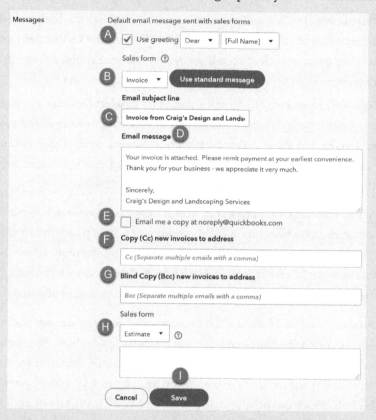

Figure 3.5: Customizing the email message for invoices, estimates, and sales receipts

To customize emails, you can choose to use a greeting (**A**), select the type of form (**B**), customize the email subject line (**C**), and customize the email message (**D**) or choose to use the standard message shown. You can have a copy of the email sent to you (**E**), send a carbon copy to someone else (**F**), and blind copy (Bcc) new invoices to multiple people (**G**). You can also customize emails for estimates and sales receipts by choosing the option from the drop-down (**H**).

After making your selections, be sure to click the **Save** button (**I**).

- **Reminders (7)**: QuickBooks allows you to send payment reminder emails to customers. You can customize the message that goes out to your customers in this section.

- **Online delivery (8)**: Online delivery allows you to select the format of all the sales forms that will go out to customers. The options are PDF, HTML, or a link to the online invoice.

The selections that are made here will affect all invoices, sales receipts, and estimates that are emailed directly from QuickBooks.

- **Statements (9)**: If you prefer to send statements to customers, you can select from two types of formats. You can have each transaction listed as a single line on the statement or you can list each transaction and the details on the statement.

Now that you know how to customize sales forms, set payment terms for customers, and turn on discounts and deposits, it's time to learn how to manage expenses. We will discuss Expenses settings next.

Expenses settings

The settings in the **Expenses** section are centered around preferences for managing bills, expenses, and purchase orders. In this section, you will determine what information you want to appear on expense and purchase forms, whether or not you want to track expenses and items by customer, and default payment terms.

The following is a screenshot of the **Expenses** settings:

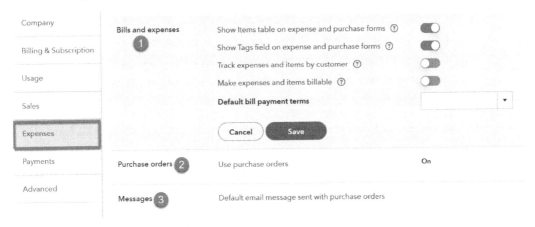

Figure 3.6: Expenses settings

The following is a brief explanation of what you can find in the **Expenses** preferences:

- **Bills and expenses (1)**: This section includes the following five options for tracking expenses:

    - **Show Items table on expense and purchase forms**: This feature is automatically turned on and it will add a *Products and services* table to your expense and purchase forms so that you can itemize your products and services.

- **Show Tags field on expense and purchase forms:** This feature is automatically turned on. If you don't use tags to track expenses, you can turn this feature off.

QBCU 3.2.1

- **Track expenses and items by customer:** This feature allows you to tag expenses with a specific customer. This is ideal for reporting purposes if you want to keep track of specific items that have been purchased but aren't billable to customers. For example, we want to track photography supplies such as paper or ink, but they are not billable to the customers of our photography business.

QBCU 3.2.2

- **Make expenses and items billable:** This feature adds a billable column on all expense and purchase forms so that you can bill customers for items you've purchased on their behalf. For example, a wedding album can be purchased on a client's behalf to put photos in as a keepsake.

QBCU 3.2.3

To see a list of unbilled expenses, you can run the Unbilled Charges report, which is located in the **Who Owes You** report group.

- **Default bill payment terms:** If most of the bills you receive have similar payment terms (for instance, Net 30), you can set payment terms for all vendors here and then change the vendor profile for those vendors whose payment terms may differ. In *Chapter 6, Managing Customer, Vendor, and Products and Services Lists*, we cover this in detail.

- **Purchase orders (2):** If you plan to create purchase orders, be sure to turn this feature on. If you don't need to create purchase orders, you can leave it turned off.

- **Messages (3):** You can email purchase orders directly from QuickBooks to vendor suppliers. This section allows you to customize the email message that your vendor supplier will receive along with the purchase orders.

Now that you are familiar with the **Expenses** settings that affect bills, purchase orders, and expenses, you can set up QuickBooks the way you need to in order to track expenses that are incurred by your business. Next, we will discuss a way for you to get paid faster by your customers by using QuickBooks Payments.

Payment settings

QuickBooks Payments allows you to accept online payments from customers in the form of wire transfers, debit cards, and credit cards. Once approved, all the invoices that you email to customers will include a payment link. Your customers can click on the link, enter their payment details, and submit a payment in just a few minutes.

To apply for a **QuickBooks Payments** account, click on the **Learn more** button shown in *Figure 3.7*:

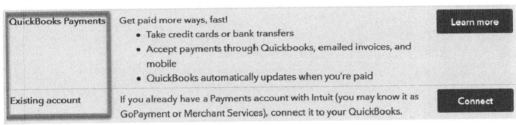

Figure 3.7: Payment settings

If you have an existing Payments account, you can connect it by clicking the **Connect** button and following the onscreen instructions.

As we mentioned previously, QuickBooks Payments makes it easier to get paid by customers in a timely manner. This will allow you to maintain a positive cash flow, which is important for your business.

Advanced settings

The **Advanced** settings page includes nine key settings: **Accounting, Company type, Chart of accounts, Categories, Automation, Projects, Time tracking, Currency**, and **Other preferences**.

The following is a screenshot of the **Advanced** settings section:

Company			
Billing & Subscription			
Usage			
Sales			
Expenses			
Payments			
Advanced			

Accounting (1)	First month of fiscal year	January
	First month of income tax year	Same as fiscal year
	Accounting method	Accrual
	Close the books	Off
Company type (2)	Tax form	Sole proprietor (Form 1040)
Chart of accounts (3)	Enable account numbers	Off
	Tips account	
Categories (4)	Track classes	Off
	Track locations	Off
Automation (5)	Pre-fill forms with previously entered content	On
	Automatically apply credits	On
	Automatically invoice unbilled activity	Off
	Automatically apply bill payments	On
Projects (6)	Organize all job-related activity in one place	On
Time tracking (7)	Add Service field to timesheets	Off
	Make Single-Time Activity Billable to Customer	On
Currency (8)	Home Currency	United States Dollar
	Multicurrency	Off
Other preferences (9)	Date format	MM/dd/yyyy
	Number format	123,456.00
	Customer label	Customers
	Warn if duplicate check number is used	On
	Warn me when I enter a bill number that's already been used for that vendor	Off
	Warn if duplicate journal number is used	Off
	Sign me out if inactive for	1 hour

Figure 3.8: Advanced settings

A brief description of what information is included in the **Advanced** settings section is as follows:

- **Accounting (1)**: In the accounting settings, you will select the first month of your fiscal year and income tax year, which may be the same. You will indicate your accounting method (for example, cash or accrual) and there is an option to close the books. Closing the books allows you to prevent any changes from being made to your financial data after a certain date. For example, once you have filed your tax returns for the year, you should enter the last day of the previous year as your closing date (for example, 12/31/2021). This will ensure that information dated 12/31/2021 and prior cannot be changed.

- **Company type (2)**: In this field, you will select the structure of your business. The common business structures are sole proprietor, partnership, limited liability, C-Corporation, and S-Corporation. Photos by Design is a sole proprietor.

- **Chart of accounts (3)**: As we discussed in *Chapter 1, Getting Started with QuickBooks Online*, the chart of accounts is a way to categorize your day-to-day business transactions. You have the option to assign account numbers to your chart of accounts list by turning on the **Enable account numbers** preference. If your business allows customers to leave tips, you can keep track of these tips in a separate account.

- **Categories (4)**: There are two types of categories in QuickBooks: classes and locations. **Classes** are generally used to track income and expenses for departments or product lines. **Locations** are used to track income and expenses for multiple locations of your business. These preferences must be turned on for you to use them.

  QBCU 1.2.4 1.2.5

- **Automation (5)**: You can save time by automating certain tasks. QuickBooks will automatically pre-fill forms based on the information you have provided in a previous transaction for a customer or vendor. You can also allow QuickBooks to automatically apply credit that's been received from vendor suppliers and bill payments.

- **Projects (6)**: The **Projects** feature allows you to keep track of all income and expenses for jobs/projects that you are working on. To view all projects, click on the **Projects** tab, which is located on the left navigation bar.

  QBCU 1.2.4 1.2.5

- **Time tracking (7)**: If you need to track hours for employees, contractors, or yourself, you can easily do this in QuickBooks. You can also bill customers for hours you've worked by transferring the hours to customer invoices.

- **Currency (8):** QuickBooks allows you to create invoices and pay bills in multiple currencies. You can do business with vendor suppliers and customers across the globe by providing invoices in their native currency. All of your financial reports can be generated in your home currency or any currency that you choose.

 Pro Tip: Once you turn on the multi-currency feature, it cannot be turned off. This is because several conversion tables are activated in the background once you turn this feature on and start using it.

- **Other preferences (9):** The **Other preferences** section involves general formatting preferences for the dates and numbers that appear throughout the program. You can also select the type of label for your customers. For example, if you are a nonprofit organization, you can select **Donors**, and if you are a real estate investor, you can select **Tenants**. This nomenclature will appear throughout the program. This preference also includes a warning if you use a duplicate check number or vendor invoice number. You should turn both of these features on to help prevent duplicate payments. A similar warning is also included when recording journal entries. A journal entry is an adjustment made to the books for transactions that are only recorded prior to closing the books, like depreciation. For security reasons, QBO will automatically sign you out after you have been inactive for 1 hour. However, you can change this setting to a maximum of 3 hours.

You now know that accounting settings affect several areas of QuickBooks. You can determine your chart of accounts structure, turn on time tracking, set your home currency, and turn on the multi-currency feature if you do business in other countries. In addition, you can turn on the projects and categories feature for additional tracking of income and expenses.

Summary

In this chapter, we have covered key information and documents required to set up a QBO account. We have also shown you how to customize the company settings, which includes billing and subscription, usage limits, sales, expenses, payments, and advanced settings. Taking the time to set up your company file will help you save time in the long run because you won't have to do it later on. Plus, you won't have to worry about customer invoices or vendor bills missing key information because your company file wasn't set up properly.

In the next chapter, we will take a look at what information you will need to convert from your existing accounting software to QBO.

This will include choosing your QuickBooks start date, the order you need to follow when bringing over historical data into QuickBooks, and various options when it comes to converting from another system to QBO.

Join our book's Discord space

Join the book's Discord workspace for a monthly *Ask me Anything* session with the author: `https://packt.link/QuickBooks`

4

Migrating to QuickBooks Online

Whether you are currently using another form of accounting software or spreadsheets to manage the books for your business, you will need to gather a few key documents and information to migrate over to **QuickBooks Online (QBO)**, a list of which we gave you at the start of the previous chapter. In addition, the date on which you decide to start implementing QuickBooks will also determine what information is required for a smooth migration. Providing all of the information required will ensure that QuickBooks is properly set up prior to you using it to track your business income and expenses. Otherwise, you could encounter inaccurate and unreliable financial statements, which will make it hard to know your business' overall health and make filing taxes difficult.

In this chapter, we will discuss questions you need to be prepared to answer before conversion regarding how you will run your business. Then, we will show you how to convert from another form of accounting software or Excel to QBO. If you are currently using **QuickBooks Desktop (QBD)**, we will show you how to convert from QBD to QBO.

In this chapter, we will cover the following five key concepts:

- Questions to ask yourself in preparation for data conversion
- Choosing your QuickBooks start date
- Converting from another accounting software or Excel to QBO
- Reasons not to convert from QBD to QBO
- Converting from QBD to QBO

The US edition of QBO was used to create this book. If you are using a version that is outside of the United States, results may differ.

Questions to ask yourself in preparation for data conversion

When setting up your QuickBooks company file, you will need to determine whether you want to bring over any data from your existing accounting program. Additionally, you need to know what features you want to use in QuickBooks. Answering the following questions will help determine what type of setup you need to manage your day-to-day business activities:

- **How much historical data do you want to bring over to QuickBooks?**

  If you are converting in the middle of the year, you need to determine whether you will bring over all of the transactions that have occurred thus far, or just start from the current month you are in. The benefit of bringing over transactions that go back to the beginning of the year is that it will allow you to run financial statements in QuickBooks for the entire year, as opposed to only part of the year. Keep in mind that it will be more time-consuming to do this, so you will need to weigh up the cost versus the benefit to determine whether or not it is worth it.

- **How much detailed information do you want to bring over to QuickBooks?**

  If you do decide to bring over the historical information for an entire year, you've got two options. First, you can enter each transaction individually into QuickBooks. Depending on how much data you have, this could be quite labor-intensive and expensive if you have to pay someone else to do it. Second, you can create a summary journal that is a lot faster than entering each individual transaction, but you will not have the details of each transaction in QuickBooks. If you have a ton of transactions, then using a summary journal is going to be the best option for you. However, if you don't have a lot of activity, then enter transactions individually.

- **Do you create estimates or proposals for existing or prospective customers?**

  If you plan to create estimates in QuickBooks, you will need to make that selection during the setup process. Once you do so, a couple of benefits are that you can easily email estimates, as well as track the status of when the estimates are approved, or not approved, by customers.

- **Do you plan to create billing statements for customers?**

  During the QBO setup process, you can select the option to create billing statements. Depending on the type of business you own, you may want to generate billing statements for customers on a weekly, monthly, quarterly, or ad hoc basis. This is common for doctor's offices and for companies that provide services to customers on a recurring basis (for example, monthly, quarterly, or annually).

- **Do you want to use invoices to bill customers?**

  If you choose to create billing statements for some customers but want to create invoices for others, you can do that in QuickBooks. Invoices are commonly used to bill customers to whom you have extended credit terms. This means that payment is not due when you provide goods and/or services. Instead, you send these customers an invoice that includes a due date, and they are expected to remit payment before or by the due date. For example, Net 30 payment terms means that the bill is due 30 days after the date on the invoice.

- **Do you want to keep track of your bills through QuickBooks?**

  During the QBO account setup process, you will need to choose whether or not you want to track and pay bills in QuickBooks. If you have a lot of bills to keep track of, you should consider entering all bills into QuickBooks. Once you enter a bill into QuickBooks, it will alert you when the bill is getting close to the due date. You can pay the bill through online banking, or you can pay the bill by writing a check directly from QuickBooks. If you don't receive a lot of paper bills, then it may not be ideal to track unpaid bills through QuickBooks. Instead, you can track bills as they are paid from your bank/credit card account.

- **Do you want to keep track of inventory through QuickBooks?**

  Inventory tracking is another feature that must be activated during the QBO account setup process. If you need to keep track of inventory purchases by tracking quantities and costs, then you need to track the inventory in QuickBooks. However, if you prefer to keep track of sales only, there is no need to turn on the inventory tracking feature in QBO.

- **Do you have employees or 1099 contractors?**

  Payroll is not automatically activated when you set up your QBO account. You will need to activate this feature and complete the setup. If you have employees who you need to track in QuickBooks, see *Chapter 15, Managing Payroll in QuickBooks Online*, on how to set up and track payroll in QuickBooks. All 1099 contractors should be set up as vendors in QuickBooks. See *Chapter 16, Managing 1099 Contractors in QuickBooks Online*, to learn how to set up and track payments to 1099 contractors.

Make sure you add them to the list of vendors that you will import into QuickBooks.

- **Do you need to track by department or location?**

  If you need to track income and expenses by department or business segment, you will need to turn on class tracking in the QBO account setup process. You can also turn on location tracking if you have more than one store or office location you need to keep track of.

Similar to the key information and documents discussed in the previous section, it's important for you to think about how you want to use QuickBooks. Answering a few simple questions can help you determine what features you need to turn on in QBO to manage your books. Another key component to getting your books set up is choosing your QuickBooks start date. We will discuss this in detail in the next section.

Choosing your QuickBooks start date

One of the most important decisions you will make is what your QuickBooks start date will be. The start date is based on how much historical information you decide to bring over from your existing accounting software into QBO. Let's take a look at a few examples:

- **Example 1**: Let's say a web designer decided to start a business in January. The start date in QuickBooks for this brand-new business would be January 1.

- **Example 2**: Let's assume it's January 2022 and you have decided to bring in data from January 1 through December 31, 2021. Your QuickBooks start date will be December 31, 2021. That way, you can bring over all 2021 balances as of this date, and transactions dated January 1, 2022 and after will be directly entered into QBO.

- **Example 3**: Let's assume it's April 16 and your tax professional has informed you that a shoebox of receipts will no longer be accepted next year and that you should start using QuickBooks as soon as possible. Since you've already filed your taxes for the previous year, there is no need to enter that information into QuickBooks. Instead, you can go back to January 1 to enter your data, or start with April 1. We recommend starting at the beginning of a month, quarter, or year to keep things simple.

After reviewing these examples, you should have an idea of how to determine your QuickBooks start date. As discussed, this is a critical decision when it comes to deciding how much historical data to bring over from your existing accounting software. If you are converting from another accounting software or Excel, we will discuss in detail how to convert your data over to QBO next.

Converting from another accounting software or Excel to QBO

There are four primary steps for converting from another accounting software or an Excel spreadsheet into QBO:

1. Complete the initial company file setup.

2. Import all of your list information for customers, vendors, and products and services. Refer to the *Importing Data into QuickBooks Online* section below for detailed instructions.

3. Import your chart of accounts list, or update the default listing in QuickBooks to match your current list.

4. Verify the accuracy of the data that has been converted.

In *Chapter 3, Company File Setup*, we covered in detail how to complete the initial company file setup.

In this chapter, we will cover the other two options you have for entering data into QuickBooks: recording details of historical data, and recording a summary journal entry of historical data. We will look at the correct order in which to enter historical transactions, and how to verify the accuracy of the data.

Recording details of historical data in QBO

As mentioned previously, the ideal method of entering historical data into QBO is to enter individual transactions. While this is more time-consuming than completing a summary journal entry, it includes all the details of each transaction.

Individual transactions must be entered in the correct order to avoid any issues. The order in which to enter historical transactions into QBO is as follows:

1. Purchase orders; bills and payments; credits from vendors; credit card charges; checks; inventory on hand

2. Employee timesheets, billable hours

3. Invoices; sales receipts; credit memos; returns

4. Customer payments; bank deposits

5. Sales taxes paid; payroll transactions

6. All banking transactions (not previously entered); credit card transactions (not previously entered); reconcile all bank and credit card accounts

It's important that you follow these steps to avoid issues later on. To help save you some time, you can import certain data into QBO.

Importing data into QBO

If you can put your data into an Excel or CSV file, you can easily import that data into QBO. Currently, you are able to import data from your financial institution, customer lists, vendor lists, chart of accounts, products and services, and invoices. Follow the steps below to import this data into QBO:

1. Click on the **gear** icon and select **Import data**, as shown in *Figure 4.1*:

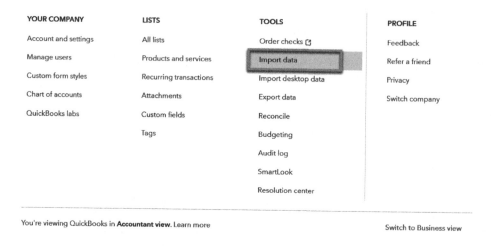

Figure 4.1: The Import data option

2. The following screen will appear:

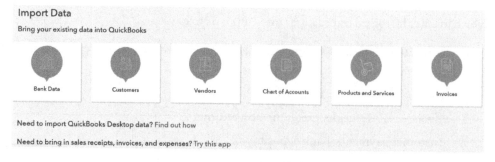

Figure 4.2: The Import Data screen

Click on the icon that represents the type of data you would like to import and follow the onscreen instructions to import the data into QBO.

For step-by-step instructions on importing bank data and a chart of accounts, refer to *Chapter 5, Customizing QuickBooks for Your Business*. Refer to *Chapter 6, Managing Customer, Vendor, and Products and Services Lists*, to learn how to import customers, vendors, and products and services data.

If you don't have the time to enter individual transactions, you can opt for recording a summary journal entry.

Recording a summary journal entry of historical data in QBO

A summary journal entry will only include lump sum total amounts. To enter balances for balance sheet accounts, you should run a balance sheet report in your current accounting system for the last day of the year for which you are bringing over data. If you would like to also bring over income and expense data, you need to print an income statement from your existing accounting system, as of the last day of the year for which you are bringing over data. Enter the totals for each account into QuickBooks.

Pro Tip: Make sure the accounts that appear on both the balance sheet and income statement reports have been created in QuickBooks before you create the journal entry. In *Chapter 5, Customizing QuickBooks for Your Business*, we show you how to create new accounts.

Follow these steps to create a journal entry in QBO:

1. Navigate to the Journal Entry screen by clicking on the **+ New** button on the left navigation bar, as indicated here:

Figure 4.3: The + New button

2. In the **OTHER** column, click on **Journal entry**, as follows:

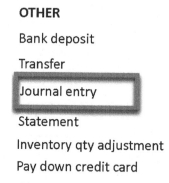

OTHER

Bank deposit

Transfer

Journal entry

Statement

Inventory qty adjustment

Pay down credit card

Figure 4.4: Navigating to the Journal Entry form

3. Complete the fields in the Journal Entry form:

Figure 4.5: The Journal Entry form

You will need to complete eight fields. Here is a brief explanation of what information to include in each field:

-   **Journal date (1)**: Enter the effective date of the journal entry. For example, you would enter the last date of the fiscal year for which you are bringing data over (for example, December 31, 20XX).

-   **Journal no. (2)**: QuickBooks will automatically assign a journal entry number, beginning with 1. However, you can start with a different number, such as 1000, and QuickBooks will automatically increment each journal number thereafter.

-   **ACCOUNT (3)**: From the drop-down menu, select the account(s) that require a debit. After all debits have been entered, you can enter the accounts that will be credited right after.

-   **DEBITS (4)**: Enter all debit amounts in this field.

- **CREDITS (5):** Enter all credit amounts in this field.
- **DESCRIPTION (6):** Enter a brief description of the purpose of the journal entry (for example, to bring over existing balances as of December 31, 2021).
- **NAME (7):** If a line item is for a specific customer, you can select the appropriate customer from the drop-down menu.

 Pro Tip: The **Name** field is used in those instances when you are making an adjustment to the accounts receivable balance for a specific customer.

Now that you know the two methods used to enter historical data into QBO, you can decide which method will work best for you. If you are a current QuickBooks Desktop user, there is some additional information you need to know. We will cover converting from QuickBooks Desktop to QuickBooks Online next.

Reasons not to convert from QuickBooks Desktop to QBO

If you are in the process of deciding whether to convert from QuickBooks Desktop to QuickBooks Online, you need to review the list of key features that you may currently use in QBD but that are not available in QBO. Additionally, you need to review the list of data that will not convert from QBD to QBO. This is important because there may be features not available in QBO that you need to run your business. You also need to determine whether you can do without the information that does not convert over to QBO. We will explore these ideas in the next two sections.

Functionality not available in QBO

QBO does not include the ability to create sales orders or manage fixed assets. Therefore, we do not recommend you convert from QBD to QBO if you need the following features:

- **Sales orders:** A form used to record and track customer orders. A sales order will commit the quantity ordered or trigger a backorder if the product is out of stock.
- **Fixed asset tracking with Fixed Asset Manager:** Fixed asset tracking includes keeping track of the cost of fixed assets purchased, and calculating depreciation and the current value of assets.

If you currently use these features in QBD, you should either find a workaround in QBO or postpone converting over to QBO if they are critical to your business.

QuickBooks Desktop data that will not convert to QBO

As we mentioned previously, QBD and QBO are two completely different products. QBD is available for Windows and iOS platforms, whereas QBO is cloud-based software. With that said, there are several data points that will not convert to QBO.

The following table provides a summary of the data that will not convert to QBO, along with a workaround in QBO. For the complete list of Desktop features and how they will (or will not) convert to QBO, read *What to expect when you switch from QBD to QBO*, an article by Intuit: `https://quickbooks.intuit.com/learn-support/en-us/convert-data-files/what-to-expect-when-you-switch-from-quickbooks-desktop-to/00/186758`.

QuickBooks Desktop data that will not convert to QuickBooks Online	Workaround in QuickBooks Online
Custom sales form templates for estimates, invoices, and sales receipts	Create new templates using the built-in template layout designer.
Bank and credit card connections, and downloaded bank activity pending review	Re-establish a connection in QBO for all bank and credit card accounts. Review all transactions prior to proceeding with the conversion.
QuickBooks users and permissions	Create each user with the appropriate permissions.
Reconciliation reports for all bank and credit card accounts previously reconciled	Since the reconciled status, **R**, will convert, do one big reconciliation, or redo them individually to recreate the reports.
Memorized reports	Re-create reports that you run often, and save them in Favorites.
Audit trail report with historical activity	Print and save the audit trail report from QBD. Refer to the backup QBD file (covered later in this chapter).
The connection to your QuickBooks Payments merchant services account	Connect your QuickBooks Payments merchant services account to QBO.
Balance sheet budgets	QBO Plus does not allow you to create balance sheet budgets. However, you can create profit and loss budgets, which only include income and expense accounts.
Closing date password and accumulated closing date exceptions	QBO will track new exceptions from the date of the conversion.

Table 4.1: Workarounds in QBO

You should determine whether the workaround is an ideal solution, or if you can run your business without bringing over certain data. After you have compiled key information, asked yourself a few questions, chosen your start date, and familiarized yourself with the data that will not convert, you are ready to convert your data. We will discuss converting QuickBooks Desktop data to QuickBooks Online next.

Converting QuickBooks Desktop data to QBO

Now that you are familiar with most of the limitations of converting data from QuickBooks Desktop to QuickBooks Online, we will walk through the steps for doing this. There are seven primary steps involved with converting data from QBD to QBO:

1. Checking the target count
2. Creating a QuickBooks Online account
3. Backing up your QuickBooks Desktop file
4. Checking for updates
5. Running the QuickBooks Desktop conversion to the QuickBooks Online tool
6. Logging in to QuickBooks Online
7. Verifying that all of your data was converted

Let's take a look at each of these steps, one by one.

Checking the target count

In order to convert your Desktop data to Online, your data limit must not exceed 350,000.

To check your target count, open your QuickBooks file. From the home page, press *F2*, which will open the **Product Information** screen. On this screen, you will find your product license number, the location of your company file, and other key data points, such as the target count.

The following screenshot includes an example of the target count on the **Product Information** screen. For this company file, the target count is 3,731, which is well below the 350,000 limit:

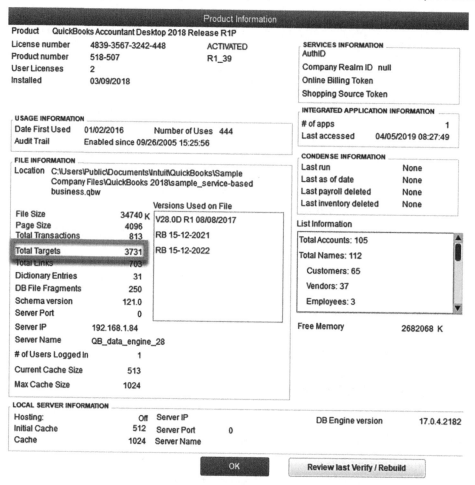

Figure 4.6: Checking the total targets

After verifying that your QuickBooks file is below the 350,000 limit, you can proceed to create a QBO account.

Pro Tip: If your file exceeds the maximum 350,000 targets, you can try to reduce the targets by condensing your QuickBooks file. Read this article by Intuit, *Condense your QBD file for import to QBO* (https://quickbooks.intuit.com/learn-support/en-us/migrate-services/condense-your-quickbooks-desktop-file-for-import-to-quickbooks/00/186240), to learn how this works.

Creating a QBO account

Prior to converting your data, you must already have a QBO account. If you don't have a QBO account, refer back to *Chapter 1, Getting Started with QuickBooks Online*, to learn how to set one up. If you have an existing account, you must convert your QuickBooks Desktop data within the first 60 days of your QBO subscription date. If you are past the 60 days, you will need to cancel your account and create a new QBO subscription.

To recap, follow these steps to create a QBO account:

1. Go to www.intuit.com.
2. Click on **Products** and choose QuickBooks.
3. Click on **Plans & Pricing**.
4. Choose one of the following versions of QBO:

   - Simple Start
   - Essentials
   - Plus
   - Advanced

5. Refer back to *Chapter 1* for a detailed guide to setting up your account.

The final step is to **log out of your account**. As we work through the *Logging into QuickBooks Online* section below, the system will prompt you to log back in when appropriate.

After creating your QBO account, you are ready to convert your data. Before converting your Desktop data, it's important to save a backup of your QuickBooks file. If there is an error with converting your data, you can always refer back to the backup file if you need to. Let's walk through backing up your QuickBooks Desktop file.

Backing up your QuickBooks Desktop file

Converting your data does not change it. However, you should always have a backup copy of your data prior to conversion.

Follow these steps to create a backup copy of your QuickBooks file:

1. Click on the **File** menu.
2. Select **Create Copy**.

3. Select **Backup copy**, as indicated in *Figure 4.7*:

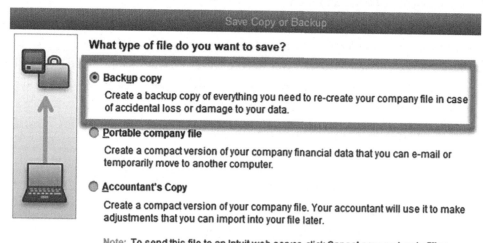

Figure 4.7: Creating a backup copy

4. Follow the onscreen instructions to save your file to a local drive.

Now that you have a backup copy of your QuickBooks Desktop data, you can proceed with the conversion. To avoid errors when converting your data, you need to ensure that you are working with the latest version of QuickBooks Desktop.

Checking for updates

Before using the conversion tool, you need to make sure you have the most recent version of the tool. For QuickBooks Pro, Premier, and Enterprise users, follow these instructions to check for updates:

1. From the **Help** menu at the very top of the home page, select **Update QuickBooks Desktop...**, as indicated here:

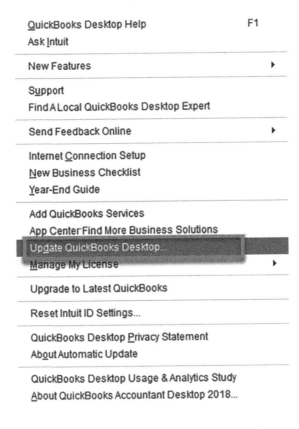

Figure 4.8: The Update QuickBooks Desktop setting

2. Next, click on the **Update Now** tab, select all the updates by putting a checkmark in the first column to select the available updates, and click **Get Updates**, as indicated in *Figure 4.9*:

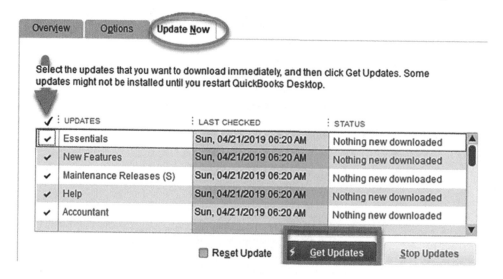

Figure 4.9: Getting all updates

Once your QuickBooks software has been updated to the most recent version, you are ready to run the QBD conversion to QBO tool. We will cover this in detail next.

Running the QuickBooks Desktop conversion to QuickBooks Online tool

There is a QuickBooks Desktop conversion tool within QuickBooks Desktop. To access it, from the **Company** menu, select **Export Company File to QuickBooks Online**, as indicated in *Figure 4.10*:

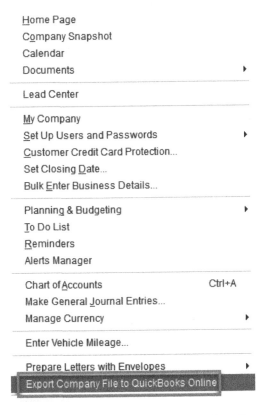

Figure 4.10: The Export Company File to QuickBooks Online option

The next screen will allow you to log in to your QBO account that you set up in the *Creating a QBO account* section. To complete the QBD data conversion, log in to your QBO account.

Logging in to QBO

After exporting your QuickBooks data file, the login screen for QBO will appear. Follow the steps outlined here:

1. Enter your secure **Email or user ID** and **Password** for your QBO account:

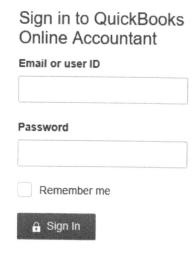

Figure 4.11: Signing into QBO

2. Follow the onscreen instructions to complete the upload. The length of time this will take will depend on how large your company file is. Once the upload is complete, you will see an onscreen notification that your data has successfully uploaded. When your data is ready, you will receive an email from the Intuit support team. This generally takes place within 1 to 24 hours, at the most.

After completing all the steps to export your QuickBooks data file to QBO, and once you have received an email from the Intuit support team confirming your data has been uploaded, the final step in converting your data is to verify that the data in your QBO file is correct.

Verifying that all of your data was converted

The final step in the conversion process is to verify that all your data was successfully imported into QuickBooks Online. To do this, you need to run a profit and loss report and a balance sheet report in both QuickBooks Online and Desktop. For instructions on how to run these reports in QuickBooks, head over to *Chapter 12, Business Overview Reports.* Be sure to use the following report parameters:

- All dates
- Accrual accounting method

Compare the reports to see if they match. If they don't, contact the Intuit support team by clicking on the **Help** menu in your QBO file and then selecting the option to chat with a support representative, or contact them by telephone. A support representative will assist you with troubleshooting any out-of-balance issues.

Once you have verified that your data was successfully converted to QuickBooks Online, you are ready to start using QBO to manage your bookkeeping. You should keep the backup file created in the previous section, in case you discover an issue later on.

Summary

We have covered the key concepts you need to know when converting your QuickBooks Desktop data to QuickBooks Online. You now know what key documents and information you need, what questions to ask yourself, how to choose your start date in QuickBooks, how to convert historical data in detail and as a summary, and the detailed steps to convert your QuickBooks Desktop data to QBO. Once all of your data has been converted and verified, you are ready for the next step.

In the next chapter, we will show you how to customize QuickBooks Online for your business.

Join our book's Discord space

Join the book's Discord workspace for a monthly *Ask me Anything* session with the author:
`https://packt.link/QuickBooks`

5

Customizing QuickBooks for Your Business

Whether you created your **QuickBooks Online (QBO)** account from scratch or you transferred your details from another accounting software program, there are some additional areas that you need to set up to further customize QBO for your business.

In this chapter, we will show you how to add, edit, and delete accounts to customize the chart of accounts for your business. We will walk through the process of connecting your bank and credit card accounts to QBO so that transactions will automatically be downloaded. By connecting your bank accounts to QuickBooks, you will reduce, if not eliminate, the need to manually enter these transactions into QuickBooks. If you need to give other users access to your QuickBooks data, you can easily do so; we will show you how to give your bookkeeper, accountant, and other users access.

The following are the key topics that will be covered in this chapter:

- Customizing the chart of accounts list
- Connecting bank accounts to QuickBooks Online
- Connecting credit card accounts to QuickBooks Online
- Giving other users access to your QuickBooks data

 The US edition of QBO was used to create this book. If you are using a version that is outside of the United States, results may differ.

QBCU
1.3.1
1.3.2
1.3.4
1.3.5

Customizing the chart of accounts list

As we saw in *Chapter 1, Getting Started with QuickBooks Online*, the chart of accounts is a list of accounts that is used to categorize your day-to-day business transactions. It is the backbone of every accounting system, and if it is not set up properly, it can result in inaccurate financial statements. One of the benefits of using QuickBooks is that you don't have to create a chart of accounts from scratch. Based on the industry that you selected when you created your QBO account, QuickBooks will include a preset chart of accounts list. You can customize the chart of accounts by adding, editing, or deleting accounts to fit your business needs. In this section, we will show you how to add, edit, delete (inactivate), and merge accounts on the chart of accounts list.

Adding a new account to the chart of accounts list

The default chart of accounts list will include a generic list of accounts used by most businesses, with a few custom accounts related to your industry. However, you will most likely need to customize the list based on your accountant's preferences or your own. For example, if you sell products and services, you may want to create an income account for each, as opposed to lumping sales for both into one account.

Go through the following three steps to add a new account to the chart of accounts list:

1. Click on the **Accounting** tab located on the left menu bar and select **Chart of Accounts**, as shown in *Figure 5.1*:

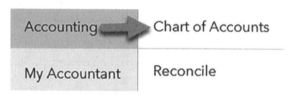

Figure 5.1: Navigating to the Chart of Accounts option

2. Click on the **New** button located in the upper right-hand corner of the screen, directly to the right of the **Run Report** button, as shown in *Figure 5.2*:

Figure 5.2: The New button

3. To create a new account, you will need to provide the account type, the detail type, the name of the account, and a description of the account, as shown in *Figure 5.3*:

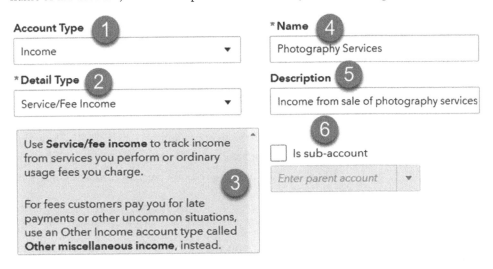

Figure 5.3: Providing account details

The following list gives brief descriptions of what information should be included in the fields that are labeled:

- **Account Type (1)**: From the drop-down menu, select the account type that the new account should be categorized as. As we saw in *Chapter 1, Getting Started with QuickBooks Online,* the five main account types are assets, liabilities, equity, income, and expenses. You will also find other account types in this list, such as fixed assets, bank, and credit card, and they should be used when appropriate.

- **Detail Type (2)**: From the drop-down menu, select the detail type that most accurately describes the type of account you are setting up. The options in the drop-down menu will differ based on the account type selected. The detail type can be used to filter reports and link to tax software.

- **Description of detail type(3)**: In this box, QuickBooks will provide you with a detailed explanation of the account type selected. This should help guide you as to which account type you should select.

- **Name (4)**: This field will automatically be populated with the detail type you selected. However, you can (and should) change it to something more descriptive, as we have done in the preceding example.

- **Description (5):** This field is self-explanatory, and should include a brief description of the types of transactions that should be posted to this account.

> **Pro Tip:** While you may be tempted to leave the **Description** field blank, we recommend that you don't. It can be useful to include a detailed description so that a bookkeeper or someone who you have hired to manage your books will know what type of transactions belong in this account. If you don't think a description is needed, copy and paste the account name into this field. That way, this field will not appear blank on reports. You can also use this field to enter more details about the accounts, such as account numbers or other useful information.

- **Is sub-account (6):** Sub-accounts are used to provide a more detailed breakdown of an account that is used for multiple types of transactions. For example, it is a good idea to create a main account for car expenses and a sub-account for repairs, registration, and gasoline. Having a detailed breakdown of each type of expense will allow you to easily run a report to see how much you have spent on each account.

> **Pro Tip:** Sub-accounts must have the same account type as the parent account. For example, the account type for the car expenses account is expenses. Therefore, all sub-accounts such as repairs, registration, and gasoline must also be set up as expenses.

4. Once you have completed all of the fields for the new account and saved it, the new account will appear on your chart of accounts list, as shown in *Figure 5.4*:

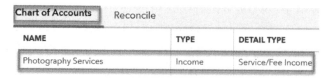

Figure 5.4: The Chart of Accounts list

As you can see, adding a new account to the chart of accounts list is pretty straightforward. If you need to add more than five accounts, you may want to consider importing new accounts instead of manually entering them.

In the next section, we will show you how to import a chart of accounts list from an Excel file.

Importing a chart of accounts list

If your accountant has given you a chart of accounts list that they prefer you to use, you can import that list into QBO. Go through the following steps to import a chart of accounts list. The sample template can be found at `https://github.com/PacktPublishing/Mastering-Quickbooks-2022-Third-Edition/tree/main/Chapter05`:

1. Format your Excel spreadsheet to include the following columns (**Account Number, Account Name, Type, Detail Type**) and save it in .csv format:

Account Number	Account Name	Type	Detail Type
112720	Checking Account - Bank of America	Bank	Checking
112721	Money Market - First National Bank	Bank	Money Market
410790	Product Sales Revenue	Income	Sales of Product Income
500780	Cost of Materials	Cost of Goods Sold	Supplies & Materials

Figure 5.5: Chart of accounts spreadsheet

2. Navigate to the **Chart of Accounts**, as indicated below:

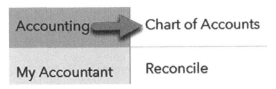

Figure 5.6: Navigating to the Chart of Accounts

3. Click on the arrow to the right of the **New** button and select **Import**, as shown in *Figure 5.7*:

Figure 5.7: Clicking Import

4. Follow the onscreen prompts to complete the import.

Next, we will show you how to edit the chart of accounts list.

Editing accounts on the chart of accounts list

On occasion, you may want to make changes to an existing account on the chart of accounts list. You can change the account name and description at any time; however, you can only make changes to the account type and detail type if you have *not* used the account in a transaction. If you have used the account and then realize that you selected the wrong account type, you will not be able to change it.

Instead, you will need to create the account again from scratch with the correct account or detail type. Once the new account has been created, you'll need to transfer the transactions that were coded to the wrong account to the new account. After transferring all the recorded transactions to the new account, you can inactivate the old account.

You can edit accounts on the chart of accounts list by going through the following steps:

1. Click on the **Accounting** tab located on the left menu bar and select **Chart of Accounts**, as shown in *Figure 5.8*:

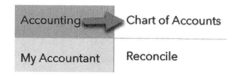

Figure 5.8: Selecting the Chart of Accounts option

2. Scroll through the chart of accounts list to find the account you want to edit. The following screenshot shows the **ACTION** column on the far right. Click on the arrow located to the right of **Run report**, as shown in *Figure 5.9*:

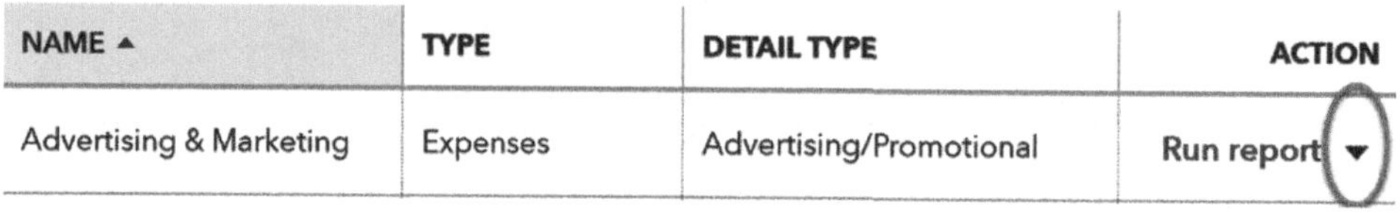

NAME ▲	TYPE	DETAIL TYPE	ACTION
Advertising & Marketing	Expenses	Advertising/Promotional	Run report ▼

Figure 5.9: Editing an account

3. On the next screen, you will see two options: **Edit** and **Make inactive**, as shown in *Figure 5.10*:

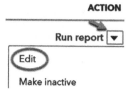

Figure 5.10: Choosing the Edit option

The following is a brief explanation of when you should edit an account and when you should make an account inactive:

- **Edit**: To make changes to the account name, account description, or sub-account, click on the **Edit** button. As we mentioned previously, the only time you can edit the account type and detail type is if you have not used the account in any transactions that you have recorded in QuickBooks. However, you can edit the name of the account and description even if an account has been used in a transaction.

- **Make inactive**: Once you have created an account in QuickBooks, there is no way to delete it. Instead, you will need to inactivate the account. When you inactivate an account in QuickBooks, it will still exist, but it will disappear from the chart of accounts list and will not appear in any drop-down lists. The primary reason for this is that if you have recorded transactions to an account that you decide to stop using, then your transactions will remain in QuickBooks. This is very important in order to maintain accurate financial records.

4. When you click **Edit**, the current account setup will be displayed. Make the necessary changes, as shown in *Figure 5.11*:

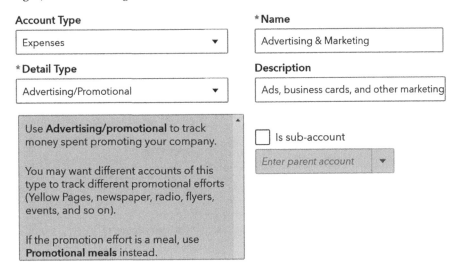

Figure 5.11: Editing the account details

 If you have not used the account in a transaction, the **Account Type** and **Detail Type** fields will also be editable.

In this section, we covered how to make changes to an existing account on your chart of accounts list. We also explained the difference between editing an account and making an account inactive. As previously mentioned, you cannot delete an account, but you can make it inactive. In the next section, we will show you how to inactivate an existing account.

Inactivating an account on the chart of accounts list

Once you add an account to the chart of accounts list, you cannot delete it; however, if you decide that you no longer want to use an account, you can inactivate the account. Inactivating an account will remove the account from the chart of accounts list and the drop-down menus, but it will still exist in the program. This will ensure that any transactions that have been recorded will remain intact, which will also ensure that you have accurate financial statements.

To inactivate an account, go through the following steps:

1. Click on the **Accounting** tab located on the left menu bar and select **Chart of Accounts**, as shown in *Figure 5.12*:

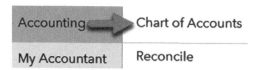

Figure 5.12: Navigating to the Chart of Accounts option

2. Scroll through the chart of accounts list to find the account you want to edit. In the **ACTION** column on the far right, click on the arrow located to the right of **Run report**, as shown in *Figure 5.13*:

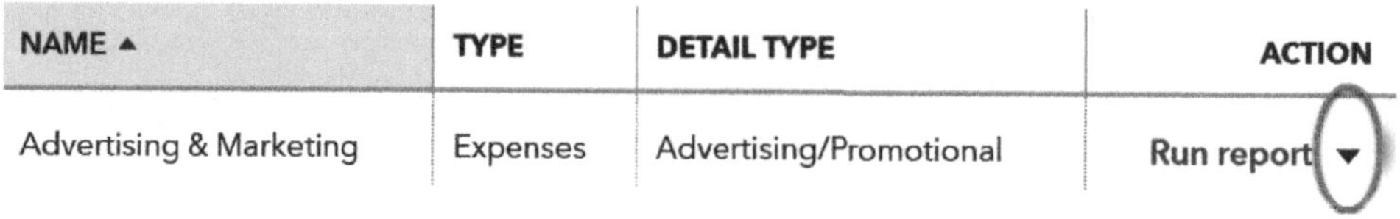

NAME ▲	TYPE	DETAIL TYPE	ACTION
Advertising & Marketing	Expenses	Advertising/Promotional	Run report ▼

Figure 5.13: Editing an account

3.   Select **Make inactive** from the drop-down arrow, as shown in *Figure 5.14*:

Figure 5.14: Making an account inactive

4.   You will then receive a message similar to the one shown in the following screenshot, asking you to confirm that you would like to inactivate the account:

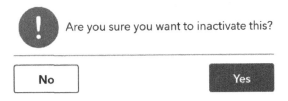

Figure 5.15: Inactivation confirmation message

5.   Click **Yes** to proceed with the inactivation or **No** to leave the account active.

Reactivating an account on the chart of accounts list

If you decide to reactivate an account that was previously made inactive, you can easily do this:

1.   From the chart of accounts list, click on the gear icon located directly above the **ACTION** column, as indicated below:

Figure 5.16: The gear icon

2. Put a checkmark in the box that says **Include inactive** so that all inactive accounts appear on the chart of accounts list, as indicated below:

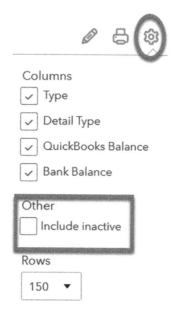

Figure 5.17: The Include inactive option

3. Next to the inactive accounts, click the link that says **Make active** to the right of the account, as shown in *Figure 5.18*:

NAME ▲	TYPE	DETAIL TYPE	ACTION
Advertising & Marketing (deleted)	Expenses	Advertising/Promotional	Make active ▼

Figure 5.18: The Make active option

Merging accounts in QuickBooks Online

An issue that you may encounter at some point is duplicate accounts. For example, you may end up having accounts with similar names like "office supplies" and "office supplies expense". This can happen if you have more than one person adding accounts to the chart of accounts, or if you have not documented a procedure for creating new accounts. However, you can easily fix this issue by merging the accounts, which will combine all of the data from both accounts into one.

Follow the steps below to merge accounts:

1. Navigate to the account list and identify the duplicate accounts:

NAME	TYPE ▲	DETAIL TYPE
Office Supplies	Expenses	Office/General Administrative Expenses
Office Supplies & Software	Expenses	Office/General Administrative Expenses

Figure 5.19: Identifying duplicate accounts in the chart of accounts

In the image above, **Office Supplies** and **Office Supplies & Software** are the same accounts.

2. Click once on the account you plan to remove and choose Edit from the Run report drop-down in the far right column. In our example, this is Office Supplies.

3. The following account information will appear:

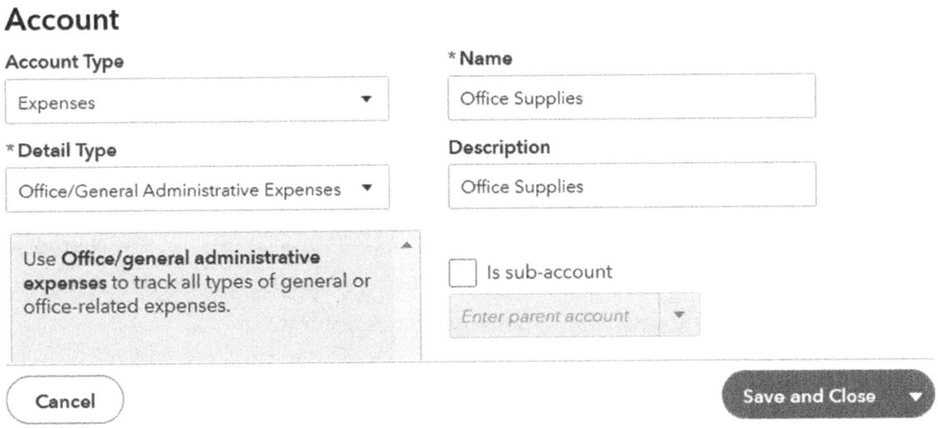

Account

Account Type		*Name
Expenses ▼		Office Supplies

*Detail Type		Description
Office/General Administrative Expenses ▼		Office Supplies

Use **Office/general administrative expenses** to track all types of general or office-related expenses. ▲

☐ Is sub-account

Enter parent account ▼

(Cancel)   Save and Close ▼

Figure 5.20: Displaying account information

Type the name of the account you wish to keep in the **Name** field. In our example, this would be **Office Supplies & Software**.

Click the **Save and Close** button.

4. The following message will appear:

Figure 5.21: Confirm that you would like to merge the duplicate accounts

Choose **Yes** and the two accounts will be consolidated into one:

Figure 5.22: Chart of accounts list with the duplicate account removed

As you can see, the duplicate account (**Office Supplies**) is no longer on the chart of accounts list. All transactions recorded for this account have been transferred to the **Office Supplies & Software** account.

You now know how to add an account, import a chart of accounts list, edit an account, inactivate and reactivate an account, and merge accounts on the chart of accounts list. The chart of accounts is the backbone of the system. Now that you know how to manage your chart of accounts list, you can be confident that your financial statements will be accurate.

In the next section, we will show you how to reduce the number of transactions entered manually by connecting your bank accounts to QuickBooks. In the long run, this will save you a lot of time.

QBCU
4.1.1

Connecting bank accounts to QuickBooks Online

One of the best features of using cloud accounting software such as QBO is the ability to connect your bank account to the software, so that your books are always up to date with the most recent deposits and withdrawals that have been made to your bank accounts.

There are two ways in which you can update QuickBooks with your banking activity. You can connect your bank account to QuickBooks so that transactions are imported automatically into QuickBooks, or you can upload transactions from an Excel spreadsheet. We will walk you through each of these processes in more detail now.

Importing banking transactions automatically

There are several benefits to importing your banking transactions automatically. First, you will save a ton of time because you won't have to enter transactions manually. Second, QuickBooks will be updated on a *daily* basis with the most recent banking activity on your account. And finally, it will be a breeze to reconcile your bank account on a daily, weekly, or monthly basis.

QBCU
4.1.2

Go through the following steps to import banking transactions automatically into QBO:

1. Select **Banking** from the left menu bar on the home page, as shown in *Figure 5.23*:

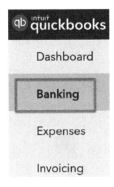

Figure 5.23: Selecting Banking

2. If you have never connected a bank/credit card account, you will get the following screen. Click on the **Connect account** button, as shown in *Figure 5.24*:

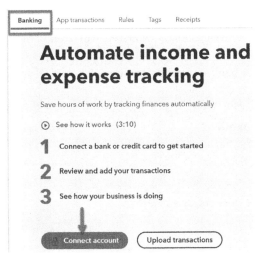

Figure 5.24: Clicking on Connect account

3. If you have connected a bank/credit card account previously, you will see the **Link account** option. Click on it:

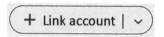

Figure 5.25: The Link account button

4. To connect your bank account, select your bank by clicking on the icon or typing the name of the bank in the search box, as shown in *Figure 5.26*:

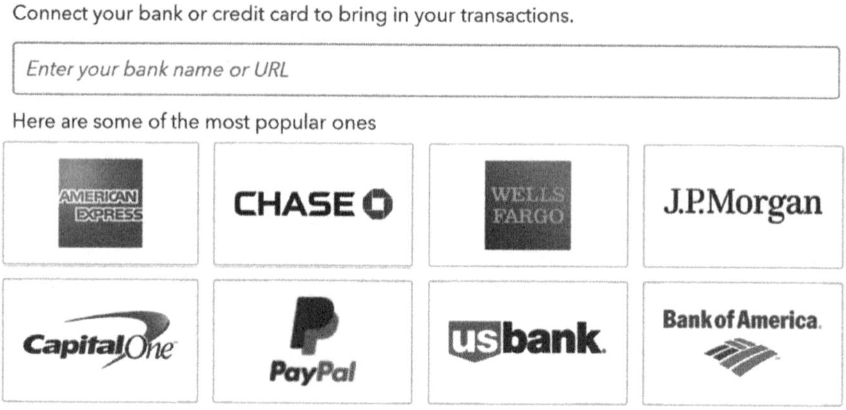

Connect your bank or credit card to bring in your transactions.

Enter your bank name or URL

Here are some of the most popular ones

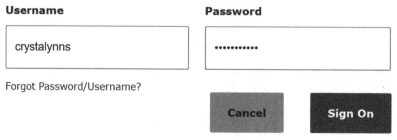

Figure 5.5.26: Selecting your bank

 If you cannot locate your bank, you will not be able to connect your account to QuickBooks; however, you can still download your banking information into QuickBooks, which we will cover in the next section.

5. Sign in to your bank account using the secure user ID and password issued by your bank:

Enter your Wells Fargo Online® username and password.

Username

crystalynns

Password

···········

Forgot Password/Username?

Cancel   **Sign On**

Figure 5.5.27: Signing in to your bank account

6. Before connecting your bank account to QBO, you will be required to consent to the terms and conditions set by your bank. This consent confirmation is documentation that proves you agree to share your financial data with QuickBooks:

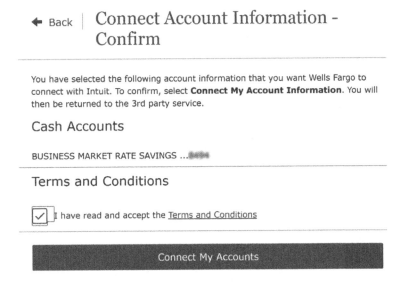

Figure 5.28: Consenting to your bank's terms and conditions

7. Follow the remaining onscreen instructions to connect your bank account to QuickBooks. If you have more than one account with the same financial institution, you will have the option to connect all bank accounts or select specific bank accounts to connect with QuickBooks.

 Pro Tip: Make sure that you only connect business bank accounts to QuickBooks and not personal bank accounts; otherwise, you will have personal banking activity co-mingled with business transactions, which is not a best practice.

You can save yourself a lot of time by connecting your bank account to QuickBooks so that your transactions automatically download. However, if your bank does not allow you to connect your account, you can still save time by obtaining an Excel CSV file from your bank so that you can upload the transactions to your QuickBooks file.

Uploading banking transactions from an Excel CSV file

If your financial institution does not integrate with QuickBooks, then you need to download your banking transactions as an Excel CSV file. Most banks allow you to download your transactions as a PDF or CSV file. Log in to your bank account and look for the **Download Transactions** option, or other data download options. If you don't see this option, contact your bank and inform them that you need your banking transactions in a CSV file so that you can download them to QuickBooks.

To upload banking transactions from an Excel CSV file to QuickBooks, go through the following instructions:

1. At the beginning of this chapter, we showed you how to add a new account to the chart of accounts list. Follow those step-by-step instructions and add your bank account to QuickBooks.

2. Your bank account setup screen should resemble the one in *Figure 5.29*:

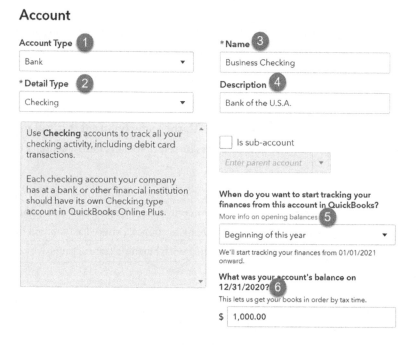

Figure 5.29: Bank account setup screen

Here is a brief explanation of how to fill in the new bank account fields:

-   **Account Type (1):** The account type will be **Bank** for all checking, savings, and money market accounts.

- **Detail Type (2):** From the drop-down, select the type of bank account you want to add. Your choices are cash-on-hand, checking, money market, savings, and trust account.

- **Name (3):** The name of the bank account belongs in this field. In our example, we have created a business checking account and named it accordingly. This will work if all of your bank accounts are at the same financial institution; however, if you have multiple bank accounts set up at different financial institutions, you should include the name of the bank along with the type of account in this field; for example, **Wells Fargo Business Checking, Bank of America Business Savings,** and so on.

- **Description (4):** You can include a brief description of the account that you are adding in this field.

- **Date to start tracking in QuickBooks (5):** From the drop-down, select the date you want to begin tracking your finances for this account.

- **Opening balance (6):** Enter the current balance in your bank account as of your QuickBooks start date from *step 5*. For example, if you are starting to use QuickBooks as of January 1, enter the balance of your bank account as of the last day of the previous period, which would be December 31 of the previous year.

 Pro Tip: It's important to have your bank statements handy as you are adding bank accounts to QuickBooks. This is to ensure that you enter the correct balance and effective dates. It will also help you to balance later on when you are ready to reconcile the account.

3. From the gear icon, select **Import Data**, which is located in the **Tools** column, as shown in *Figure 5.30*:

Tools

Import Data

Import Desktop Data

Export Data

Reconcile

Figure 5.30: The Import Data option

4. The **Import Data** screen is where you can import banking transactions, customers, vendors, a chart of accounts list, products and services, and invoices. Select the **Bank Data** option to display the setup screen, as shown in *Figure 5.31*:

Figure 5.31: The Import Data screen

5. The following screen appears. Click on **select files** to select the file that includes your bank data, as indicated below:

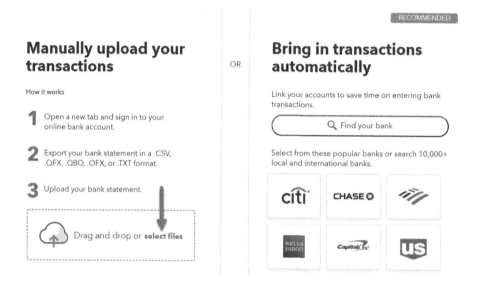

Figure 5.32: Clicking select files

The selected filename will appear in the field, as shown below:

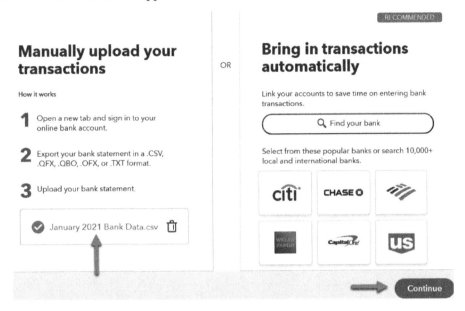

Figure 5.33: Checking the filename

6. Click the **Continue** button to proceed to the next step.

7. In this step, you will select the bank account for which you want the transactions to be uploaded to QuickBooks. Select the **Business Checking** account from the drop-down menu, as shown in *Figure 5.34*:

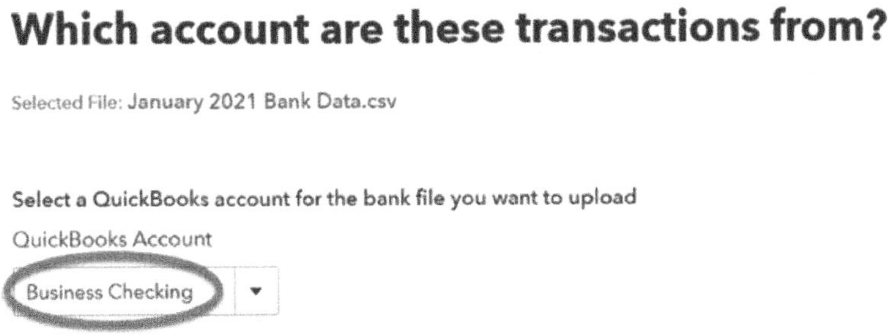

Which account are these transactions from?

Selected File: **January 2021 Bank Data.csv**

Select a QuickBooks account for the bank file you want to upload

QuickBooks Account

Business Checking ▾

Figure 5.34: Selecting the bank account

Click **Continue**.

Pro Tip: If you have more than one bank account, you will need to set up an account on the chart of accounts for each bank account and link them.

8.   The following setup screen will appear:

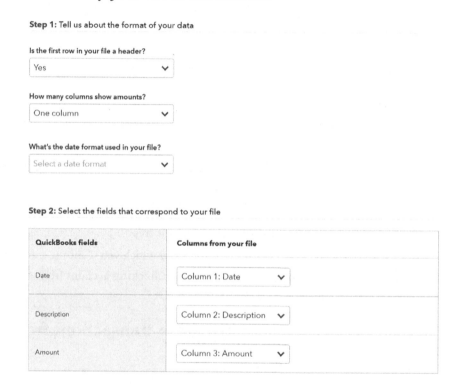

Figure 5.35: Setup screen

In this step, you will map the columns in your CSV file to a field in QuickBooks. This is a very important step to ensure that the information is entered into the correct fields in QuickBooks.

For each QBO field located on the left, select the column from your import file that includes the corresponding data, as shown in the screenshot above. There are three fields that need to be populated in QuickBooks: the transaction date, a brief description, and the transaction amount. You will need to indicate what column in your CSV file includes this information:

- **Date (1)**: From the drop-down, select the column in the CSV file that includes the date of the banking transactions. You can also select the format that the date is in (for example, mm/dd/yyyy).

- **Description (2)**: Select the column in the CSV file that includes descriptions of the transactions.

- **Amount (3)**: From the drop-down, select the column in the CSV file that includes the transaction amounts. Amounts can be formatted into one column that includes both positive and negative numbers, or into two separate columns, one for positive numbers (deposits) and one for negative numbers (withdrawals). In our example, both positive and negative numbers are formatted into one column.

Click **Continue**.

9. A preview of how your data will be uploaded to QuickBooks will appear. It's important to review the data to ensure that the correct fields are populated:

Which transactions do you want to add?

Select the transactions to import

	DATE	DESCRIPTION	AMOUNT
☐	1/4/2021	QT 921 12/31 PURCHASE GRAND PRAIRIE TX	-27.65
☐	1/4/2021	CHICK-FIL-A # 00 12/31 PURCHASE GRAND PRAIRIE TX	-7.12
☐	1/4/2021	COMET CLEANERS 12/31 PURCHASE MANSFIELD TX	-52.47
☐	1/4/2021	KROGER #0594 01/04 PURCHASE MANSFIELD TX	-14.00
☐	1/5/2021	WELLS FARGO IFI DES:DDA TO DDA ID:F209KMG2W7 INDN:CI	-700.00
☐	1/7/2021	TARGET 000 01/06 MOBILE PURCHASE MANSFIELD TX	-22.17
☐	1/8/2021	BizUnion Inc DES:DIR DEP ID:00000001 INDN:Crystalynn Shelto	2,443.04
☐	1/8/2021	VICTORIA'S SEC 01/08 PURCHASE ARLINGTON TX	-8.15
☐	1/8/2021	DISCOVER CARD Bill Payment	-339.00
☐	1/11/2021	GIV*VALENCIACHRIS 01/08 PURCHASE 661-296-4822 CA	-268.00
☐	1/11/2021	QT 921 01/08 PURCHASE GRAND PRAIRIE TX	-30.26
☐	1/11/2021	CHEESECAKE PARKS 01/08 PURCHASE ARLINGTON TX	-30.32
☐	1/11/2021	GEICO AUTO 01/09 PURCHASE WASHINGTON DC	-85.90

Figure 5.36: A preview of your data

To select all transactions for import, put a checkmark in the box circled in the above screenshot. Alternatively, you can put a checkmark next to each individual transaction you wish to import into QBO.

Click the **Next** button in the lower-right corner to proceed to the next screen.

10. On the next screen, QuickBooks will provide you with the number of transactions to be uploaded. This is your final opportunity to confirm that the data is correct. Once you confirm this, there will be no option to undo it. To proceed with the upload, click the **Yes** button, as shown in *Figure 5.37*:

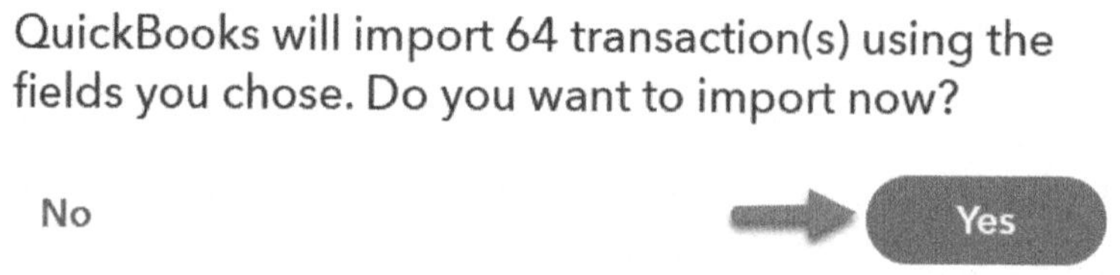

QuickBooks will import 64 transaction(s) using the fields you chose. Do you want to import now?

No   Yes

Figure 5.37: Confirming the import

11. After confirming the number of transactions to import, your transactions will be added to QuickBooks. To verify the data was imported correctly, head over to the banking center where you can see the number of transactions that were successfully imported from your CSV file, along with their dates, descriptions, and dollar amounts. In *Chapter 10, Reconciling Downloaded Bank and Credit Card Transactions*, we will show you what to do with this data after it has been imported.

Now that we know how to connect our bank accounts to QBO, let's learn how to connect our credit card accounts in the next section.

Connecting credit card accounts to QuickBooks Online

Similar to bank accounts, you can connect your credit card accounts to QBO. There are two ways that you can update QuickBooks with your credit card activity. You can connect your credit card account to QuickBooks so that transactions are imported automatically into QuickBooks. The other option is to upload transactions from an Excel spreadsheet. We will walk you through each process in more detail in the following sections.

Importing credit card transactions automatically

There are several benefits to importing your credit card transactions automatically. First, you will save a lot of time because you won't have to manually enter transactions. Second, QuickBooks will be updated on a *daily* basis with the most recent credit card activity on your account. Third, it will be much easier to reconcile your credit card accounts.

QBCU 4.1.2

Listed below are the steps required to import credit card transactions automatically into QBO:

1. Select **Banking** from the left menu bar, as shown in *Figure 5.38*:

Figure 5.38: The Banking option

2. On the following screen, you will see a link to a short video tutorial, which is a demo of how the banking center works. Click on the **Connect account** button, or the **Link account** button if you have previously connected a bank/credit card account:

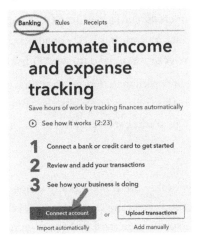

Figure 5.39: Connecting an account

3. To connect your credit card account, select your credit card company by clicking on the icon or typing the name of the financial institution in the search box, as shown in *Figure 5.40*:

Connect your bank or credit card to bring in your transactions.

Here are some of the most popular ones

Figure 5.40: Selecting your bank

 If you cannot locate your financial institution, you will not be able to connect your account to QuickBooks.

4. Sign in to your credit card account using the secure user ID and password issued by your bank.

5. Before connecting your credit card account to QBO, you will be required to consent to the terms and conditions set by your bank. This consent is used as documentation proving that you agree to share your financial data with QuickBooks.

6. Follow the remaining onscreen instructions to connect your credit card account to Quick-Books. If you have more than one account with the same financial institution, you will have the option to connect all credit card accounts or just select specific credit card accounts to connect.

 Pro Tip: Make sure that you only connect business credit card accounts to QuickBooks and not personal credit card accounts; otherwise, you will have personal credit card activity co-mingled with business transactions, which is not ideal.

After connecting your credit card accounts to QuickBooks, they will appear in the banking center. From the banking center, you can see the date of the most recent download along with a description and the amount of each transaction downloaded. If your financial institution does not allow you to connect your credit card account to QuickBooks, you will need to upload credit card transactions from an Excel CSV file.

Uploading credit card transactions from an Excel CSV file

If your financial institution does not integrate with QuickBooks, you need to download your credit card transactions to an Excel CSV file. Most banks allow you to download your transactions as a PDF or CSV file. Log in to your credit card account and look for a **Download Transactions** option. If you don't see this option, contact the credit card company and inform them that you need your transactions in a CSV file so you can download them to QuickBooks.

To upload credit card transactions from an Excel CSV file to QuickBooks, follow these instructions:

1. At the beginning of this chapter, we showed you how to add a new account to the chart of accounts list. Follow those step-by-step instructions and add your credit card account to QuickBooks.

2. Your credit card account setup screen should resemble the one in *Figure 5.41*:

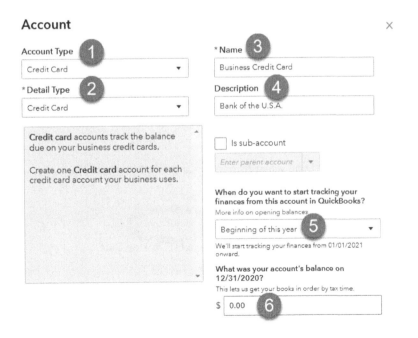

Figure 5.41: Adding account details

The following is a brief explanation of the new credit card account fields:

- **Account Type (1)**: The account type will be **Credit Card**.
- **Detail Type (2)**: This field will automatically be populated with your selection for the account type.
- **Name (3)**: The name of the credit card belongs in this field. If you have multiple credit card accounts at the same financial institution, you may want to consider entering the last four digits of each account in the **Name** field. This will make it easier when you are entering transactions and reconciling accounts.
- **Description (4)**: You can include a brief description of the account that you are adding in this field or enter the name of the account.
- **Date to start tracking in QuickBooks (5)**: From the drop-down, select the date you want to begin tracking your finances for this account.
- **Open balance (6)**: Enter the current outstanding balance due on your credit card account as of your QuickBooks start date (in *step 5*). For example, if you began to use QuickBooks as of January 1, enter the balance owed on your credit card as of the last day of the previous period, which would be December 31 of the previous year.

 Pro Tip: It's important to have your credit card statements handy as you are adding credit card accounts to QuickBooks. This is to ensure that you enter the correct balance and effective dates. If you leave this field blank, you will not be able to access this field later on; instead, you will have to make a balance adjustment directly in the credit card register.

3. From the gear icon, select **Import Data** in the **Tools** column, as shown in *Figure 5.42*:

Figure 5.42: The Import Data option

4. The **Import Data** screen is where you can import bank and credit card transactions, cus-
    tomers, vendors, a chart of accounts list, a products and services list, and invoices. Select
    the **Bank Data** option to display the setup screen, as shown in *Figure 5.43*:

Figure 5.43: The Import Data screen

5. The following screen appears. Click on **select files** to choose the file that includes your
    bank data, as indicated below:

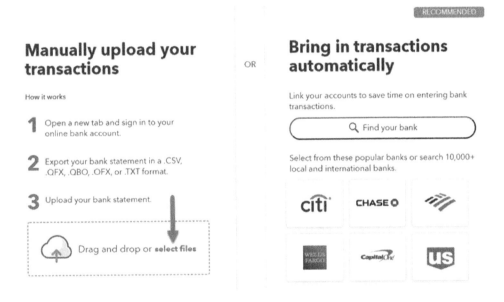

Figure 5.44: Clicking select files

The filename will appear in the field as shown below:

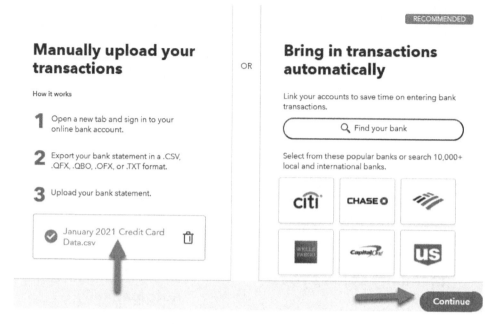

Figure 5.45: Checking the filename

6. Click the **Continue** button to proceed to the next step.

7. In this step, you will select the credit card account for which you want the transactions to be uploaded to QuickBooks. Select the **Business Credit Card** account from the drop-down menu, as shown in *Figure 5.46*:

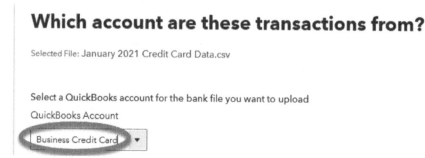

Figure 5.46: Selecting the account

Click **Continue**.

8. The following screen appears:

Let's set up your file in QuickBooks

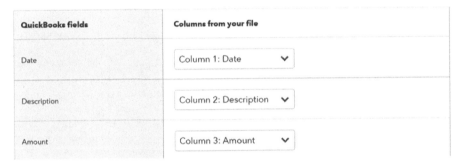

Step 1: Tell us about the format of your data

Is the first row in your file a header?

Yes ⌄

How many columns show amounts?

One column ⌄

What's the date format used in your file?

Select a date format ⌄

Step 2: Select the fields that correspond to your file

QuickBooks fields	Columns from your file
Date	Column 1: Date ⌄
Description	Column 2: Description ⌄
Amount	Column 3: Amount ⌄

Figure 5.47: Setting up your file in QuickBooks

In this step, you will map the columns in your CSV file to a field in QuickBooks. This is a very important step to ensure that the information is entered into the correct fields in QuickBooks.

For each QBO field located on the left, select the column from your import file that includes the corresponding data as shown in the screenshot above. There are three fields that need to be populated in QuickBooks: the transaction date, a brief description, and the transaction amount. You will need to indicate what column in your CSV file includes this information:

- **Date (1):** From the drop-down, select the column in the CSV file that includes the dates of the credit card transactions. You can also select the format that the date is in (for example, mm/dd/yyyy).

- **Description (2)**: Select the column in the CSV file that includes descriptions of the transactions.
- **Amount (3)**: From the drop-down, select the column in the CSV file that includes the transaction amounts. Amounts can be formatted into one column that includes both positive and negative numbers or into two separate columns, one for positive numbers (credit card charges) and one for negative numbers (credit card payments and credits).

Click **Continue**.

9. On the next screen is a preview of how your data will upload to QuickBooks. It's important to review the data to ensure that the correct fields are populated.

Which transactions do you want to add?

Select the transactions to import

	DATE	DESCRIPTION	AMOUNT
☐	1/4/2021	QT 921 12/31 PURCHASE GRAND PRAIRIE TX	-27.65
☐	1/4/2021	CHICK-FIL-A # 00 12/31 PURCHASE GRAND PRAIRIE TX	-7.12
☐	1/4/2021	COMET CLEANERS 12/31 PURCHASE MANSFIELD TX	-52.47
☐	1/4/2021	KROGER #0594 01/04 PURCHASE MANSFIELD TX	-14.00
☐	1/5/2021	WELLS FARGO IFI DES:DDA TO DDA ID:F209KMG2W7 INDN:CI-	700.00
☐	1/7/2021	TARGET 000 01/06 MOBILE PURCHASE MANSFIELD TX	-22.17
☐	1/8/2021	BizUnion Inc DES:DIR DEP ID:00000001 INDN:Crystalynn Shelto	2,443.04
☐	1/8/2021	VICTORIA'S SEC 01/08 PURCHASE ARLINGTON TX	-8.15
☐	1/8/2021	DISCOVER CARD Bill Payment	-339.00
☐	1/11/2021	GIV*VALENCIACHRIS 01/08 PURCHASE 661-296-4822 CA	-268.00
☐	1/11/2021	QT 921 01/08 PURCHASE GRAND PRAIRIE TX	-30.26
☐	1/11/2021	CHEESECAKE PARKS 01/08 PURCHASE ARLINGTON TX	-30.32
☐	1/11/2021	GEICO AUTO 01/09 PURCHASE WASHINGTON DC	-85.90

Figure 5.48: Checking your data

Click the **Next** button to proceed.

10. On the next screen, QuickBooks will provide you with the number of transactions to be uploaded. This is your final opportunity to confirm that the data is correct. Once you confirm this, there will be no option to undo it. To proceed with the upload, click the **Yes** button, as shown in the following screenshot:

QuickBooks will import 64 transaction(s) using the fields you chose. Do you want to import now?

No   Yes

Figure 5.49: Confirming the import

After confirming the number of transactions to import, your transactions will be added to Quick-Books. To verify the data was imported correctly, head over to the banking center where you should see the dates, descriptions, and number of transactions that were successfully imported from your CSV file.

Giving other users access to your QuickBooks data

QBCU
1.1.4

The ability to give other users access to your data is one of the many benefits of using QBO. With the exception of QBO Advanced, which includes three accountant users, the other QBO subscriptions include access for two accountant users and access for one or more additional users. There are five types of users that you can create in QBO:

- Standard user
- Company administrator
- Reports-only
- Time tracking
- Accountant

We will discuss each of these in more detail in the following subsections.

Standard user

You can give the standard user full or limited access to your QBO data, excluding administrative privileges. You can choose to give the standard user full access, access to customers and vendors, access to customers only, or access to vendors only.

Go through the following steps to create a standard user:

1. From the gear icon, select **Manage Users** in the **Your Company** column, as shown in *Figure 5.50*:

Your Company

Account and Settings

Manage Users

Custom Form Styles

Chart of Accounts

QuickBooks Labs

Figure 5.50: The Manage Users option

2. Click on the **Add user** button:

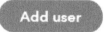

Figure 5.51: The Add user button

3. Click on **Standard user**:

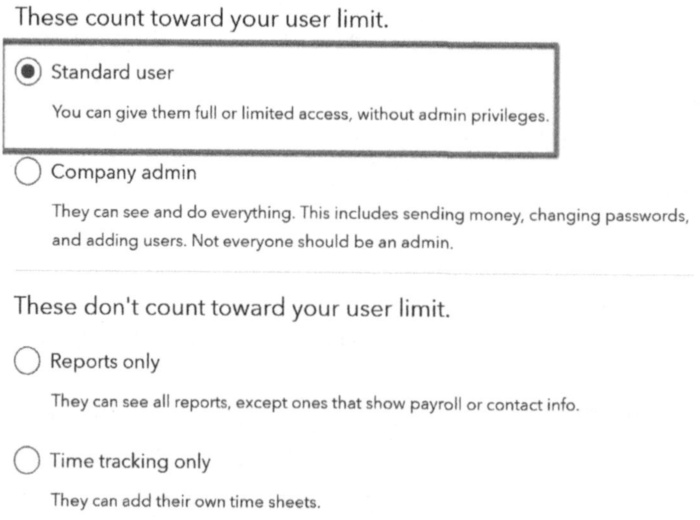

These count toward your user limit.

◉ Standard user

You can give them full or limited access, without admin privileges.

◯ Company admin

They can see and do everything. This includes sending money, changing passwords, and adding users. Not everyone should be an admin.

These don't count toward your user limit.

◯ Reports only

They can see all reports, except ones that show payroll or contact info.

◯ Time tracking only

They can add their own time sheets.

Figure 5.52: Choosing a user type

A standard user will count toward the total number of users included in your QBO subscription. To recap, the following is a summary of the number of users that are included in each plan:

- QuickBooks Online Simple Start: 2 accountants, 1 user
- QuickBooks Online Essentials: 2 accountants, 3 users
- QuickBooks Online Plus: 2 accountants, 5 users
- QuickBooks Online Advanced: 3 accountants, 25 users

4. Click the **Next** button in the lower right corner.

5. The following is a snapshot of the access rights you can choose from: **All**, **None**, or **Limited**:

Figure 5.53: Selecting access rights for the user

Selecting **All** access rights gives the user the ability to manage all customers, sales, vendors, and purchase transactions. **Limited** access rights allow you to give someone access to customers and/or vendor transactions.

The following is a snapshot of the access rights for **Customers**:

Figure 5.54: Access rights for customers

Limited customer access rights give the user the ability to manage all customers and sales transactions. This level of access would be ideal for an accounts receivable clerk who only needs access to customers and sales.

The following is a snapshot of the access rights for **Vendors**:

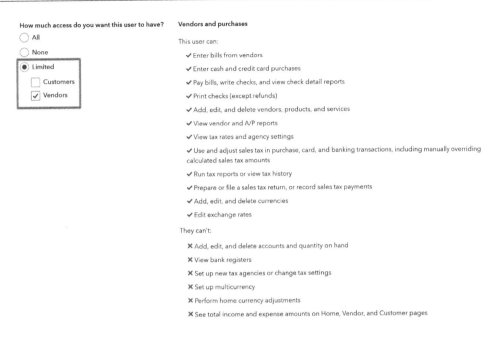

Figure 5.55: Access rights for vendors

Limited vendor access rights give the user the ability to manage all vendor and purchasing transactions. This level of access would be ideal for an accounts payable clerk who needs access to vendors and purchasing transactions.

6. Once you have specified how much access you want the user to have, click **Next** to complete the steps for adding a standard user.

The standard user category is ideal for users who need access to customers and vendor transactions. All-access rights are ideal for someone who manages accounts payable or accounts receivable.

Company administrator

The company administrator role includes access to every aspect of QuickBooks. This includes adding new users, changing passwords, and having control of your QBO subscription. Because there are no limitations to what this user can do, we recommend that you limit this role to owners of the business, IT personnel, or an officer of the company. Similar to the standard role, the company administrator role counts toward your user limit. To add a company administrator, follow *steps 1* and *2* in the *Standard user* section. In *step 3*, select **Company admin** and follow the onscreen prompts to complete the setup.

Reports-only user

The reports-only role is very limited. This role can generate just about any report in QuickBooks except payroll or vendor and customer contact information; however, the reports-only user cannot add, edit, or change any QuickBooks data. They also do not have the ability to view anything outside of reports. This role is ideal for a partner who wants to periodically review reports but has no day-to-day responsibilities. Unlike the standard and company admin roles, the reports-only role does not count toward your user limit, which means you can give reports-only access to an unlimited number of users. To add a reports-only user, follow *steps 1* and *2* in the *Standard user* section. In *step 3*, select **Reports only** and follow the onscreen prompts to complete the setup.

Time tracking user

Similar to the reports-only role, the time tracking user role is also very limited. This role is limited to entering timesheets. It is ideal for employees and contractors who don't need access to any other areas of QuickBooks. Similar to the reports-only role, the time tracking user does not count toward your user limit. This means that you can add an unlimited number of time tracking users. To add a time tracking user, follow *steps 1* and *2* in the *Standard user* section. In *step 3*, select **Time tracking only** and follow the onscreen prompts to complete the setup.

Accountant user

Each QBO plan includes at least two accountant users, at no additional cost. The level of access the accountant user has is identical to that of the company administrator. Accountant users can access all areas of QuickBooks.

This includes adding users, editing passwords, and managing your QuickBooks subscription. You should be extremely careful with who you give this level of access to; ideally, it should be limited to your CPA, tax preparer, or bookkeeper.

Go through the following steps to invite an accountant to access your QuickBooks data:

1. Click on the gear icon and select **Manage Users** from the company info column, as shown in *Figure 5.56*:

Figure 5.56: The Manage Users option

2. On the **Manage users** page, click on **Accounting firms**, as shown in *Figure 5.57*:

Figure 5.57: The Accounting firms tab

3. The following screen appears. Type your accountant's email address in the field and click the **Invite** button, as shown in *Figure 5.58*:

Figure 5.58: Inviting your accountant to your QBO account

4. Your accountant will receive an email inviting them to access your QBO account. They will need to accept the invitation and create a secure password. Their user ID will be the email address that you entered in the screenshot above.

You should now have a better understanding of the five types of users you can set up in Quick-Books (standard, company admin, reports-only, time tracking only, and accountant). Using the detailed information we have provided on the level of access each user has, you can start inviting your accountant, bookkeeper, and other users to access your QuickBooks data.

Summary

In this chapter, we showed you how to customize the chart of accounts by adding, editing, deleting, and merging accounts. We covered how to connect your bank and credit card accounts to QuickBooks so that transactions are automatically downloaded into QuickBooks. We also covered how to import banking transactions into QuickBooks from a CSV file.

Finally, we showed you how to give other users, such as a bookkeeper, partner, or CPA, full or limited access to your QuickBooks data. By now, you should know how to manage your chart of accounts, bank, and credit card accounts, and how to add additional users.

In the next chapter, we will show you how to manage customers, vendors, and products and services in QBO. This will include how to add, edit, and inactivate new customers, vendors, and products and services.

Join our book's Discord space

Join the book's Discord workspace for a monthly *Ask me Anything* session with the author:
https://packt.link/QuickBooks

6

QBCU
1.3.1
1.3.2
1.3.3
1.3.4

Managing Customer, Vendor, and Products and Services Lists

Now that you've created your company files, it's time to add the people you do business with on a regular basis. This includes your customers to whom you sell your products and services, and the vendors from whom you purchase services and supplies. We will also cover how to create your products and services list in QuickBooks Online so that you can keep track of your sales.

In this chapter, we will cover the following key concepts:

- Managing customer lists in QuickBooks Online
- Managing vendor lists in QuickBooks Online
- Managing products and services lists in QuickBooks Online

By the end of this chapter, you will understand how to add, edit, delete, and merge customers, vendors, and products and services that you sell.

 The US edition of QBO was used to create this book. If you are using a version that is outside of the United States, results may differ.

Managing customer lists in QuickBooks Online

A customer is anyone that you sell products or services to. A customer can be an individual or a business.

Some of the information QuickBooks Online allows you to keep track of in relation to customers includes contact information, such as their telephone number and email address, payment terms, invoicing, and payment history. You can enter customer information manually or import it from an Excel spreadsheet. If you need to make changes to the contact information for a customer, you can do so easily. If you stop doing business with a customer, you can make customers inactive so that they no longer appear in the customer listing. You can also merge customers if you have duplicates. In this section, we will show you how each of these works, beginning with manually adding customers.

Manually adding customers in QuickBooks Online

In order to add new customers to **QuickBooks Online (QBO)**, you need to have the basic contact details about your customer. This includes their company name, billing address, business telephone number, and the first and last name of the primary contact. You should also know what payment terms you will extend to customers (for example, net 30 days or net 60 days).

Follow these steps to add a new customer in QuickBooks Online:

1. Navigate to **Customers** by selecting **Sales** from the left menu bar and then **Customers**, as shown in *Figure 6.1*:

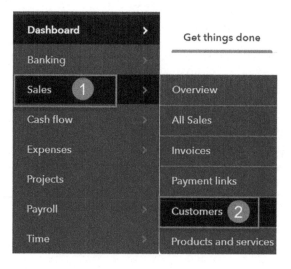

Figure 6.1: Navigating to Customers

2. The following screen will appear:

Figure 6.2: The Add customer manually button

Click on the **Add customer manually** button.

3. Fill in the fields on the **Customer information** screen, as shown in *Figure 6.3*:

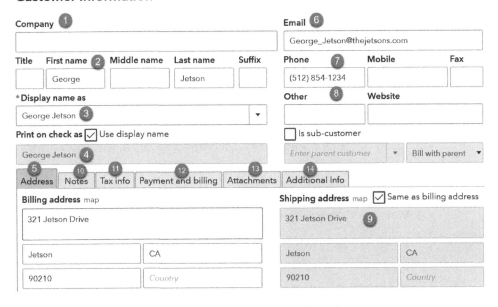

Figure 6.3: Filling in customer information

The following is a brief description of the 14 fields of information you can enter for new customers; the only required field is the **Display name as** field:

- **First name** and **Last name (1)**: If the customer is an individual, enter their first and last names in these fields. If the customer is a business, leave these fields blank.

- **Company (2)**: If the customer is a business, enter the business name in this field. If the customer is an individual, leave this field blank.

QBCU 2.1.1

- **Display name as (3)**: There is no need to input anything in this field; it will automatically be populated with the information you entered in the **Company** or **First name** and **Last name** fields. This field is important because the information will be displayed in the customer list found in the Customer center.

- **Print on check as (4)**: Similar to the **Display name as** field, this field will automatically be populated with the information that you entered in the **Company** or **First name** and **Last name** fields. If you need to change the payee name, simply remove the checkmark above this field and enter the name you would like to appear on checks.

QBCU 2.1.2

- **Address (5)**: Enter the address where your customers would like their invoices to be mailed to and/or where correspondence should be sent. Even if you plan to email all the invoices and other correspondence, we recommend that you keep an address on file for all of your customers. The address entered in the **Billing address** field will automatically be copied to the **Shipping address** field. This can be edited if necessary. The billing address will be used to mail invoices to customers and the shipping address is where products are shipped, if applicable.

- **Email (6)**: Enter the business email address for customers in this field.

- **Phone (7)**: Enter the business telephone number for customers in this field.

- **Other (8)**: Enter an additional contact phone number in the **Other** field.

- **Website (9)**: Enter the website address for the business if you have one.

QBCU 2.1.5

- **Is sub-customer (10)**: If you have more than one job or project you are working on for the same customer, you can create sub-customers to keep track of the income and expenses for each job separately. This will allow you to easily run reports by sub-customer (job, project) so that you can see the profitability of each one.

QBCU
2.1.5

- **Is sub-customer (11)**: The field to the right of **Is sub-customer** allows you to select how you would like to bill the customer. If you have a different bill to address for jobs, you can choose to bill the sub-customer. Otherwise, you can choose to invoice the parent customer for the job.

- **Notes (12)**: This field can be used to enter additional information about your customers, such as any preferences they have, or even to document previous incidents or issues. This information is for internal use only and is not visible to the customer.

QBCU
2.1.4

- **Tax info (13)**: For tax-exempt customers, you will mark the box that says **Tax exempt**. In addition, you should request a copy of their resale certificate and enter the resale number in the field. This will cover you if you ever have a sales tax audit and need to provide supporting information on why you did not charge a customer sales tax. For customers who are subject to sales tax, you will select the tax rate that is applicable to them.

- **Payment and billing** (14): There are four fields in this section: **Preferred payment method**, **Preferred delivery method**, **Payment terms**, and **Opening A/R balance**.

Let's take a look at the options we have here:

  - **Preferred payment method**: Select the preferred method by which the customer likes to make a payment. If it's a credit card, you can enter the credit card details and keep them on file for future payments. However, you must be **PCI compliant** (`https://www.investopedia.com/terms/p/pci-compliance.asp`) when it comes to sensitive information such as this.

  - **Preferred delivery method**: Select the preferred manner in which the customer likes to receive invoices (for example, US mail or email).

QBCU
2.1.3

  - **Payment terms**: This is the number of days a customer has to pay an invoice. From the drop-down, select the payment terms for your customer. The most common payment term is net 30, which means invoices are due 30 days after the invoice date. It's important that you select payment terms for all your customers so that QuickBooks can alert you when invoices are due or past due. Staying on top of unpaid invoices is the key to maintaining a positive cash flow.

- **Opening A/R balance**: Generally, you wouldn't use this field unless converting from another accounting software. This field is useful for recording the existing accounts receivable balance that customers have with you at the time of converting from your old accounting system to QuickBooks. However, if you plan to enter unpaid invoices into QuickBooks, leave this field blank.

- **Language (15)**: From the drop-down, you can select the language you would like to invoice customers in. Currently, the choices are English, French, Spanish, Italian, Chinese (Traditional), and Portuguese (Brazil).

- **Attachments (16)**: You can store important documents such as contracts, engagement letters, or proposals in QuickBooks. Simply scan the document into your computer and attach it to the customer with whom it is associated.

- **Additional info (17)**: There is a field called **Customer Type** in this section. If you need to categorize your customers into different types (for example, wholesaler, retailer), you can create custom types and assign each customer to a type. This will allow you to run reports and filter by customer type to get detailed information, such as sales by customer type.

If you have more than a handful of customers to add to QuickBooks, I recommend you put the customer information into an Excel spreadsheet and import the data into Quickbooks.

Importing customers into QuickBooks Online

You can import all of your customer details from a CSV file into QuickBooks. This template can be found here: `https://github.com/PacktPublishing/Mastering-Quickbooks-2022-Third-Edition/blob/main/Chapter06/QuickBooks_Online_Customer%20Import%20Template.xls`.

Follow these steps to import customers into QuickBooks Online:

1. Navigate to **Customers** by selecting **Sales** from the left-hand menu bar and then **Customers**, as shown in *Figure 6.4*:

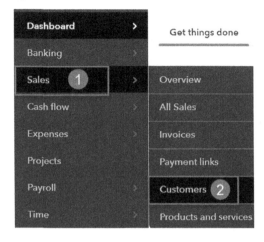

Figure 6.4: Navigating to Customers

2. Click the drop-down arrow next to the **New customer** button located in the upper-right corner and select **Import customers**, as shown in *Figure 6.5*:

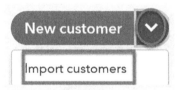

Figure 6.5: The Import customers option

3. On the **Import customers** screen, click the **Browse** button to upload the CSV file from your computer, as shown in *Figure 6.6*:

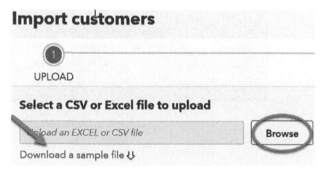

Figure 6.6: Uploading a CSV or Excel file

You can click on the blue link to download the sample file (shown in the preceding screen-shot). This file includes all of the fields of information you can upload for customers. Save this file and use it as your template.

4. Follow the onscreen instructions to import your customer data into QBO.

A common error made when importing data is the use of special characters. QuickBooks will not accept the use of special characters (for example, &, !, $), so be sure to avoid doing this.

Making changes to existing customers in QuickBooks Online

There may be times when you need to correct or update a customer's information. For example, if a customer's address changes or their primary contact changes, you will need to update your records with the new information. Updating customer information is easy to do in QuickBooks – all you need to do is navigate to the **Customers** center and select the customer that you need to make changes to.

Follow these steps to edit an existing customer in QuickBooks Online:

1. Navigate to **Customers** by selecting **Sales** from the left-hand menu bar and then **Customers**, as shown in *Figure 6.7*:

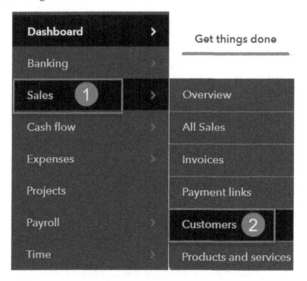

Figure 6.7: Navigating to Customers

2. The detailed customer record will appear on the next screen. Click on the **Customer Details** tab and then the **Edit** button to make changes:

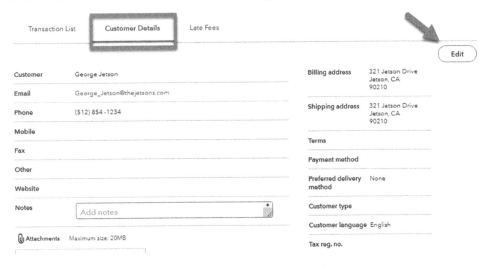

Figure 6.8: Editing customer details

You can update the information you have on file for your customers at any time. Having up-to-date information will ensure that invoices, sales receipts, and other documents contain the most recent contact information, such as billing and shipping address information, on file.

Inactivating customers in QuickBooks Online

Unlike QuickBooks Desktop, which allows you to delete customers, vendors, or products as long as you have *not* used them in a transaction, you cannot delete customers, vendors, or products in QBO. However, similar to accounts on the chart of accounts, you can inactivate customers, vendors, and products, which will keep the existing transactions recorded in QuickBooks, but "hide" the customer, vendor, or item from the drop-down list.

Follow these steps to inactivate customers in QuickBooks Online:

1. Navigate to **Customers** by selecting **Sales** from the left-hand menu bar and then **Customers**, as shown in *Figure 6.9*:

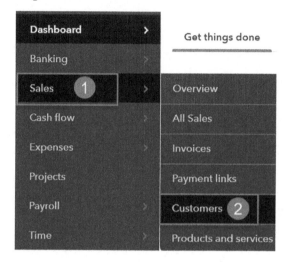

Figure 6.9: Navigating to Customers

2. Put a checkmark next to the customer you want to inactivate, click the arrow next to **Batch actions**, and select **Make inactive**, as shown in *Figure 6.10*:

Figure 6.10: The Make inactive option

Similar to accounts and customers, you can inactivate vendors and items that have been used in a transaction from their drop-down lists. This action is called **Make inactive** and it will prevent someone from selecting customers, vendors, and items you no longer wish to use, while preserving the historical transactions that have been recorded for each customer, vendor, and item at the same time. We will cover how to make vendors and items inactive later on in this chapter.

Pro Tip: To review the steps we have covered in this section, watch this Intuit video tutorial, *How to add customers to QuickBooks*: `https://www.youtube.com/watch?v=49yRB6zgBg4`.

Merging customers in QuickBooks Online

A common issue that you may encounter is duplicate customers. If you have more than one person setting up customers in QuickBooks or you don't have an established way of adding new customers, you will have this issue. The best way to avoid having duplicate customers is to establish a specific process for adding new customers. For example, have only one person who is responsible for adding customers in QuickBooks and establish whether you will enter customers by first name, last name, or last name, first name.

If you do encounter duplicate customers, you can combine the information entered for the two customers to create one customer profile.

Follow the steps below to merge customers:

1. Navigate to the **Customer** center and identify the duplicate customers:

CUSTOMER ▲ / COMPANY	PHONE	OPEN BALANCE	ACTION
Astro Jetson Astro Jetston & Associates	(818) 678-2345	$0.00	Create invoice ▼
Elroy Jetson ✉ Elroy Jetson, Inc	(818) 876-5432	$0.00	Create invoice ▼
George Jetson ✉	(512) 854 -1234	$21.90	Receive payment ▼
Jane Jetson ✉ Jane Jetson Industries	(818) 234-5678	$0.00	Create invoice ▼
Jetson, Astro		$0.00	Create invoice ▼

Figure 6.11: Identifying duplicate customers in the Customer center

In the screenshot above, **Astro Jetson** and **Jetson, Astro** are the same customer. Since the owner would like all customer information entered as first name, last name, the customer profile we want to keep is the one at the top of the list, **Astro Jetson**.

2. Click once on the customer profile you plan to remove. In our example, this is **Jetson, Astro**.

3. The following appears once we click on **Jetson, Astro**:

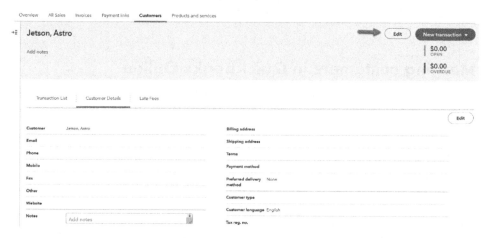

Figure 6.12: Viewing customer information

Click the **Edit** button as indicated above.

4. The **Customer information** screen will appear:

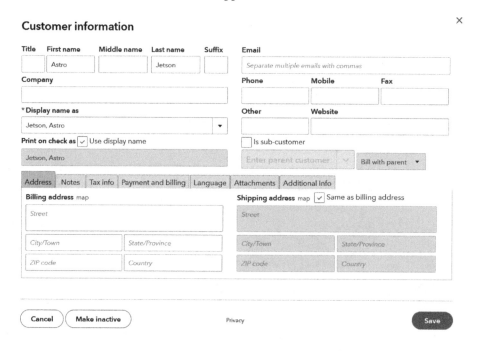

Figure 6.13: Editing information for an existing customer

Click once in the **Display name as** field and type the name exactly as it appears in the customer profile that you wish to keep. In our example, this would be **Astro Jetson**, as shown below:

Figure 6.14: Editing the Display name as field

Click the **Save** button in the lower-right corner.

5. The following message will appear:

Figure 6.15: Confirming the merging of customers

Click **Yes** and the customer profiles will be combined into one:

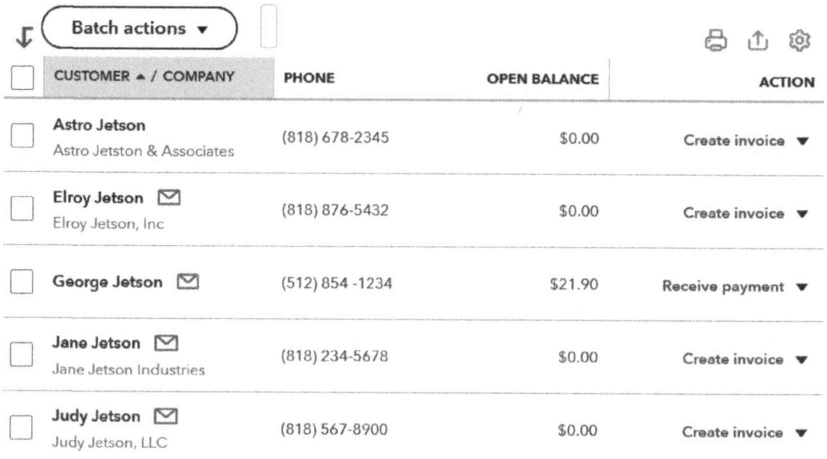

Figure 6.16: The Customer center with both profiles combined

As you can see, the duplicate profile (Jetson, Astro) is no longer on the customer list. All of the transactions recorded for that customer have been moved to the **Astro Jetson** profile.

In this section, we have shown you how to manually add customers, how to import customers, how to edit customer information, how to inactivate customers, and how to merge customers. In the next section, we will show you how to add, import, edit, inactivate, and merge vendors.

Managing vendor lists in QuickBooks Online

A vendor is an individual or a business that you pay. Vendors can be 1099 contractors, utility companies, or businesses you purchase products from. Similar to customers, you can keep track of all vendor information, such as the company's address, telephone number, email address, and federal tax ID number for 1099 reporting. 1099 reporting is required for contractors who you have paid $600 or more to within a calendar year.

In this section, we will show you how to add new vendors, edit existing vendors, inactivate vendors, and merge vendors in QuickBooks.

Manually adding vendors in QuickBooks Online

To add new vendors to QBO, you need to have each vendor's contact details. This includes a business telephone number, remit to address, email address, and tax ID number (or social security number) for 1099 vendors. You can also enter the payment terms your vendor has extended to you. Entering these payment terms will allow QuickBooks to remind you when bills are due or past due.

Follow these steps to manually add vendors in QuickBooks Online:

1. Navigate to **Vendors** by clicking on **Expenses** on the left-hand menu bar and selecting **Vendors**, as shown in *Figure 6.17*:

Figure 6.17: Selecting Vendors

2. Click the **New vendor** button located in the upper-right corner, as shown in *Figure 6.18*:

Figure 6.18: The New vendor button

If this is the first time you are accessing the vendor center, you will see the option to **Add vendor manually** instead of the **New vendor** button.

3. Fill in the fields in the **Vendor Information** window, as shown in *Figure 6.19*:

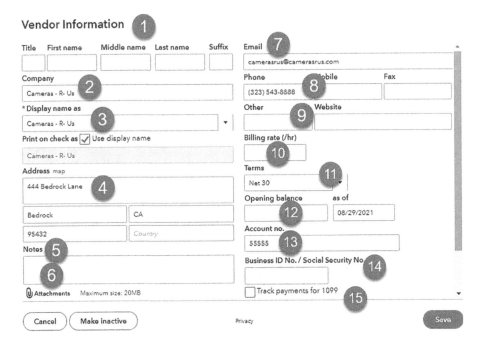

Figure 6.19: Filling in Vendor Information

The following is a brief description of the 15 fields of information you can enter for new vendors:

- **First name** and **Last name** (1): Enter the name of the individual you are purchasing goods or services from.

- **Company** (2): Enter the name of the business that you are purchasing from. If the vendor is an individual, such as a 1099 contractor, leave this field blank and complete the **First name** and **Last name** fields instead.

QBCU 3.1.1

Pro Tip: If you have an existing customer who is also a vendor, you will need to set them up as a vendor in QuickBooks. Since QuickBooks does not allow you to use duplicate names, we recommend you add additional verbiage after the name, such as **V** or **Vend**, to differentiate between the customer profile and the vendor profile. For example, if Cameras-R-Us is already set up in QuickBooks, we would set it up as a vendor as: **Cameras-R-Us-V** or **Cameras-R-Us-Vend**.

- **Display name as** (3): QuickBooks will automatically populate this field with the information that was entered in either the **Company** field or the **First name** and **Last name** fields.

- **Address** (4): Enter the address where you send payments to.

Pro Tip: If you make your payments online or via credit card, it's still a good idea to keep an address on file for each vendor. This is especially important to do for 1099 contractors because you are required to mail a 1099 form to them at the end of the year for tax reporting purposes.

- **Notes** (5): This field can be used to record internal notes about vendors.

- **Attachments** (6): Similar to customers, you can attach key vendor documents to a vendor record, such as proposals, contracts, a W9 form, or any other documents.

- **Email** (7): Enter the primary email address for the vendor in this field. This email address will be used to send purchase orders and other vendor-related documents directly from QuickBooks.

- **Phone (8)**: Enter the business telephone number, cellphone, and fax number in these fields.

- **Other** and **Website (9)**: Use the **Other** field to enter any additional information you would like to keep track of. If the vendor has a website, enter that information in the **Website** field.

- **Billing rate (10)**: If you have an agreed-upon billing rate that does not change, enter that information in this field. However, if the billing rate varies, leave this field blank.

QBCU 3.1.3

- **Terms (11)**: Select the payment terms the vendor has extended to you (for example, net 30 days, net 15 days, or due upon receipt). It's important to select payment terms so that QuickBooks can use this information to remind you when bills are due or past due.

- **Opening balance (12)**: If you are converting from another accounting software to QuickBooks, you can enter the outstanding accounts payable balance for suppliers in this field. However, if you plan to manually enter unpaid bills into QuickBooks, leave this field blank.

- **Account no. (13)**: If your vendor has given you an account number, enter it into this field. Otherwise, you can leave this field blank.

- **Business ID No. (14)**: Enter the social security number or federal tax ID number for all 1099 vendors in this field. If a business is incorporated, there is no need to obtain this information.

Pro Tip: It's good practice to request a W9 form from all 1099 contractors before you remit payment. A W9 form includes the individual's first and last names, their company name **Doing Business As (DBA)**, mailing address, business entity (for example, sole prop, LLC), and social security or federal tax ID number. This form will give you all of the information you need to add them to QuickBooks as a new vendor and complete 1099 reporting at the end of the year.

QBCU
3.1.4

- **Track payments for 1099 (15):** Select this checkbox for any individuals you purchase goods and services from that are *not* incorporated. By marking this box, QuickBooks will flag these vendors so that they appear on the 1099 report at the end of the year.

Pro Tip: In the US, if you pay $600 or more to a 1099 contractor during the year, you are required to provide each contractor with a 1099 form at the end of the year. If total payments during the year do not equal $600 or more, you are not required to provide a 1099 form.

Similar to customers, you can include a wealth of information in QuickBooks pertaining to your vendors. By including this information in QuickBooks, you can easily create purchase orders, bills, and other forms and documents without the need to enter this information over and over.

Importing vendors into QuickBooks Online

If you have more than a few vendors to add to QuickBooks, you may want to consider importing the information instead of manually inputting it into QuickBooks. Similar to customers, you can import your vendor details from a CSV file. This template can be found here: `https://github.com/PacktPublishing/Mastering-Quickbooks-2022-Third-Edition/blob/main/Chapter06/QuickBooks_Online_Vendor%20Import%20Template.xls`.

Follow these steps to import vendors into QuickBooks Online:

1. Navigate to **Vendors** by clicking on **Expenses** on the left-hand menu bar and selecting **Vendors,** as shown in *Figure 6.20*:

Figure 6.20: Selecting Vendors

2. Click on the arrow to the right of the **New vendor** button located in the upper-right corner and select **Import vendors**, as shown in *Figure 6.21*:

Figure 6.21: The Import vendors option

3. On the **Import vendors** screen, click the **Browse** button to upload the CSV file from your computer, as shown in *Figure 6.22*:

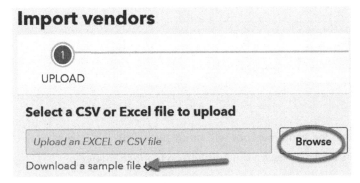

Figure 6.22: Uploading a CSV or Excel file

You can click on the blue link to download the sample file (shown in the preceding screenshot). This file includes all of the fields of information you can upload for vendors. Save this file and use it as your template.

4. Follow the onscreen prompts to import your vendors into QBO.

Review the vendor information to ensure accuracy. If you do find errors, you can easily fix them.

Making changes to existing vendors in QuickBooks Online

QBCU 3.1.3

Similar to customers, the information that you have on file for vendors can change. For example, the **remit to** address where payments are mailed could change, or the telephone number may need to be updated. When it does, you can quickly update your records in QuickBooks. You will need to navigate to the **Vendors** center and select the vendor that you need to make changes to.

Follow these steps to edit an existing vendor in QuickBooks Online:

1. Navigate to **Vendors** by clicking on **Expenses** on the left-hand menu bar and selecting **Vendors**, as shown in *Figure 6.23*:

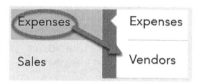

Figure 6.23: Selecting Vendors

2. Select the vendor you want to edit by clicking on the vendor's name, as shown in *Figure 6.24*:

Figure 6.24: Clicking on a vendor name

3. The detailed vendor record will be displayed on the next screen. Click on the **Vendor Details** tab and then on the **Edit** button to make changes:

Figure 6.25: Editing a vendor

QuickBooks makes it easy to update vendor contact information. Having up-to-date vendor information will ensure that all purchase orders, bills, and reports are accurate. If you decide you no longer want to do business with a vendor, but you have existing transactions in QuickBooks, you can inactivate vendors. We will look at this next.

Inactivating vendors in QuickBooks Online

Similar to customers, you can inactivate vendors you no longer do business with. This will maintain your existing vendor transactions that were previously recorded but remove the vendor from the Vendors Center.

Follow these steps to inactivate vendors in QuickBooks Online:

1. Navigate to **Vendors** by clicking on **Expenses** on the left-hand menu bar and selecting **Vendors**, as shown in *Figure 6.26*:

Figure 6.26: Selecting Vendors

2. Put a checkmark in the box next to the vendor you want to inactivate and select **Make inactive**, as shown in *Figure 6.27*:

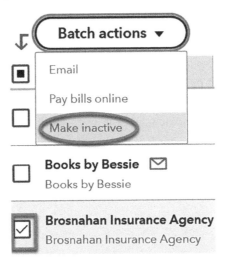

Figure 6.27: Making a vendor inactive

As mentioned previously, you cannot delete vendors but you can inactivate them. When you inactivate a vendor, QuickBooks will preserve the existing historical transactions but remove the vendor from the drop-down list so that it cannot be used in future transactions, such as purchase orders and bills.

Pro Tip: To review the information covered in this section, watch this Intuit video tutorial, *How to add vendors to QuickBooks Online*: `https://www.youtube.com/watch?v=U-Y7Vf0sBnE`.

QBCU
3.1.2

Merging vendors in QuickBooks Online

Similar to customers, you could run into an issue where you have inadvertently added a vendor twice. Like customers, you can easily merge duplicate vendors. Follow the steps below to merge two vendor profiles:

1. Navigate to the **Vendors** Center and identify the duplicate vendors:

Figure 6.28: Duplicate vendors in the Vendors center

Notice we have one vendor that includes a period after each letter in U.S.A. and the other vendor without the periods in-between. These are duplicate vendors and we will keep the vendor that does not include the periods, **Bank of the USA**.

2. Click once on the vendor you do *not* wish to keep. In our example, that would be **Bank of the U.S.A.**

3. The following appears after clicking once on **Bank of the U.S.A.:**

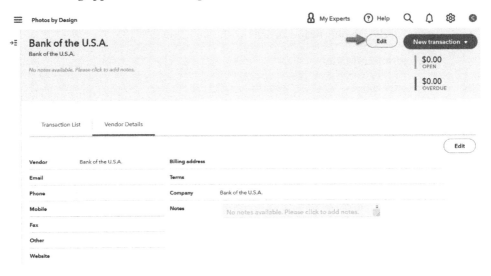

Figure 6.29: Viewing vendor information

Click on the **Edit** button as indicated above.

4. The **Vendor Information** window will appear:

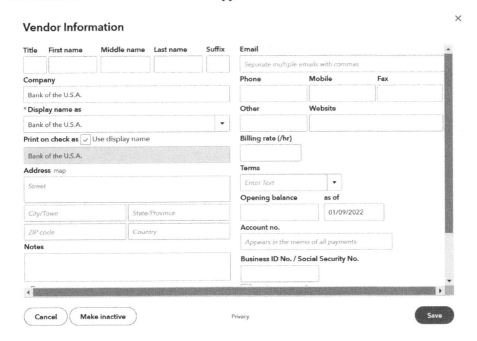

Figure 6.30: Editing information for an existing vendor

Click once in the **Company** field, and type the name exactly as it appears in the vendor profile that you wish to keep. In our example, this would be **Bank of the USA**. Repeat these steps for the **Display name as** field as shown below:

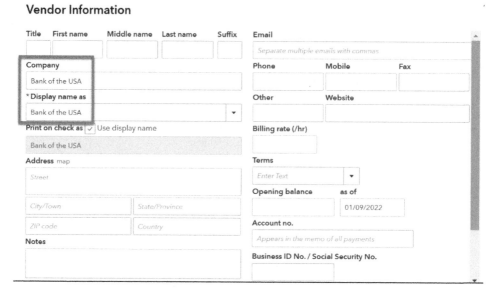

Figure 6.31: Editing the Company and Display name as fields

5. Click the **Save** button in the lower-right corner.

6. The following message will appear:

Figure 6.32: Confirming the merge of duplicate vendors

Click **Yes** and the two vendor profiles will be combined into one:

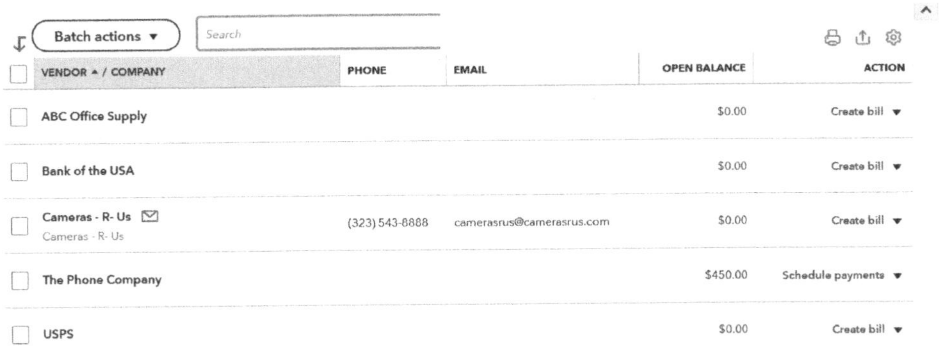

Figure 6.33: The Vendors center with the vendors merged

As you can see, the duplicate profile (**Bank of the U.S.A.**) is no longer on the vendor list. All of the transactions recorded for that vendor have been moved to the **Bank of the USA** profile.

In this section, we have covered how to manually add vendors, how to import vendors, and how to make changes to vendors, as well as how to inactivate and merge vendors. Next, we will cover how to add, import, edit, inactivate, and merge products and services that you sell.

Managing products and services lists in QuickBooks Online

The products and services that you sell are referred to as **items** in QuickBooks. You can track all of the products and services that you sell in QuickBooks Online. This includes the product name, product (item) number, product description, cost, selling price, and quantity on hand. It's important to set up products and/or services so that you can easily invoice customers for their purchases. In addition, these items are linked to an account on the chart of accounts so that QuickBooks can do the accounting behind the scenes for you. Once you have added products and services to QuickBooks, you will be able to run detailed reports on the products and services you sell.

In this section, we will cover how to manually add items, how to import items, how to modify existing items, how to inactivate items, and how to merge items in QuickBooks Online. You will need to create items in order to invoice customers.

Pro Tip: Keep in mind that you must have a QuickBooks Plus or QuickBooks Advanced subscription to track inventory items.

Manually adding products and services in QuickBooks Online

In order to add products and services in QuickBooks, you need to have a list of the products or services you plan to sell, along with the cost, sales price, and a brief description that you want to appear on invoices.

Follow these steps to add a new item in QuickBooks Online:

1. Navigate to the **Products and Services** list by clicking on the gear icon and selecting **Products and Services**, as shown in *Figure 6.34*:

Figure 6.34: Selecting Products and Services

2. Click on the **New** button, as indicated here:

Figure 6.35: The New button

If this is your first time adding a product/service, you will see the **Add a product or service** button instead.

3.   On the next screen, select the appropriate item type, as shown in *Figure 6.36*:

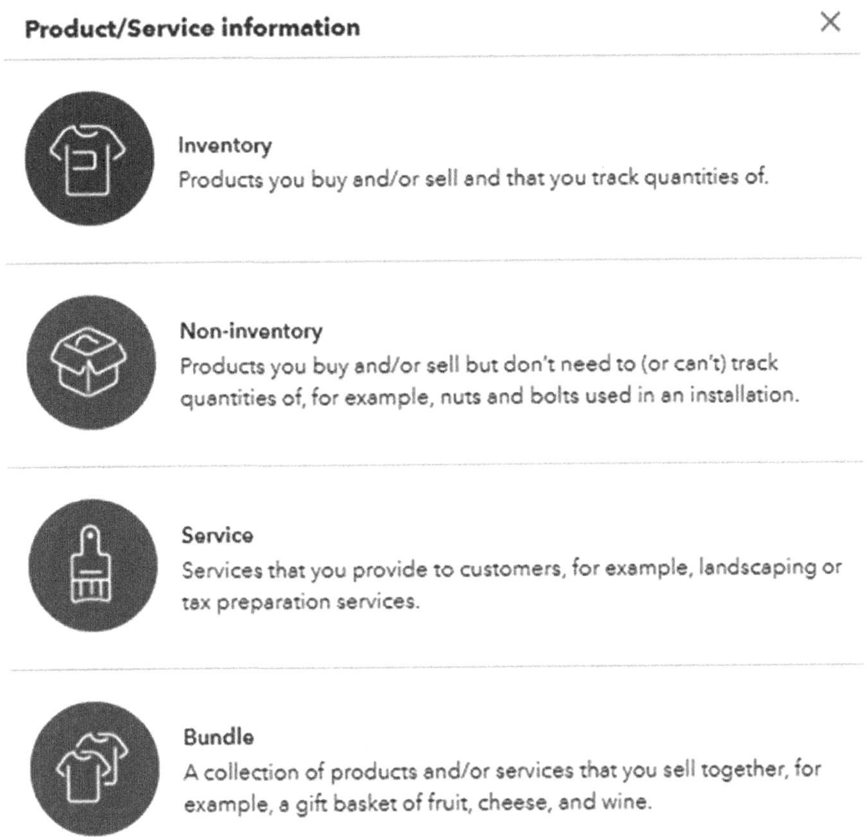

Product/Service information   ✕

Inventory
Products you buy and/or sell and that you track quantities of.

Non-inventory
Products you buy and/or sell but don't need to (or can't) track quantities of, for example, nuts and bolts used in an installation.

Service
Services that you provide to customers, for example, landscaping or tax preparation services.

Bundle
A collection of products and/or services that you sell together, for example, a gift basket of fruit, cheese, and wine.

Figure 6.36: Selecting an item type

QBCU 2.2.1 2.2.4

There are four item types to choose from. A brief description of each item type follows:

- **Inventory:** Products that you buy and sell and want to track in inventory should be set up as **Inventory** items; for example, a retail T-shirt store that purchases T-shirts and resells them or a grocery store that needs to keep track of the items they've purchased and sold.

- **Non-inventory:** The **Non-inventory** type is used to track items you sell but don't keep in inventory. For example, a photographer may purchase photo paper to print pictures, but does not keep track of the quantity of photo paper they've purchased.

QBCU
2.2.1
2.2.4

- **Service: Service** is typically used for services that you sell; for example, bookkeeping services, photography services, or landscaping.
- **Bundle:** A bundle is a collection of products that are sold together; for example, a gift set that includes all of the James Bond movies.

Fill in the following fields to add a new **Service** item:

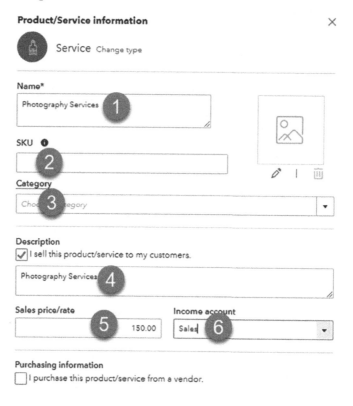

Figure 6.37: Adding a new product or service

A brief description of the six fields you will complete in order to add a new **Service** item in QuickBooks Online follows:

- **Name (1)**: Enter the name of the service you will be selling to customers.

- **SKU (2)**: A **stock-keeping unit (SKU)** is a scannable bar code printed on product labels in a retail store. If applicable, enter the SKU for the product you are selling. In general, an SKU applies to products and not service items.

- **Category (3)**: This field is *optional*. If you want to categorize the products and services you sell, you can do so by creating categories. For example, if you sell T-shirts in three different colors – red, blue, and green – you could create a category for each color to track the sales separately.

- **Description (4)**: Enter a brief description of the item in this field. This description will appear on all customer invoices and sales receipts.

- **Sales price/rate (5)**: Enter the sales price for the item if it generally is the same for all customers. However, if the price varies by customer, you can leave this field blank and complete it when you create an invoice to bill your customers.

- **Income account (6)**: This is a required field. From the drop-down, select the appropriate income account where you want sales for this item to be recorded on the financial statements.

 Pro Tip: Every item you create in QuickBooks will be mapped to an account. Using this information, QuickBooks will record the debits and credits for you in the background so that you don't have to.

Fill in the following fields to set up an **Inventory** item:

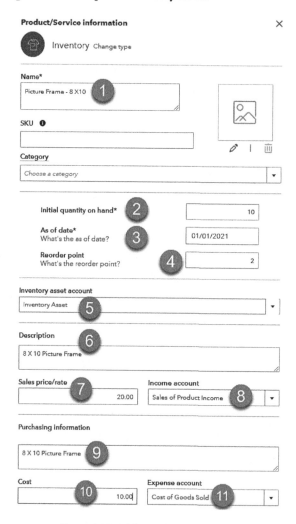

Figure 6.38: Adding an inventory item

Brief descriptions of the fields you will fill in when setting up an **Inventory** item are as follows:

- **Name (1)**: Enter the name of the product or item.
- **Initial quantity on hand (2)**: This should represent the total quantity for each item you have in your inventory.

Pro Tip: You need to perform a physical inventory count before setting up inventory items in QuickBooks Online. If you don't have the inventory quantity when setting up the item, you won't be able to add it to this screen later on. Instead, you will have to create an inventory adjustment journal to record the inventory. You will learn how to record inventory adjustments in *Chapter 17, Closing the Books in QuickBooks Online*.

- **As of date (3)**: Enter the date when the inventory was counted.

- **Reorder point (4)**: The reorder point is the minimum you want your inventory count to go to before QuickBooks alerts you to place an order. In our example, when the inventory goes down to two T-shirts, QuickBooks will alert us to place an order.

- **Inventory asset account (5)**: All our inventory is recorded as an asset and the default account is **Inventory Asset**, as indicated in our example.

- **Description (6)**: Enter the description that you want to appear on customer sales receipts and invoices.

- **Sales price/rate (7)**: Enter the price you sell the item for. If it varies, leave it blank and you can complete it when you create the customer invoice.

- **Income account (8)**: Enter the account you want to track all sales of for this product.

- **Purchasing information (9)**: Enter the description that you want to appear on purchase orders when placing an order with your supplier.

- **Cost (10)**: Enter the amount that you pay your vendor/supplier for this item. The cost reflected here is for information purposes only and will be determined by QuickBooks after bills are entered.

- **Expense account (11)**: The default expense account is the **Cost of Goods Sold** for products. However, if you prefer to track these costs in a different account, you can click on the dropdown and add a new account.

If you don't have the time to enter your products and services manually, you can import this data into QuickBooks, as we have demonstrated already for accounts, customers, and vendors.

Importing products and services in QuickBooks Online

Similar to customers and vendors, you can import a products and services list in QuickBooks. This can save you a lot of time if you have a sizeable list of products or services that you sell. You can import this information from a CSV file into QBO. This template can be found here: https://github. com/PacktPublishing/Mastering-Quickbooks-2022-Third-Edition/blob/main/Chapter06/ QuickBooks_Online_Prod%20and%20svs%20import%20template.xls.

Follow these steps to import products and services into QuickBooks Online:

1. Navigate to the **Products and Services** list by clicking on the gear icon and selecting **Products and Services**, as shown in *Figure 6.39*:

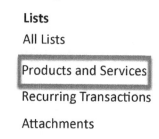

Figure 6.39: Selecting Products and Services

2. Click on the arrow next to the **New** item button located in the upper-right corner and then click on **Import**, as shown in *Figure 6.40*:

Figure 6.40: The Import option

3. Click the **Browse** button to upload the CSV file from your computer, as shown in *Figure 6.41*:

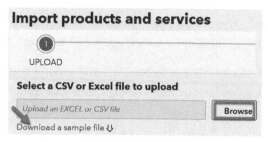

Figure 6.41: Uploading a CSV or Excel file

You can click on the blue link to download the sample file (shown in the preceding screen-shot). This file includes all of the fields of information you can upload for items. Save this file and use it as your template.

4. Follow the onscreen prompts to import your products and services into QuickBooks Online.

Be sure to review the data imported to ensure accuracy. If you do find that corrections are needed, you can easily make them.

Making changes to existing products and services in QuickBooks Online

You can change any fields in existing products and services except the item type. If you have already used an item in a transaction, QuickBooks will not allow you to change the item type. Instead, you will need to inactivate the old item and add a brand-new item with the correct item type.

Follow these steps to make changes to existing products and services in QBO:

1. Navigate to the **Products and Services** list by clicking on the gear icon and selecting **Products and Services**, as shown in *Figure 6.42*:

Lists

All Lists

Products and Services

Recurring Transactions

Attachments

Figure 6.42: Selecting Products and Services

2. Select the product or service you would like to make changes to by clicking on the **Edit** button in the far-right column, as shown in *Figure 6.43*:

NAME ▲	TYPE	SALES DESCRIPTION	SALES PRICE	COST	ACTION
Hours	Service				Edit ▼
Photography Services	Service	Photography Services	150		Edit ▼
Picture Frame - 8 X10	Inventory	8 X 10 Picture Frame	20	10	Edit ▼
Sales	Service				Edit ▼

Figure 6.43: Editing a product or service

As we mentioned previously, you can change an item type if you haven't used it in a transaction in QuickBooks. However, if you have used an item in a transaction and the item type is incorrect, you will need to create a new item with the correct item type and inactivate the old item.

Inactivating products and services in QuickBooks Online

As we discussed when we talked about customers and vendors, you cannot delete products and services in QBO once you have created them; however, you can inactivate them. This will preserve the existing transactions and remove the product or service from the items list so it cannot be used in new transactions.

Follow these steps to inactivate a product or service in QuickBooks Online:

1. Navigate to the **Products and Services** list by clicking on the gear icon and selecting **Products and Services**, as shown in *Figure 6.44*:

Figure 6.44: Selecting Products and Services

2. Scroll down the items list to the product (or service), click on the **Edit** button, and select **Make inactive**, as shown in *Figure 6.45*:

Figure 6.45: Making a product or service inactive

Similar to customers and vendors, inactivating a product or service will remove it from selection for future transactions. However, the existing data will remain intact to ensure reports are accurate for tax and other reporting purposes.

Pro Tip: To recap the steps covered in this section, watch this Intuit video tutorial, *How to create inventory products in QuickBooks Online*: `https://www.youtube.com/watch?v=PkKKZwtkNeM`.

Merging products and services in QuickBooks Online

Like vendors and customers, you can also merge duplicate services that have been entered into QuickBooks by mistake. Unfortunately, you cannot merge duplicate inventory items because of the complexity of inventory tracking. Instead, you will need to inactivate one of the duplicate inventory items and record inventory adjustments to manage the transactions that have been recorded. Consult with your accountant before making any inventory adjustments.

Follow the steps below to merge duplicate services:

1. Navigate to the **Products and Services** list and identify the duplicate items:

NAME ▲	SKU	TYPE	SALES DESCRIPTION	SALES PRICE	COST	TAXABLE	QTY ON HAND	REORDER POINT
8 X 10 Picture Frame		Inventory	8 X 10 Picture F...	20		✓	0	
Hours		Service						
Photo Services		Service	Photo Services	150		✓		
Photography Services		Service	Photography Se...	150				
Picture Frame - 8 X10		Inventory	8 X 10 Picture F...	20	10		8	2
Sales		Service						

Figure 6.46: Identifying duplicate services in the Products and Services list

As you can see in the image above, there is an item called **Photo Services** and a duplicate item called **Photography Services**. In order to maintain accurate inventory records, we must merge them into one. The item we will keep in our example is **Photography Services**.

2. Click on the item that you wish to remove – **Photo Services** in our example.

3. After you click on **Photo Services**, the **Product/Service information** window will appear:

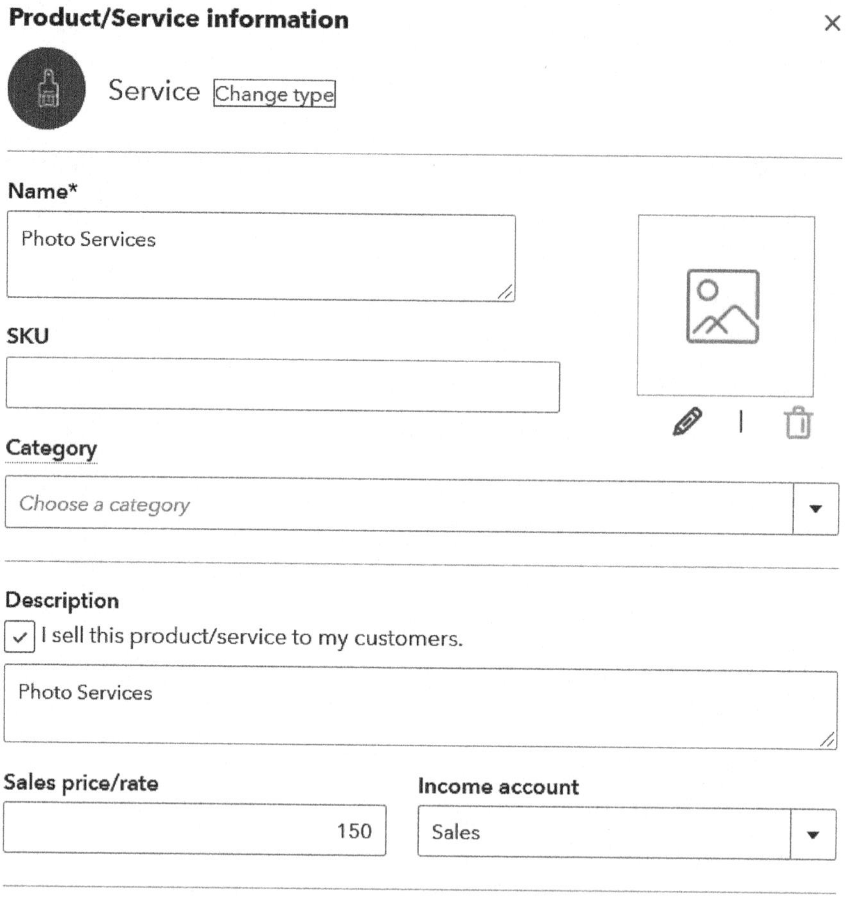

Product/Service information   ×

Service Change type

Name*

Photo Services

SKU

Category

Choose a category   ▼

Description

✓ I sell this product/service to my customers.

Photo Services

Sales price/rate   **Income account**

150   Sales   ▼

Figure 6.47: Displaying products and services information

Click once in the **Name** field and type in the item name you want to merge with –
Photography Services in our case. Type this also in the **Description** field, as shown below:

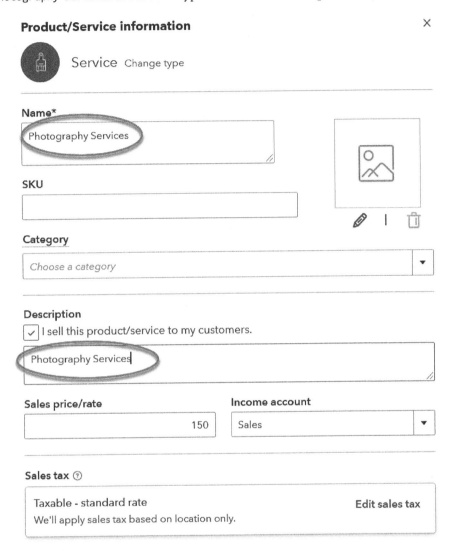

Figure 6.48: Editing product and services information

4.   Click the **Save and Close** button in the lower-right corner.

5.   The following message will appear:

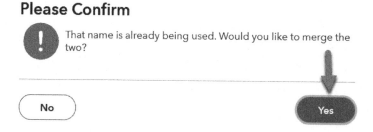

Figure 6.49: Confirming the merging of duplicate service items

Click **Yes** and the two service items will be combined:

	NAME ▲	SKU	TYPE	SALES DESCRIPTION	SALES PRICE	COST	TAXABLE	QTY ON HAND	REORDER POINT	ACTION
☐	8 X 10 Picture Frame		Inventory	8 X 10 Picture F...	20		✔	0		Edit ▾
☐	Hours		Service							Edit ▾
☐	Photography Services		Service	Photography Se...	150					Edit ▾
☐	Picture Frame - 8 X10		Inventory	8 X 10 Picture F...	20	10		8	2	Edit ▾
☐	Sales		Service							Edit ▾

Figure 6.50: The Products and Services list with the merged item

Notice the **Photo Services** item is no longer shown because it has been merged with **Photography Services**.

We have now covered how to manually add products and services, import products and services, make changes to existing products and services, inactivate products and services (also known as items), and merge services.

Summary

In this chapter, we covered how to manage customer data by manually adding and importing the information, editing existing customers, and inactivating customers you no longer do business with.

In addition, we covered how to manage vendor data by manually adding and importing the information, editing existing vendors, inactivating vendors you no longer do business with, and merging duplicate customer and vendor records.

Finally, we showed you how to manage products and services, also referred to as items, including how to add and import data, how to edit existing products and services, how to inactivate products and services, and how to merge service items in QuickBooks Online.

Now that you understand how to manage your customers, it's time to learn how to set up and manage sales tax. In the next chapter, we will show you how to set up sales tax, create an invoice that includes sales tax, and run sales tax reports.

Join our book's Discord space

Join the book's Discord workspace for a monthly *Ask me Anything* session with the author:
`https://packt.link/QuickBooks`

Section 2: Recording Transactions in QuickBooks Online

7

Managing Sales Tax

In this chapter, we will cover how to manage sales tax in QuickBooks Online. In the United States, sales tax is typically applied to the sale of products. However, some states and local tax jurisdictions also apply sales tax to certain types of services. You need to consult with your CPA or accountant to determine which laws apply in your geographical location.

We will cover the following topics in this chapter:

- Setting up sales tax in QuickBooks Online
- Creating an invoice that includes sales tax
- Sales tax reports
- Paying sales tax when it comes due

 The US edition of QuickBooks Online was used to create this book. If you are using a version that is outside of the United States, results may differ.

Setting up sales tax in QuickBooks Online

If you are required to collect sales tax from customers, it is important to complete the sales tax setup in QuickBooks prior to invoicing customers. If you create an invoice without sales tax, you will ultimately underpay the sales tax you are required to submit to your local tax authority. This could lead to additional taxes and penalties, which can add up quickly. Setting up sales tax in QuickBooks from the start allows QuickBooks to automatically calculate and keep track of sales tax that you owe.

Perform the following steps to set up sales tax:

1. Click **Taxes** on the left menu bar, as indicated in the following screenshot, to navigate to the Sales Tax Center screen:

Figure 7.1: Navigating to the Sales Tax Center

2. The following message will appear. Click the **Use Automatic Sales Tax** button, as indicated in *Figure 7.2*:

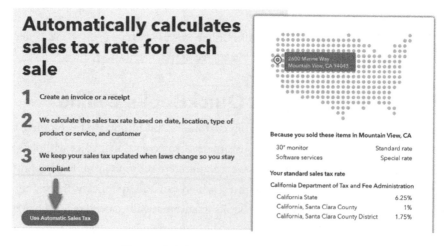

Figure 7.2: Sales Tax Center welcome page

3. The following window will appear:

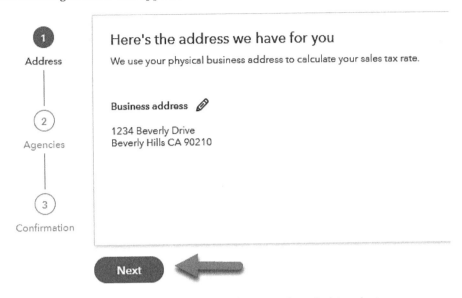

Figure 7.3: Entering the business address used to calculate sales tax

Your business address should automatically populate the fields (as indicated in the preceding screenshot). If it does not, click the pencil icon and type the information into the appropriate fields.

Click **Next.**

4. The following screen will appear:

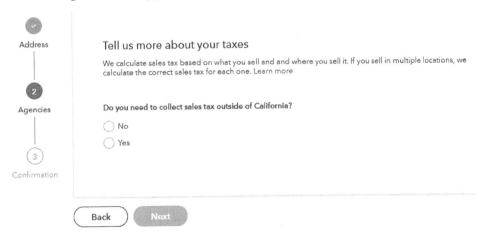

Figure 7.4: Sales tax information outside of your state

If you are required to collect sales tax outside of your state, select **Yes** to the question on this screen; otherwise, select **No**, and click **Next**.

 Pro Tip: Most businesses are not required to collect sales tax outside their state. If you are not sure, you need to consult with your tax professional or CPA on this matter.

5. Click **Next** and the following screen will appear, indicating that the automatic sales tax setup is complete:

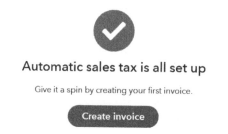

Figure 7.5: Confirmation that automatic sales tax is set up

6. Click the **X** in the upper-right corner of the screen to bypass the preceding message and navigate to the **How often do you file sales tax?** screen:

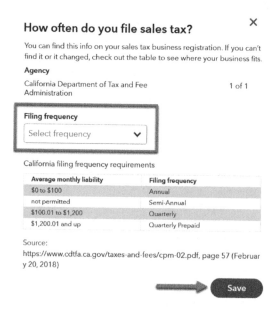

Figure 7.6: Filing frequency for sales tax

Based on the state where your business is located, the **Agency** field will automatically be populated.

From the drop-down menu, select the frequency with which you file sales tax. The options are monthly, quarterly, and yearly.

 Pro Tip: If you are not sure how often you need to submit sales tax, refer to the chart that appears below the **Filing frequency** field or click the link below **Source:** in the preceding screenshot.

Click the **Save** button to keep your changes.

7. The following sales tax window will appear:

Figure 7.7: Sales tax due

This window is where you can find the amount of sales tax that is currently due, or coming due. You can change the time period you wish to look at in the from/to fields.

Since we don't currently have any taxable sales recorded, we will create an invoice with sales tax next.

Creating an invoice that includes sales tax

After completing the setup for sales tax, you are ready to create invoices and sales receipts with sales tax. In this section, we will create an invoice and show you how to include sales tax.

Perform the following steps to create an invoice with sales tax:

1. From the left menu bar, click on **Sales** and then select **Invoices**, as indicated in *Figure 7.8*:

Figure 7.8: Navigating to Invoices

2. Click the **Create invoice** button located on the right side of the screen, as indicated in *Figure 7.9*:

Figure 7.9: Creating an invoice

3. A blank invoice template will appear. Complete the fields as follows:

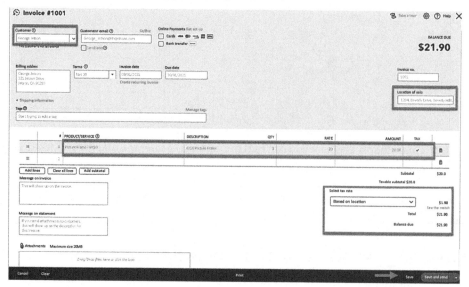

Figure 7.10: Invoice template

- **Customer:** From the dropdown, select the customer/client you are invoicing (in our example, **George Jetson**). Press *Tab* and the email, billing address and payment terms, and due date fields will be populated automatically.

- **PRODUCT/SERVICE:** From the dropdown, select the product/service you are invoicing the customer for.

 If you have previously added products and services to QuickBooks the **DESCRIPTION** and **RATE** fields will automatically be populated.

- **QTY:** Enter the quantity sold in this field.

- **AMOUNT:** QuickBooks will automatically multiply the quantity by the rate to calculate the total amount.

- **TAX:** To mark this item as taxable, put a checkmark in the **TAX** column if it does not already appear. If you marked items as taxable when you set them up, this field will automatically be populated.

Based on the city/state for your business, the sales tax rate for that geographical location will be applied. In the bottom-right corner, you can see that sales tax of **$1.90** was calculated on this sale of **$20.00**. The total amount due with tax is **$21.90**.

4. Click the **Save** button to save the invoice, and click the **X** in the upper-right corner to close out of the invoice.

5. Navigate back to the Sales Tax Center by clicking on **Taxes** from the left menu bar. The following window will appear:

Figure 7.11: Sales Tax Center with updated sales tax amount

As you can see, the tax of **$1.90** now shows up as upcoming sales tax that will be due sometime in the future. Once the sales tax becomes due, the amount will show up in the **SALES TAX DUE** field.

QBCU
5.1.1

Sales tax reports

QuickBooks makes it easy to stay on top of the sales tax collected, which will ensure that you pay the correct amount when it comes due. There are two reports available to help you stay on top of the sales tax you owe: a tax liability report and a taxable customer report.

Perform the following steps to access the sales tax reports:

1. Within the Sales Tax Center, click on the **Reports** link, as indicated in *Figure 7.12*:

Figure 7.12: Sales tax reports

- **Tax liability report**: This report will show you the sales tax collected as of a specific period of time. The report will show gross sales, taxable sales, non-taxable sales, and the tax amount.

  In the report shown below, there are four columns: **GROSS AMOUNT, NON TAXABLE AMOUNT, TAXABLE AMOUNT**, and **TAX AMOUNT**. The gross amount is $20.00, the non-taxable amount is $0, the taxable amount is $20.00, and the total tax amount is $1.90.

Figure 7.13: Sales tax liability report

- **Taxable customer report**: This report will list all customers who are subject to sales tax, along with their billing address, shipping address, taxable sales, and tax rate. Below is a snapshot of what this report looks like:

Figure 7.14: Taxable customer report

As you can see, it is easy to keep track of sales tax in QuickBooks. You can use the tax liability report and the taxable customer report to prepare your sales tax return. In addition, you will use these reports to determine the amount owed.

Paying sales tax when it comes due

Unfortunately, you cannot pay sales tax within QuickBooks Online. You must visit the website of your state tax authority and submit payment online or mail a check before the due date. The following Intuit video tutorial provides a recap of what we have covered in this chapter, plus the steps you need to take to make a payment and record it in QuickBooks Online: `https://youtu.be/Rns_R4fRros`.

Summary

In this chapter, we have discussed the importance of setting up sales tax in QuickBooks so it can automatically calculate sales tax for you. We have shown you how to create an invoice and include sales tax and we have covered the key reports available to help you stay on top of your sales tax liability. Since you cannot make sales tax payments in QuickBooks, we have also included a video that explains how to make your sales tax payments outside of QuickBooks. It's important to make sure you set up sales tax and use the correct sales tax rate. This will help you to avoid penalties or fees for under-reporting and underpaying sales tax to your state tax office. In the next chapter, we will cover how to record invoices and sales receipts in QuickBooks Online.

Join our book's Discord space

Join the book's Discord workspace for a monthly *Ask me Anything* session with the author:
`https://packt.link/QuickBooks`

8

QBCU 2.4.1

Recording Sales Transactions in QuickBooks Online

In *Chapter 6, Managing Customer, Vendor, and Products and Services Lists*, you learned how to customize QuickBooks by adding customers, vendors, and the products and services you sell to QuickBooks. Now that you have completed your QuickBooks setup, it's time to learn how to record transactions. In this chapter, we will focus on recording sales transactions in **QuickBooks Online (QBO)**. We will cover the three types of sales transactions, when you should use each, how to record each transaction, and the behind-the-scenes accounting that QuickBooks does for you. We will also show you how to record customer payments and how to issue credit memos and refunds to customers. Recording sales transactions will allow you to keep track of how much money your business is making. This information is important and will help you to determine whether or not your business is profitable.

In this chapter, we will cover the following key concepts:

- Entering sales forms—sales receipts, deposits, and sales invoices
- Recording payments received from customers
- Recording payments to the undeposited funds account
- Issuing credit memos and refunds to customers

 The US edition of QBO was used to create this book. If you are using a version that is outside of the United States, results may differ.

Understanding sales forms

Recording income for a business can be accomplished in a variety of ways. There are three primary ways to record income in QuickBooks Online. First, a **sales receipt** is used when you receive payment at the same time you provide products and/or services to your customers. Second, you can use a **deposit** to record income for a specific customer or to record income from multiple customers at any one time. Third, you can use a **sales invoice**, which allows you to bill a specific customer, who will pay you based on payment terms that are agreed upon upfront.

In the following sections, we will cover when and how to record income using a sales receipt, a deposit, and a sales invoice. We will also show you the accounting that takes place behind the scenes for each transaction. This will include the debits and credits recorded for each transaction.

QBCU 2.4.2

Recording income using a sales receipt

A sales receipt is used when the sale of a product or service and receipt of the customer payment take place simultaneously. For example, retail businesses such as restaurants or clothing stores will receive payment at the same time they provide their service (for example, serving food to customers) or products (for example, clothing items for purchase). You can record a sales receipt in QuickBooks by completing a couple of simple steps.

Follow these steps to record a sales receipt:

1.　From the **+ New** menu, select **Sales receipt**, as indicated in *Figure 8.1*:

Figure 8.1: Navigating to the Sales Receipt form

2. The following screenshot shows a snapshot of a completed sales receipt:

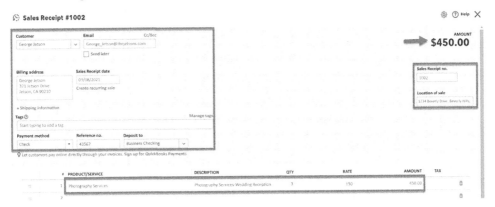

Figure 8.2: Completing the Sales Receipt form

There are several fields of information that need to be completed on the Sales Receipt form. The following is a brief description of the information you need to include in each field:

- **Customer:** Select the customer you sold the product or service to by clicking on the drop-down arrow in this field. **George Jetson** is the customer in our example. If you have not added any customers yet, you can add a new customer by typing the customer name in this field.

 Pro Tip: If you need to record sales for an event for multiple customers at once, you can enter the event name and date or the week instead of a specific customer; for example, Sales for the week of 2/1/21 to 2/7/21.

- **Email:** This field will automatically be populated with the email address you have on file for the customer. The email address in our example is `George_Jetson@ thejetsons.com`. If the field is blank, you can type an email address directly in this field.
- QuickBooks will email the sales receipt to the email address you include in this field.
- **Billing address:** This field will automatically be populated with the billing address you have on file for this customer. The billing address in our example is **321 Jetson Dr., Jetson, CA 90210**. If you don't have an address on file, you can enter one directly in this field.

- **Sales Receipt date:** Enter the date of the sale in this field, which is **09/08/21** in our example.

- **Payment method:** Select the payment method by clicking the drop-down arrow. We have selected **Check** in our example.

- **Reference no.:** If your customer paid by check, enter the check number in this field. If payment was made by cash or credit card, you can enter a reference number, or leave this field blank. The reference no. is **43567** in our example.

- **Deposit to:** From the drop-down menu, select the bank account to which you will deposit this payment. In our example, the funds will be deposited into the **Business Checking** account.

> **Pro Tip:** If you plan to deposit payments for multiple customers on the same day, select the **Undeposited funds** account instead of the Business Checking account as the Deposit to account. Later on, you will be able to select the specific deposits made on each day. This will make it much easier to reconcile the bank account.

- **Sales Receipt no.:** QuickBooks will automatically generate this number, which is **1002** in our example.

- **Location of sale:** For sales tax purposes, this field will automatically be populated with the business address of our sample company, Photos by Design. The business address in our example is **1234 Beverly Drive, Beverly Hills, CA 90210.**

- **PRODUCT/SERVICE:** From the drop-down menu, select the type of service (or product) sold to the customer. In our example, it is photography services.

- **DESCRIPTION:** This field will automatically be populated based on the product/service selected. In our example, the description is **Photography services – Wedding reception.**

- **QTY:** Enter the quantity of items sold or the total hours of service provided. In our example, the quantity is **3.**

- **RATE:** Enter the hourly rate for your services or the unit cost of the product sold. In our example, the rate is **$150.**

- **AMOUNT:** You don't need to enter anything in this field. QuickBooks will multiply the quantity by the rate to automatically calculate the total amount of the sales receipt. In our example, the total amount is **$450.**

Pro Tip: This Intuit video tutorial summarizes the steps we have covered on *How to create a sales receipt*: https://quickbooks.intuit.com/learn-support/en-us/sales-receipts/how-to-record-a-sales-receipt/00/344860.

As mentioned in *Chapter 1, Getting Started with QuickBooks Online*, one of the benefits of using QuickBooks is that you don't need to have knowledge of debits and credits to use the software. QuickBooks will automatically debit and credit the appropriate accounts for you. However, it is important for you to understand the impact of recording transactions in QuickBooks.

The following screenshot shows the journal entry that is recorded behind the scenes in Quick-Books for the sales receipt displayed previously:

Date	Account Name	Debit	Credit
9/8/2021	Business Checking	450	
	Sales		450

Figure 8.3: Automatic journal entry recorded for a sales receipt

When you create a sales receipt in QuickBooks, it has an impact on the balance sheet and the income statement. You can find both of these reports in the Report Center. In *Chapter 12, Business Overview Reports*, we show you how to generate these reports. In our example, the checking account is increased by $450, which increases the total assets on the balance sheet report. Sales has also increased by $450, which increases the total income on the profit and loss (income statement).

Now that you know how to use a sales receipt to record income, we will show you how to record income using a deposit, and the impact deposits have on financial statements.

Recording income using a deposit QBCU 2.4.3

Another method used to record income in QuickBooks is that of a deposit. The downside to using this method is that you won't have a detailed record of the type of service that was performed, since there is no field to select the service or product provided. This method should be used if you don't need to record your sales by the type of product or service that was sold. An example of a business that might use this method is a real estate agent recording commission income. You can record a lump-sum deposit amount for multiple sales, or you can record deposits for a specific customer. Recording a deposit in QuickBooks can be done in just a couple of steps.

Follow these steps to record income in QuickBooks using a deposit:

1. From the **+ New** menu, select **Bank deposit** in the **OTHER** column, as indicated in *Figure 8.4*:

Figure 8.4: Navigating to Bank Deposit

2. The following screenshot shows a snapshot of the Bank Deposit form:

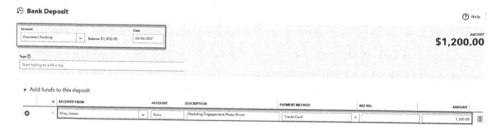

Figure 8.5: Bank Deposit form

Brief descriptions of the fields that need to be completed in a deposit slip are given here. All fields are required except for the **DESCRIPTION, PAYMENT METHOD**, and **REF NO.** fields:

*   **Account:** Use the drop-down arrow to select the bank account to which the deposit will be made. In our example, we have selected the **Business Checking** account.

*   **Date:** Enter the date on which you will make the deposit with your bank. This deposit was made on **09/08/2021**.

- **RECEIVED FROM:** Click in this field and select the customer from whom you received the payment. If you prefer not to track income according to the customer, you can leave this field blank. Our deposit was received from **Elroy Jetson**.

- **ACCOUNT:** From the drop-down menu, select the appropriate account to which this income should be categorized. This should be based on the type of product or service provided. The account in our example is **Sales**.

- **DESCRIPTION:** This field is optional. You can type a brief description of the product or service provided. The description in our example is **Wedding Engagement Photo Shoot**.

- **PAYMENT METHOD:** In this field, you can indicate the method of payment received (that is, by credit card, cash, or check). The payment method is credit card.

- **REF NO.:** If the payment method was **Check**, enter the check number in this field. For all other payment methods, you can leave this field blank.

- **AMOUNT:** Enter the amount of the sale in this field. The total amount of the above deposit is **$1200**.

When you create a deposit transaction in QuickBooks, it affects the balance sheet and profit and loss (income statement) reports. The bank account where the deposit will be made goes up, which increases the assets section of the balance sheet report. The profit and loss report is increased by the product or service that was sold.

The following screenshot shows the journal entry recorded for the deposit transaction displayed previously:

Date	Account Name	Debit	Credit
9/8/2021	Business Checking	1200	
	Sales		1200

Figure 8.6: Automatic journal entry to record bank deposit

In our example, the business checking account increased by $1,200, which will increase the total assets on the balance sheet report. Sales also increased by $1,200, which will increase the total income on the profit and loss (income statement).

Now that you know how to record income using a deposit, we will show you how to record income using a sales invoice.

QBCU
2.4.2

Recording income using a sales invoice

A sales invoice is used to record income from customers who have been given extended payment terms. This means the customer does not pay at the time the product is sold or services are rendered; instead, they pay you sometime in the future. The most common payment term is net 30, which means the invoice is due 30 days from the sales date or the invoice date.

Unlike the sales receipt and deposit forms, which record both the sale and the receipt of payment in a single transaction, recording a sales invoice and payment is done in two steps. In this section, we will cover the first step: recording a sales invoice. We will cover recording customer payments in the next section.

To record a sales invoice in QuickBooks Online, follow these steps:

1. Navigate to the **+ New** menu and select **Invoice** under **CUSTOMERS**, as indicated here:

Figure 8.7: Navigating to the Invoice form

2. The following screenshot shows a snapshot of the sales invoice form, along with an example of what information should be included:

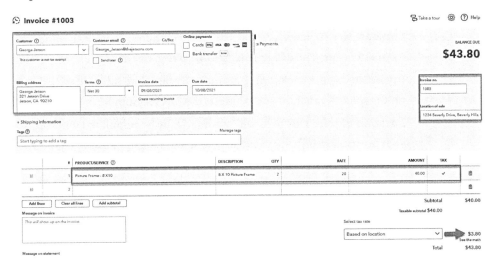

Figure 8.8: The Invoice form

Here are brief descriptions of the fields that need to be completed in a sales invoice. All fields are required except for **DESCRIPTION**, **QTY**, and the **Message on invoice** fields:

- **Customer**: Select the customer from the drop-down menu. **George Jetson** is the customer selected in our example.

- **Customer email**: This field will automatically be populated with the email address on file for the customer. If you want to be able to send the invoice directly to the customer via email, you will need to enter the email address in this field. The email address for George Jetson is George_Jetson@thejetsons.com.

- **Billing address**: This field will automatically be populated with the address information you have on file for your customer. If you have not set up the address information, you can type it directly in this field. The billing address in this field is **321 Jetson Drive, Jetson, CA 90210**.

- **Terms**: This field will automatically be populated with the payment terms you have set up for your customer. In our example, we have set payment terms of **Net 30**, which means the invoice is due 30 days from the invoice date. If you have not set up payment terms, you can select these from the drop-down menu.

- **Invoice date:** Enter the date of the sale in this field. The invoice date is **09/08/2021** in our example.

- **Due date:** This field is automatically calculated by QuickBooks. Since the payment terms are **Net 30**, it adds 30 days to the invoice date in order to compute the date payment is due. The due date is **10/08/2021** in our example.

- **Invoice no.:** QuickBooks will automatically populate this field with the next available invoice number. In our example, the invoice number is **1003**.

- **Location of sale:** This field will automatically be populated with the address of your business in order to calculate the sales tax, if applicable. The address in this field is **123 Beverly Drive, Beverly Hills, CA 90210**.

- **PRODUCT/SERVICE:** From the drop-down menu, select the product and/or services provided to the customer. **Picture frame – 8X10** is the product sold in our example.

- **DESCRIPTION:** This field will automatically be populated based on the product/ service selected in the previous field. **8X10 Picture Frame** is our description of the product sold.

- **QTY:** Enter the quantity of the product, or the total hours to bill the customer. There were **2** picture frames sold in our example.

- **RATE:** This field will automatically be populated based on the product/service selected. However, if you don't have a rate set up, you can enter the price per unit or the hourly rate in this field. Each picture frame costs **$20** in our example.

- **AMOUNT:** QuickBooks will automatically calculate the total invoice amount by taking the quantity and multiplying it by the rate. In our example, the total amount due is **$40** for the two picture frames.

- **Message on invoice:** This field is optional. You can type a personal thank you message to your customer and it will appear on the invoice.

You have the option to print the sales invoice, email it, or save it as a PDF document. If you would like to allow customers to pay their invoices online, you can sign up for the Intuit Payments service. This service allows you to accept payments from customers via credit card, debit card, or ACH bank transfer.

Pro Tip: You can now send invoices in one of six languages: English, French, Spanish, Italian, Portuguese (Brazil), and Chinese (Traditional). To select the preferred language for a customer, navigate to the customer profile and click on the **Language** tab.

This Intuit video tutorial summarizes the steps we have covered on *How to create an invoice in QuickBooks Online*: https://www.youtube.com/ watch?v=o56z20jLzas.

When you create a sales invoice in QuickBooks, it has an impact on the balance sheet as well as the profit and loss statement. The accounts receivable account will increase, which will result in an increase in the total assets on the balance sheet report. Income will also increase the profit and loss statement. In our example, we have sold a product that is subject to sales tax. Therefore, inventory, sales tax, and cost of goods sold are also affected.

The following screenshot shows the journal entry that will be recorded in QuickBooks for our sample sales invoice shown previously:

Date	Account Name	Debit	Credit
9/8/2021	Accounts Receivable	43.8	
	Cost of Goods Sold	20	
	Inventory		20
	Sales Tax Payable		3.8
	Sales		40

Figure 8.9: Automatic journal entry recorded for invoice

The amount owed by customers—also known as accounts receivable—goes up by $43.80, and sales is increased by $40.00. Since the product we sold is taxable, sales tax payable is increased by $3.80. There is also a reduction in inventory, which results in an increase to the cost of goods sold account of $20. In the next section, we will show you how to apply payments to open accounts receivable balances.

Now that you know how to record income using a sales invoice, we will cover the second step, which is receiving customer payments. You must correctly apply customer payments to outstanding sales invoices to ensure that your accounts receivable balance is always up to date.

Recording customer payments

If you record income using a sales invoice, you will receive payment based on the terms you have agreed with your customer. When customer payments are received, you must apply payments to an outstanding sales invoice in order to reduce the accounts receivable balance. You can accept multiple payment methods in QuickBooks, including check, cash, and credit card. To learn more about managing credit card payments, refer to *Chapter 18, Handling Special Transactions in QuickBooks Online.*

Follow these steps to receive payment from a customer:

1. Click on the **+ New** button.

2. Navigate to **Receive payment**, located below **CUSTOMERS**, as indicated in *Figure 8.10*:

Figure 8.10: Navigating to Receive payment

3. Complete the fields, as indicated in the following screenshot, to record the customer payment:

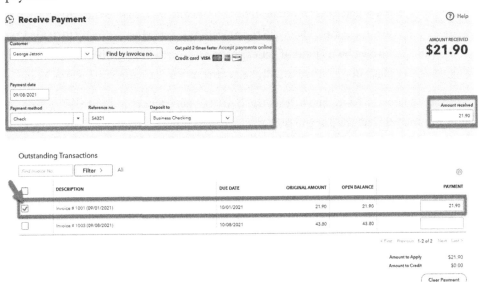

Figure 8.11: The Receive Payment window

The following are brief descriptions of the key fields for receiving customer payments:

- **Customer**: Select the customer by clicking the drop-down arrow. **George Jetson** is the customer selected in our example.

- **Payment date**: Enter the date payment was received. The payment date is **09/08/2021** in our example.

- **Payment method**: From the drop-down menu, select the payment method received (that is, by credit card, check, or cash). The payment method is **Check** in our example.

- **Reference no.**: If payment was made by check, enter the check number in this field. If another payment method was used, you can leave this field blank. The reference number is **54321** in our example.

- **Deposit to**: Select the bank account to which you will deposit this payment. **Business Checking** is the **Deposit to** account in our example.

- **Amount received**: Enter the amount of the payment received. The amount received in our example is **$21.90**.

- **Outstanding Transactions**: A list of unpaid invoices will appear in this section. Based on the amount entered in the **Amount received** field, QuickBooks will select the invoice that matches that amount and is closest to the date of the transaction. In our example shown in the preceding screenshot, invoice #**1001** for **$21.90** is the invoice being paid. If QuickBooks selects the wrong invoice, you can remove the checkmark and manually select the invoices to apply the payment to.

Recording customer payments affects the balance sheet report but not the income statement. Since income was recorded at the time the invoice was created, there is no impact on profit and loss (income statement).

The following screenshot shows the journal entry that will automatically be recorded in Quick-Books for a customer payment of $21.90:

Date	Account Name	Debit	Credit
9/8/2021	Business Checking	21.9	
	Accounts Receivable		21.9

Figure 8.12: Automatic journal entry recorded for customer payment received

The business checking account is increased by $21.90, which will result in an increase in the assets section of the balance sheet report. Accounts receivable will decrease by $21.90, which will result in a decrease in the assets section of the balance sheet report.

Pro Tip: The Receive payments method should be used when an invoice has previously been issued. Using Receive payments without an invoice will result in a credit balance on the customer account. The **Accounts receivable aging summary** should be reviewed periodically to capture any credits on customer accounts.

Recording payments to the undeposited funds account

In the previous examples, each of the payments that have been recorded from customers, whether on a sales receipt, deposit slip, or invoice, were all deposited to the business checking account. This is ideal if you don't deposit more than one check (customer payment) at a time. However, like most businesses you will probably wait until you have multiple checks before you head to the bank to make a deposit. In that case, you will need to record all customer payments to an account called **undeposited funds**.

The undeposited funds account is an account that is automatically created by QuickBooks. It acts like a "cash drawer" where all customer payments are held until you record a deposit in QuickBooks.

After you make a deposit with the bank, you need to record that deposit in QuickBooks. Follow the steps below to record a deposit that includes multiple checks (customer payments):

1. Click on the **+ New** button and select **Bank deposit**, as shown below:

Figure 8.13: Navigating to Bank deposit

2. The Bank Deposit form will appear:

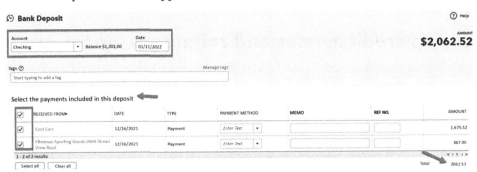

Figure 8.14: The Bank Deposit form

3. Select the bank account the deposit will be made to. **Checking** is the account selected in our example. In the **Date** field, select the date of the deposit; in our example, it is **01/11/2022**.

4. Below the **Select the payments included in this deposit** heading, put a checkmark next to each payment included in this deposit. In our example, we have put a checkmark next to all payments listed in this section, which total **$2,062.52**.

5. Click the Save button to record the deposit.

When this deposit is recorded in QuickBooks, the following journal entry is created behind the scenes:

Date	Account Name	Debit	Credit
1/11/2022	Checking	2062.52	
	Undeposited Funds		2062.52

Figure 8.15: Journal entry to transfer payments from undeposited funds to the checking account

When this deposit is recorded in QuickBooks, it only affects the balance sheet report. The checking account (an asset) increases by the total deposit amount, and the undeposited funds account, also an asset, decreases by the total deposit amount. To ensure you are in balance when you reconcile your bank accounts, always make sure that you have recorded all deposits in QuickBooks. If you have any payments sitting in the undeposited account (and they were actually deposited), you will be out of balance. To learn more about how to reconcile bank accounts, head over to *Chapter 10, Reconciling Downloaded Bank and Credit Card Transactions*.

Now that you know how to record income and apply payments to outstanding customer invoices, we will show you how to handle customer returns and refunds in the next section.

Issuing credit memos and refunds to customers

There may be times when a customer returns merchandise, or you need to refund a customer due to an issue with the services or products you have provided.

When that happens, you can create a credit memo in QuickBooks that can be applied to a future invoice, or you can refund the customer instead by clicking on + **New**, selecting **Refund receipt**, and following the onscreen instructions.

Follow these steps to create a credit memo in QuickBooks Online:

1. Click on the + **New** menu and select **Credit memo** below **CUSTOMERS**, as indicated in *Figure 8.16*:

Figure 8.16: Navigating to the Credit Memo form

2. Complete the key fields indicated here for the credit memo:

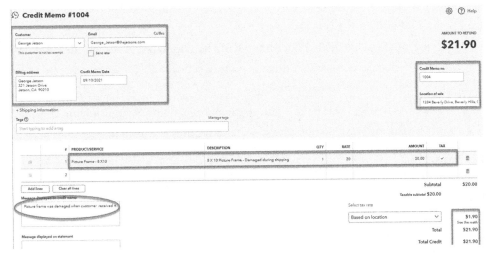

Figure 8.17: Credit Memo form

The following are brief descriptions of the key fields to complete for a credit memo. All fields are required except for the **QTY, DESCRIPTION**, and **Message displayed on credit memo** fields:

- **Customer:** From the drop-down menu, select the customer you need to refund. **George Jetson** is the customer selected in our example.

- **Email:** This field will automatically be populated with the email address you have on file. If you don't have an email address on file, you can enter the email address in this field if you would like to email the credit memo to the customer. The email address for George Jetson is George_Jetson@thejetsons.com.

- **Billing address:** This field will automatically be populated with the billing address you have on file. If you don't have a billing address on file, you can enter it directly in this field. The billing address for George Jetson is **321 Jetson Drive, Jetson, CA 90210.**

- **Credit Memo Date:** Enter the date for which you are creating this credit memo. The credit memo is dated **09/10/2021.**

- **PRODUCT/SERVICE:** From the drop-down menu, select the product or service for which you are providing a refund. The product is **Picture Frame – 8X10.**

- **DESCRIPTION:** This field will be populated automatically, based on the product/service selected. The description in our example is **8X10 Picture Frame – Damaged during shipping.**

- **QTY:** Enter the number of items or hours for which you are refunding the customer. The quantity is **1.**

- **RATE:** This field will automatically be populated based on the product/service selected. However, if there is no rate set up, you can enter the rate in this field. The rate is **$20** in our example.

- **AMOUNT:** This field is automatically calculated by multiplying the quantity by the rate. You do not have to enter anything in this field. The total amount to be refunded back to the customer is **$21.90** in our example.

- **Message displayed on credit memo:** In this field, you can add the original invoice number for which you are providing a full or partial credit, or a brief description of the reason for the credit. The message on our credit memo is **Picture frame was damaged when customer received it.**

Pro Tip: This Intuit video tutorial recaps the steps we've covered on *How to give custom-ers credit in QuickBooks Online*: https://www.youtube.com/watch?v=oi3WaGrUHK0.

Recording a credit memo in QuickBooks will have an impact on the balance sheet and income statement reports. The income account (sales) will decrease, which will reduce the total income on the profit and loss report. If the original invoice has not been paid, the credit memo can be applied to that invoice to reduce the total amount due from the customer. The accounts receivable account will decrease since the amount due from the customer has been reduced. Since this was a sale of product, we will also increase inventory for the damaged item that will be returned to the warehouse. Finally, the cost of goods sold account also goes down.

The journal entry for the preceding credit memo will automatically be recorded in QuickBooks as follows:

Date	Account Name	Debit	Credit
9/10/2021	Sales Tax Payable	1.9	
	Sales	20	
	Inventory	10	
	Cost of Goods Sold		10
	Accounts Receivable		21.9

Figure 8.18: Automatic journal entry recorded for credit memo

 Pro Tip: If you do not invoice customers through QuickBooks, you can issue a refund check by going to **+ New** and selecting **Check**, listed below the **Vendors** column.

Summary

In this chapter, you have learned how to record sales transactions for both the sale of products and services using a sales receipt, a deposit, and a sales invoice. You now know when to use each sales transaction, and how to record them in QuickBooks Online. We have also covered the journal entry recorded behind the scenes by QuickBooks for each transaction. In addition, you have learned how to record customer payments so that they are correctly applied to open invoices, and how to issue credit memos and refunds to customers. In the next chapter, we will look at how to record the money that flows out of your business to cover expenses.

Join our book's Discord space

Join the book's Discord workspace for a monthly *Ask me Anything* session with the author:
https://packt.link/QuickBooks

9

Recording Expenses in QuickBooks Online

Managing expenses incurred by a business is one of the primary reasons why many businesses decide to use QuickBooks. Most businesses know when they are generating income, but when it comes to where their money is going, it's a whole different story. For a business to be profitable, it must be able to control expenses that directly affect the bottom line.

In this chapter, we will show you four ways to record expenses (also known as **money-out** transactions): (1) entering and paying bills, (2) managing recurring expenses, (3) writing and printing checks, and (4) capturing and categorizing receipts and bills.

QBCU
3.3.2

Entering a bill is ideal for suppliers who have extended credit to you. You receive your purchases immediately and payment is due sometime in the future. However, expenses that require immediate payment should be paid via check. Entering a check allows you to record both the expense and the payment at the same time.

QBCU
3.3.3

Using one or more of these methods will give you access to detailed reports that will give you insight into all of your money-out transactions. This is a key component in having the ability to control expenses.

In this chapter, we will cover the following topics:

- Entering and paying bills
- Managing recurring expenses
- Writing checks

- Printing checks

- Editing, voiding, and deleting expenses

- Capturing and categorizing receipts and bills

By the end of this chapter, you will know how to enter and pay your bills, and how to create recurring expenses for rent, utilities, and other recurring costs. Plus, you will understand how to write a check and print it directly from QuickBooks and you will become familiar with the various ways in which you can upload receipts and bills in QuickBooks.

 The US edition of QBO was used to create this book. If you are using a version that is outside of the United States, results may differ.

Entering and paying bills

For purchases made on account, entering bills into QuickBooks and paying them a few days before they become due is the best way to manage your cash flow. If you enter bills into QuickBooks as you receive them, you can run reports that will show you which bills are due or are nearly due so that you can plan ahead, to ensure you have sufficient cash on hand to pay them. Unpaid bills are also referred to as **accounts payable**, or **A/P** for short. In the following sections, we will first cover how to enter bills, and then we will discuss how to pay a bill in **QuickBooks Online (QBO)**.

Entering bills into QuickBooks Online

Entering your bills into QuickBooks before they come due will help you to manage your cash flow. You can easily run reports, such as the Unpaid Bills report or the A/P Aging report, to see which bills are coming due or are past due.

To enter bills into QuickBooks Online, you will need to complete the following steps:

1. Click on the **+ New** button and select **Bill** in the **Vendors** column, as indicated in *Figure 9.1*:

Figure 9.1: Navigating to Bill from the Vendors menu

2. Complete the key fields in the Bill form, as indicated in *Figure 9.2*:

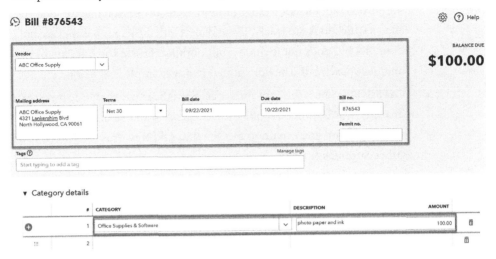

Figure 9.2: Completing the Bill form for a vendor

The following is a brief description of the key fields in the Bill form. All fields must be completed, except for the **DESCRIPTION** field:

- **Vendor**: Select a vendor from the drop-down menu, or add a new vendor if they have not been previously set up in QuickBooks. You can do this by selecting **Add New** from the drop-down menu. In our example, **ABC Office Supply** is the vendor.

- **Mailing address**: This field will automatically be populated for vendors you have previously created in QuickBooks. If this is a new vendor, you can enter the address in this field. In our example, the address is **4321 Lankershim Blvd, North Hollywood, CA 90061**.

- **Terms**: This field will automatically be populated with the vendor terms you have set up. If you have not previously set up vendor terms, you can select the appropriate payment terms from the drop-down menu. **Net 30** are the payment terms for ABC Office Supply.

- **Bill date**: Enter the date that appears on the vendor bill. Our bill date is **09/22/2021**.

- **Due date**: The due date will be calculated automatically based on the payment terms selected. If payment terms were not selected, you can also enter the due date directly in this field. The due date in our example is **10/22/2021**.

- **Bill no.:** The bill number is the invoice number assigned by the vendor supplier. If the bill does not include a unique number, create one. Having a unique bill number allows QuickBooks to track bills and alert you if there is a duplicate bill number used. If a bill does not include a bill number, utilize the bill date or something unique for each bill. The bill number in our example is **876543**.

- **CATEGORY:** Select the appropriate account the expense should be categorized to (in other words, office supplies, rent expenses, and so on). If you need to create a new account, you can do so by selecting **Add New** from the drop-down menu. **Office Supplies & Software** is the category selected in our example.

- **DESCRIPTION:** Enter a brief description of what was purchased in this field. Photo paper and ink are included in the description of our example.

- **AMOUNT:** Enter the amount of the bill in this field. The total amount is **$100** for the bill from ABC Office Supply.

When you complete a Bill form in QuickBooks, it has an impact on the balance sheet and the profit and loss (income statement) reports. A/P increases, which in turn increases current liabilities on the balance sheet report, expenses on the income statement for non-product purchases, and inventory on the balance sheet report, if you purchased a product for resale.

The journal entry that is recorded in QuickBooks for the preceding bill is shown in *Figure 9.3*:

Date	Account Name	Debit	Credit
9/22/2021	Office Supplies & Software	100	
	Accounts Payable		100

Figure 9.3: Journal entry to record a vendor bill

In our example, the debit to Office Supplies & Software increases the total expenses on the income statement by $100. In addition, the credit to A/P increases the total liabilities by $100 on the balance sheet report. In order to stay on top of your bills, it's a good idea to enter them as soon as you receive them. Be sure to enter a due date, so that QuickBooks can alert you when a bill is coming due.

Entering vendor credits into QuickBooks Online

If you overpay a vendor or receive a credit for damaged or returned merchandise, you can enter the credit memo into QuickBooks and apply it to future purchases. However, if you don't plan to order from that vendor again, you should request a refund.

To enter vendor credits into QuickBooks Online, you will need to complete the following steps:

1. Click on the **+ New** button and select **Vendor Credit** in the **Vendors** column, as indicated in *Figure 9.4*:

Figure 9.4: Navigating to the Vendor credit Form

2. Complete the key fields in the Vendor Credit form, as indicated below:

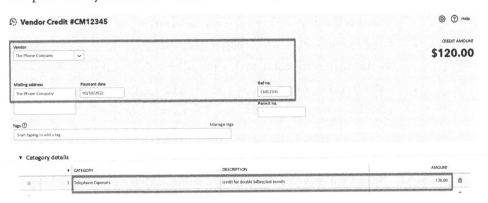

Figure 9.5: Complete Vendor Credit form

The following is a brief description of the key fields in the Vendor Credit form. All fields must be completed, except for the **DESCRIPTION** field:

- **Vendor**: Select a vendor from the drop-down menu, or add a new vendor if they have not been previously set up in QuickBooks. You can do this by selecting **Add New** from the drop-down menu. In our example, **The Phone Company** is the vendor.

- **Mailing address:** This field will automatically be populated for vendors you have previously created in QuickBooks. If this is a new vendor, you can enter the address in this field. In our example, the address is **123 Telephone Way, North Hollywood, CA 90061.**

- **Payment date:** Enter the date that appears on the vendor credit memo. Our bill date is **01/10/2022.**

- **Reference no.:** The reference number is the credit memo number assigned by the vendor supplier. If the credit memo does not include a unique number, create one. Having a unique credit memo number allows QuickBooks to track vendor credits and alert you if there is a duplicate number used. If a credit memo does not include a number, utilize the payment date or something unique for each bill. The credit memo number in our example is **CM12345.**

- **CATEGORY:** Select the appropriate account the expense should be categorized to (in other words, office supplies, rent expenses, and so on). If you need to create a new account, you can do so by selecting **Add New** from the drop-down menu. **Telephone Expenses** is the category selected in our example.

- **DESCRIPTION:** Enter a brief description of what was purchased in this field. **Credit for double billing last month** is included in the description of our example.

- **AMOUNT:** Enter the amount of the vendor credit in this field. The total amount is **$120** for the vendor credit from The Phone Company.

When you complete a vendor credit in QuickBooks, it has an impact on the balance sheet and the profit and loss (income statement) reports. A/P decreases, which in turn decreases current liabilities on the balance sheet report. Expenses on the income statement for non-product purchases decrease, and inventory on the balance sheet report decreases, if you purchased a product for resale.

The journal entry that is recorded in QuickBooks for the preceding vendor creditl is shown in *Figure 9.6*:

Date	Account Name	Debit	Credit
9/22/2021	Accounts Payable	100	
	Business Checking		100

Figure 9.6: Journal entry to record a vendor credit

In our example, the debit to Accounts Payable decreases the current liabilities on the balance sheet report, and the credit to Telephone Expenses decreases total expenses on the income statement by $120.

Paying bills in QuickBooks Online

After you enter a bill in QuickBooks, you will need to pay it before the due date. Paying bills in QuickBooks will ensure that the A/P balance is always up to date and will allow you to run reports, and to see which bills have been paid or need to be paid.

Follow these steps to pay bills in QuickBooks Online:

1. Click on the **+ New** button and select **Pay Bills** in the **Vendors** column, as indicated in *Figure 9.7*:

Figure 9.7: Navigating to Pay Bills from the Vendors menu

2. Complete the key fields in the Pay Bills form, as indicated in *Figure 9.8*:

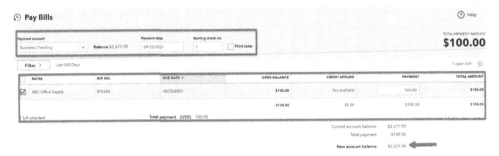

Figure 9.8: Completing the Pay Bills form

The following is a brief description of the fields in the Pay Bills form; all fields must be completed:

- **Payment account**: Select the bank or credit card account from which you want to deduct this bill payment. **Business Checking** is the account selected in our example.
- **Payment date**: Select the date on which you will pay for this bill. If writing a check, this will be the check date. The payment date is **09/22/2021** in our example.

- **Starting check no.:** If you are writing a check, make sure the check number is the next available number. The starting check number is **1** in our example.

- **Print later:** Put a check in this box if you don't plan to print the check now, but will print it later on. We will show you how to print checks later in this chapter.

- **PAYEE:** This field will include a list of the payees with open bills. To select a bill for payment, put a checkmark in the box to the left of the **PAYEE** field. In our example, **ABC Office Supply** is the payee.

> **Pro Tip:** If your vendor prefers separate checks for each invoice, select the first invoice and save it, and then select each individual invoice one at a time, clicking **Save** in-between each. Then, when you print checks, there will be separate checks for each invoice. An example where this might be useful is paying utility bills. Many utility companies prefer separate checks for each account that you are paying a bill for.

- **REF NO.:** This field will include the invoice number (or bill number) that was entered when the bill was saved in QuickBooks. In our example, **876543** is the reference number.

- **DUE DATE:** This field will automatically be populated with the due date that was entered when the bill was saved in QuickBooks. The due date for this bill is **10/22/2021** in our example.

- **OPEN BALANCE:** This field will automatically be populated with the unpaid amount of the bill. The open balance is **$100.00** in our example.

- **CREDIT APPLIED:** If you have open credits for a vendor, you will see them listed in this column. For example, if you overpaid a vendor or returned an item that was previously purchased, you will have a credit on your account that can be used toward future purchases.

- **PAYMENT:** Enter the amount you would like to pay in this field. You can pay the bill in full, or make a partial payment. If you make a partial payment, QuickBooks will keep the remaining balance due on file for you to pay in the future. The payment amount is **$100.00** in our example. However, if you wish to pay less than the bill amount, you can do so by entering the amount you want to pay in this field.

- **TOTAL AMOUNT**: This column is automatically calculated for you. It will always match the amount you entered in the **PAYMENT** field. The total amount is **$100.00** in our example.
- **New account balance**: In the lower-right corner, QuickBooks calculates the new balance in the business checking account after deducting the amount of the bill payment. The new account balance is **$2571.90** in our example.

 Pro Tip: To reinforce the steps covered for entering and paying bills in QuickBooks, watch this Intuit video tutorial, *How to manage your bills in QuickBooks Online*: `https://youtu.be/p4FPKQ8Bf5M`.

When you pay a bill in QuickBooks, it only has an impact on the balance sheet report. The A/P balance goes down because you no longer owe your vendor for the bill, and the business checking account goes down because a payment has been made. If you paid the bill with a credit card, the credit card balance goes up, which increases liabilities.

The following screenshot shows the journal entry recorded for the preceding bill:

Date	Account Name	Debit	Credit
9/22/2021	Accounts Payable	100	
	Business Checking		100

Figure 9.9: Journal entry to record a bill

In our example, the debit to A/P decreases total liabilities on the balance sheet report by $100. In addition, the credit to the business checking account decreases total assets on the balance sheet report by $100. Paying bills in QuickBooks will give you access to detailed information about your expenses. You can run reports to show how much you are spending, which vendors you purchase from, and how often. These reports will help you to control what you are spending your money on, which allows you to properly manage your expenses. In *Chapter 14, Vendor and Expenses Reports*, we cover reports in detail.

Creating recurring expenses in QuickBooks can save you a lot of time. We will cover how to manage recurring expenses next.

Managing recurring expenses

In this section, we will show you how to create a template for recurring (repeat) expenses. Most businesses purchase goods and services from the same vendors. For example, rent and utilities are examples of recurring expenses that are generally paid monthly. Instead of creating these expenses from scratch each month, you can create a recurring expense, which is a template you can save with the vendor, amount, account, and other pertinent information.

When you are ready to pay a recurring expense, you can schedule the expense to be recorded automatically on a certain day. You can manually generate the expense when you need to pay it, or have QuickBooks send you an alert when it's time to make a payment. Using recurring expense templates will save you time, and will reduce the amount of manual data entry required.

Follow these steps to create a recurring expense in QuickBooks:

1. Navigate to the gear icon and select **Recurring Transactions** from the **Lists** column, as indicated in *Figure 9.10*:

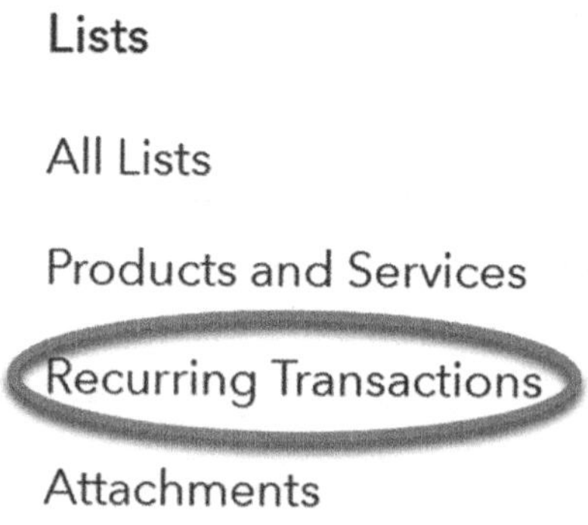

Lists

All Lists

Products and Services

Recurring Transactions

Attachments

Figure 9.10: Selecting Recurring Transactions from the Lists menu

2. Click the **New** button in the upper-right corner, as indicated in *Figure 9.11*:

Figure 9.11: Clicking New to create a new Recurring Transactions template

3. Select the transaction type from the drop-down menu, as indicated in *Figure 9.12*, and click the **OK** button:

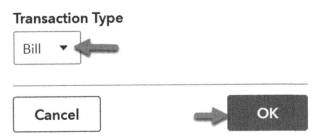

Figure 9.12: Selecting the Transaction Type for a Recurring Transactions template

You can create a recurring transaction for a number of different types of transactions besides a bill. The other options available from the drop-down include check, credit card credit, credit memo, deposit, estimate, expense, invoice, and journal entry. While the screens may differ slightly, they will be very similar to what you see in this example.

4. A blank Recurring Transactions template will appear. Complete the fields as indicated in *Figure 9.13*:

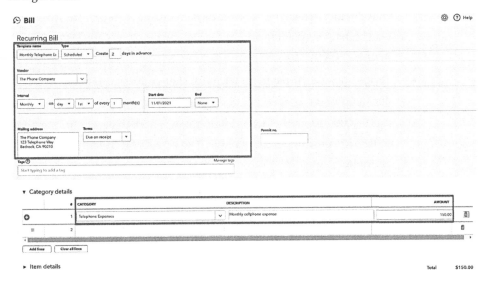

Figure 9.13: Completing the Recurring Bill template

The following is a brief description of the information required to complete the Recurring Transactions template:

- **Template name**: This field should include the type of expense or the payee's name. **Monthly Telephone Expense** is the template name in our example.

- **Type**: From the drop-down menu, you can select **Scheduled**, **Reminder**, or **Unscheduled**. **Scheduled** is the type of template we are setting up.

- **Create X days in advance**: QuickBooks will create the transaction in advance of the due date. **2** days in advance is selected in our example.

- **Vendor**: Select the payee from the drop-down menu. If you have not added vendors to QuickBooks, you can add a new vendor by selecting **Add new** in the drop-down field. **The Phone Company** is the vendor in our example.

- **Interval**: This field refers to how often you would like to create this recurring transaction. The options are **Daily**, **Weekly**, **Monthly**, or **Yearly**. **Monthly** is the interval selected in our example.

- **Start date/End**: Select the date on which you would like to start using the recurring transaction and, if applicable, you can select an end date, or select **None**. The start date is **11/01/2021** and the end date is **None** in our example.

- **Mailing address**: If you plan to mail your payment, you need to add a mailing address to this field. However, if the payment is automatically deducted from your business checking account or made using a credit card, you can leave this field blank. The mailing address for The Phone Company is **123 Telephone Way, Bedrock, CA 90210**.

- **Terms**: Include the payment terms for the vendor in this field. Payment terms are due upon receipt.

- **CATEGORY**: From the drop-down menu, select the account that accurately describes the type of purchase made. The category is **Telephone Expenses** for our example.

- **DESCRIPTION**: Include a brief description of the expense in this field. **Monthly cellphone expense** is the description in our case.

- **AMOUNT**: Enter the amount of the expense in this field. The amount is **$150.00** in our example.

5. Be sure to **Save** the template when you are done.

6. After saving the template, the Recurring Transactions template list will appear, as indicated in *Figure 9.14*:

TEMPLATE NAME ▼	TYPE	TXN TYPE	INTERVAL	PREVIOUS DATE	NEXT DATE	CUSTOMER/VENDOR	AMOUNT	ACTION
Monthly Telephone Expense	Scheduled	Bill	Every Month		11/01/2021	The Phone Comp...	150.00	Edit ▼

Figure 9.14: Recurring Transactions template (Expense)

In the Recurring Transactions template list, you will see the information previously entered in the template. The following info appears in the screenshot above:

- **TEMPLATE NAME:** Monthly Telephone Expense
- **TYPE:** Bill
- **INTERVAL:** Monthly
- **NEXT DATE:** 11/01/2021
- **CUSTOMER/VENDOR:** The Phone Company
- **AMOUNT:** 150.00
- **ACTION:** From the drop-down menu, you can **Edit, Use, Duplicate, Pause, Skip,** or **Delete. Edit** simply allows you to make changes to the template; **Duplicate** allows you to create a template with the same information; **Pause** allows you to stop the recurring transaction temporarily; **Skip** allows you to skip a recurring transaction; and **Delete** allows you to delete the template.

In addition to creating recurring transactions such as bills to pay expenses, you can also create the following types of recurring transactions:

- **Check:** Payments made via check for products or services purchased.
- **Credit card credit:** Credit card credit is money that was refunded to you from a previous credit card charge. This could also be a cashback rebate given to you by your credit card merchant for meeting a certain spending threshold.
- **Credit memo:** A credit memo is issued to customers for a product they have returned or for services that were not provided.
- **Deposit:** A deposit is money received from customers, which is then deposited into your bank account. If you have customers who pay via wire transfer or **Automated Clearing House (ACH)** bank transfer on a periodic basis, you could set these deposits up as recurring.
- **Estimate:** An estimate is a bid or quote, created to provide customers with an approximate cost of your products or services.

- **Expense**: An expense is a payment for services received from a vendor/supplier.

- **Invoice**: An invoice is a sales form, used to record the sale of products or services provided on credit.

- **Journal entry**: A journal entry form is used to make adjustments to the financial statements before closing the books.

- **Refund**: A product returned by you or your customer will result in a refund of the payment that was made for the returned goods or unfulfilled services.

- **Sales receipt**: A sales receipt is used to record sales whereby payment is made immediately by the customer (for example, businesses such as clothing stores or restaurants).

- **Transfer**: A transfer is used to move money between bank accounts, such as business checking and savings accounts.

- **Vendor credit**: A vendor credit is a refund issued to you by a vendor supplier for a product you have returned or for services that were not performed.

 Pro Tip: Recurring transactions are ideal for loan payments or other cash disbursements that you may not receive a monthly bill for.

If you need to pay a bill that was unexpected or past due, you don't need to enter it as a bill and then pay it. Instead, you can go directly to the check register and write a check. We will cover writing checks in the next section.

QBCU 3.3.3 Writing checks

So far, we have discussed how to pay expenses by entering them as bills and paying them at a later date, and how to set up recurring expenses. A third way in which you can record expenses for your business is by writing checks. The benefit of writing checks directly in QuickBooks is that you don't have to waste time manually writing a check. Instead, you can create checks and print them directly from QuickBooks. This is ideal for purchases that require payment right away. For example, if you go to the office supply store to purchase office supplies, you will need to pay for the supplies before leaving the store.

Follow these steps to write checks in QuickBooks Online:

1. Click on the **+ New** button and select **Check** in the **Vendors** column, as indicated in *Figure 9.15*:

Figure 9.15: Navigating to Checks

2. The following screenshot shows the fields of information to be completed in the Check form:

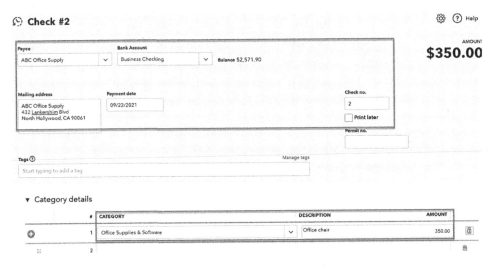

Figure 9.16: Completing the Write Checks form

The following is a brief description of the information in the Check form:

- **Payee:** From the drop-down menu, select the vendor to whom you are making a payment. If you have not added vendors, you can do so by selecting **Add new** from the drop-down menu. **ABC Office Supply** is the payee in our example.

- **Bank Account**: This field will automatically be populated with your business checking account. However, if you have more than one checking account, be sure to select the correct account from the drop-down menu. **Business Checking** is the bank account in our example.

- **Balance**: Based on the bank account selected, you will see the current balance (per QuickBooks) of the business checking account you have selected. The current balance in the business checking account is **$2,571.90** in our case.

- **Mailing address**: This field will automatically be populated with the information on file for the payee. In our case, the mailing address is **432 Lankershim Blvd, North Hollywood, CA 90061**.

- **Payment date**: This date should reflect the check date. In our example, the payment date is **09/22/2021**.

- **Check no.**: The check number will automatically be populated with the next available check number. The check number is **2** in our example.

 Pro Tip: You can also use the **Write Checks** form to record expenses paid with a debit card. Instead of entering a check number in the **Check no.** field, you would use DB or Debit, indicating the expense was paid with a debit card. To record ACH transactions, you would put ACH in the check number field.

- **CATEGORY**: Select the category (account) that best describes the items purchased.
- **DESCRIPTION**: Enter a detailed description of the items purchased.
- **AMOUNT**: Enter the amount of the purchase.

When entering a check into QuickBooks, it can have an impact on accounts that appear on both the balance sheet and the profit and loss (income statement). The balance sheet will always be affected because the bank account is included in the assets section of the balance sheet. However, the profit and loss will only be affected if you purchase an expense. Otherwise, if you purchase a product for resale (inventory), it will only have an impact on the balance sheet.

The following screenshot shows the journal entry recorded for the preceding check:

Date	Account Name	Debit	Credit
9/22/2021	Office Supplies & Software	350	
	Business Checking		350

Figure 9.17: Journal entry to record payment of a bill by check

In our example, Office Supplies & Software increased by $350, which increases expenses on profit and loss (income statement). The business checking account decreased by $350, which means assets have gone down on the balance sheet report.

After entering a check, you can choose to print the check immediately, or wait and print a batch of checks later on. In the next section, we will show you how to print checks.

Printing checks

In order to print checks, you must purchase check stock that is compatible with QuickBooks Online. You can order checks from a variety of places, such as your financial institution, or directly from Intuit. Visit the **Intuit Checks and Supplies** (`https://intuitmarket.intuit.com/checks`) website to learn more.

Follow these steps to print checks:

1. Click on the **+ New** button and select **Print Checks** in the **Vendors** column, as indicated in *Figure 9.18*:

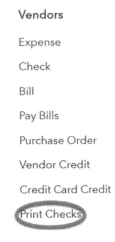

Figure 9.18: Navigating to Print Checks

2. Follow these steps on the next screen to ensure that your printer is set up properly:

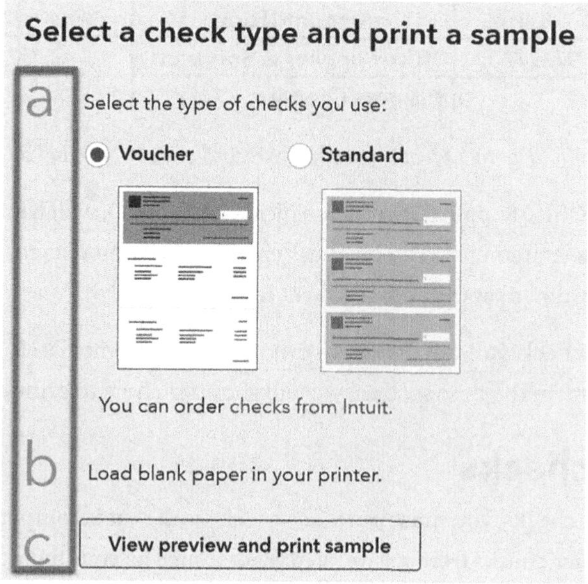

Select a check type and print a sample

a   Select the type of checks you use:

◉ **Voucher**   ◯ **Standard**

You can order checks from Intuit.

b   Load blank paper in your printer.

c   **View preview and print sample**

Figure 9.19: Selecting the check type for printing checks

The following is a brief description of the steps:

- **Select the type of checks you use:** There are two types of checks, **Voucher** and **Standard**. The **Voucher** check includes one check per page, and two printed vouchers (one for you and one for the payee). The **Standard** check has three checks per page, and no voucher.

> **Pro Tip:** A voucher is a printout of the payment details, including bill number, amount, and check number.

- **Load blank paper in your printer:** Before loading real check stock, run a test using blank paper. Draw an arrow on the top of the first sheet of paper to see how the information will print so that you know how to load the check stock in your printer.

- **View preview and print sample**: You can preview a sample check to see whether it is aligned properly. If not, follow the onscreen instructions to fix any issues before using real check stock. Checks will print to a preview screen where you can select your printer.

 Pro Tip: To recap the steps on writing and printing checks in QuickBooks, watch this Intuit video tutorial: https://quickbooks.intuit.com/learn-support/en-us/write-checks/how-to-record-print-checks/00/344866.

As discussed, printing checks directly from QuickBooks will save you time when you reconcile your bank account. Since expenses paid with a check are automatically recorded in QuickBooks when you save the check, you won't have to worry about manually entering them later on. One way to have quick access to source documents is to attach receipts and bills to transactions using the capture and categorize receipts feature. We will discuss this shortly.

 Pro Tip: Imagine you have pizza delivered to the office and you need to quickly print one check. Click the **+ New** button, select **Check**, enter the payment details, and select **Print check** at the bottom of the screen.

Editing, voiding, and deleting expenses `QBCU 3.3.8`

Like most transactions in QuickBooks, you can edit bills up until they are paid. However, after you have paid a bill you will need to either record a credit memo if you overpaid or request a new bill if you underpaid. To edit a bill, you need to go to the vendor center, select the vendor, and then click on the bill you wish to make changes to. After making the necessary changes, save the bill and close out of it. You can also edit checks in a similar manner. As long as you have not printed the check, you can make any changes necessary. Navigate to the check register, locate the check, and make the necessary changes. After you have printed a check, you will need to void it if it is incorrect. You can easily do this from the check register as well.

For expenses in general, if you have not closed the books or reconciled the bank account for the period, you can make changes to expenses that were previously recorded. **If you have closed the books or reconciled the bank account for the period, you** *cannot* **make changes to the transaction date or amount. If a correction to the books is required, you will need to consult with your accountant to discuss recording a journal entry.** See *Chapter 17, Closing the Books in QuickBooks Online*, to learn more about journal entries.

QBCU
4.3.1

Capturing and categorizing receipts and bills

Receipt capture allows you to attach receipts and bills to transactions in QuickBooks. As a result, you will be able to quickly access source documents when needed. This feature works in a couple of different ways. First, you can attach receipts and bills to transactions previously entered into QuickBooks Online. Second, you can use a receipt capture to record a transaction for the first time. Of course, you can use both methods interchangeably.

Perform the following steps to capture a receipt or bill:

1. Navigate to **Banking** and select **Receipts**, as indicated in *Figure 9.20*:

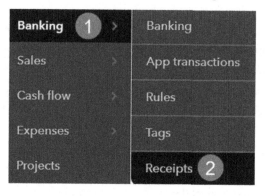

Figure 9.20: Navigating to Receipts in QBO

2. The following screen will appear (note: Make sure you are on the **Receipts** tab, as indicated here):

Figure 9.21: Uploading receipts to QBO

There are three options available to capture receipts:

- **Upload from computer**: If the bill or receipt is saved to your computer, select this option and navigate to where the receipt or bill is located on your computer.

- **Upload from Google Drive**: If the receipt/bill is located in your Google Drive account, you can access it by clicking on this icon and follow the onscreen instructions to locate the file in Google Drive.

- **Forward from email**: By selecting this option, QuickBooks will take you through a few setup screens to create a custom email address that can be used to forward receipts and bills to QuickBooks.

 Pro Tip: Keep in mind that for each of the receipt capture options, there should only be one receipt per file. If you try to include more than one receipt in a file, QuickBooks will not be able to process the receipt capture.

3. Once you add receipts to QuickBooks, they will show up in the **For review** section just below the receipt capture options, as follows:

Figure 9.22: Reviewing receipts uploaded in QBO

You can click on each receipt to review, edit, and match it to existing transactions in QuickBooks.

**QBCU
4.3.2** If you have not entered the expense into QuickBooks, you can create a new expense using receipt capture. Perform the following steps to create a brand-new expense from a receipt capture:

1. Navigate to the **Expenses** tab, as indicated in *Figure 9.23*:

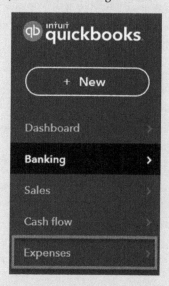

Figure 9.23: Navigating to Expenses

2. On the left menu bar, select **Expenses** and then **Expenses** again to create a new transaction with the receipt attached.

To summarize, we have covered how to use the capture and categorize receipts and bills feature, which allows you to attach source documents such as bills to existing transactions. In addition, you can create new transactions using this feature, which will save you the time you normally would have spent entering the data manually.

 Pro Tip: You can also add receipts to transactions using the paperclip (attachments) feature located at the bottom of the screen when you have an individual transaction open.

Summary

In this chapter, we have shown you how to enter and pay your bills, how to enter vendor credits, how to manage recurring expenses, how to write checks, and how to print checks. We also covered the three ways in which you can upload bills and receipts to QuickBooks.

As a result, you will be able to stay on top of your cash outflow.

In the next chapter, we will show you how to reduce or eliminate the need to manually enter bank and credit card transactions by downloading transactions automatically into QuickBooks using bank feeds.

> The primary difference between expense transactions and bank feed transactions is that expense transactions are typically entered manually through bills, checks, recurring expenses, and receipt capture, whereas bank feeds do not require manual data entry. Instead, your bank account is connected to QuickBooks and bank transactions automatically "feed" into the banking center in QuickBooks, saving you time.

QBCU 3.3.5

Join our book's Discord space

Join the book's Discord workspace for a monthly *Ask me Anything* session with the author:
`https://packt.link/QuickBooks`

10

QBCU 4.2.1

Reconciling Downloaded Bank and Credit Card Transactions

In *Chapter 5, Customizing QuickBooks for Your Business*, we showed you how to connect bank and credit card accounts to **QuickBooks Online (QBO)**, to reduce the amount of time you spend manually entering data. In this chapter, we will show you how to manage bank and credit card transactions that have been downloaded to QuickBooks.

When bank and credit card transactions are downloaded, they are organized in the Banking Center. Before these transactions can be recorded in QuickBooks, you must review them with regard to matching them with transactions that have already been entered into QuickBooks, adding payee or category information, and providing any additional details to help identify each transaction. We will also show you how bank rules can help to reduce the number of transactions requiring manual review. Last, but not least, we will show you how to reconcile your accounts. Reconciling is the process of making sure your QuickBooks data matches the monthly statements provided by your financial institution. By reconciling often, you can catch errors made by the bank or credit card company, and catch fraudulent transactions a lot sooner.

In this chapter, we will cover the following topics:

- Overview of the Banking Center
- Matching transactions
- Editing banking transactions
- Creating and using bank rules
- Reconciling accounts

By the end of this chapter, you will have a solid understanding of how the Banking Center works. You will know how to match transactions, and how to edit transactions by adding a memo or changing the category. You will be more efficient with managing banking transactions by using bank rules. Finally, you will be confident in reconciling your accounts with the statements received from your financial institution. We will start by giving you an overview of the Banking Center, which is where you will find downloaded bank and credit card transactions.

 The US edition of QBO was used to create this book. If you are using a version that is outside of the United States, results may differ.

Overview of the Banking Center

The Banking Center is where you can manage bank and credit card transactions that have been downloaded into QuickBooks from your financial institution. These transactions require your review before they are recorded in your books.

At the very top of the page, you will see tiles that represent bank and credit card accounts you have added to QuickBooks. On each tile, you will find the name of the account, the current balance (per your financial institution), the current balance (per QuickBooks), and the number of transactions that require review before they can be recorded in the QuickBooks check register.

Follow these steps to navigate to the Banking Center:

1. Click on the **Banking** tab, located on the left menu bar, and select **Banking**, as indicated in *Figure 10.1*:

Figure 10.1: Navigating to the Banking Center

2. The Banking Center will appear, as indicated in *Figure 10.2*:

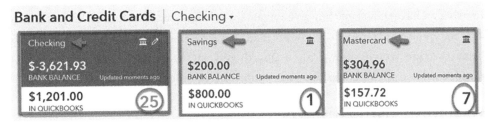

Figure 10.2: Bank and credit card accounts in the Banking Center

The following is a brief description of the information you will find in the Banking Center:

- **Bank account**: At the very top of each tile, you will find the name of the account (for example, Checking, Savings, or Mastercard).

- **BANK BALANCE**: The balance of the account per your financial institution will be displayed below the bank account name.

- **IN QUICKBOOKS**: The balance of the account per QuickBooks will be displayed right below the bank balance.

- **Transactions for review**: Transactions that have been downloaded from your financial institution and are pending review will be indicated in the lower right-hand corner of each tile. In the preceding screenshot, these numbers are **25**, **1**, and **7**.

Pro Tip: If the bank balance and the balance in QuickBooks match, this means all downloaded transactions have been reviewed. As a result, you will not see a number in the lower right-hand corner of the tile. If the balances do not match and you don't have any transactions in the review tab, that does not necessarily mean that you are missing something. A difference in the two balances can be from outstanding items that have not yet cleared the bank due to timing differences, or transactions that have not yet downloaded to QBO.

If you imported your transactions into QuickBooks from a CSV file instead of connecting your bank and credit card accounts to QuickBooks, you will only see a QuickBooks balance (not a bank balance) for each account. I recommend reviewing transactions on a daily or weekly basis so that you don't get too far behind.

Now that we have shown you how to navigate the Banking Center so you can review and manage bank and credit card transactions, you are ready to take action on the downloaded transactions. In the next section, we will show you how QuickBooks can save you time by matching downloaded transactions with transactions previously entered into QuickBooks.

Matching transactions

In this section, we will cover a process called **matching transactions**. QuickBooks will automatically attempt to match transactions that have been downloaded into QuickBooks with transactions that have already been recorded in QuickBooks. This process can help you to save time you would normally have spent trying to match transactions manually. We will show you how this process works by going through examples.

In the **For review** tab, we can see that QuickBooks has attempted to match three transactions that were previously entered into QuickBooks:

1 match found Deposit 09/03/2021 $868.15			$868.15	**Match**
1 match found Check 75 09/03/2021 -$228.75 Hicks Hardware		$228.75		**Match**
1 match found Bill Payment 6 09/02/2021 -$114.09 PG&E		$114.09		**Match**

Figure 10.3: Banking transactions in the For review tab

The following is a brief explanation of the preceding three transactions QuickBooks has found a match for:

- **Deposit for $868.15**: QuickBooks has found a deposit in the file for $868.15 (dated 09/03/21), which matches a deposit the bank has downloaded to the Banking Center for $868.15. If these transactions are one and the same, simply click **Match** in the far-right column.

- **Check for $228.75**: QuickBooks has identified Check #75 for $228.75, which matches a withdrawal downloaded from the bank for the same amount ($228.75). If these transactions are one and the same, simply click **Match** in the far-right column.

- **Bill Payment for $114.09**: QuickBooks has found a bill payment for $114.09, which matches a withdrawal downloaded from the bank for the same amount ($114.09). If these transactions are one and the same, simply click **Match** in the far-right column.

 Pro Tip: Transfers between bank accounts are also very common. If both bank accounts are connected to QuickBooks, it will most likely automatically match these bank transfers for you. Be sure to verify the accounts are correct before recording in QuickBooks.

When you select **Match**, these items will move from the **For review** tab to the **Categorized** tab in the Banking Center. These items will also be marked as cleared in QuickBooks, which will be important when we get ready to reconcile these accounts later on. If QuickBooks has not found the right match, you can replace it with the correct match.

To change the match recommended by QuickBooks, click on the transaction, and then click on the **Find other matches** button, as indicated in *Figure 10.4*:

Figure 10.4: Matching transactions in the Banking Center

In addition to matching transactions, you will need to provide additional information, such as payee and category (account), before the transaction can be recorded in QuickBooks. Banking transactions that have not been matched will remain in the Banking Center to be categorized and added to your books. Some examples are debit card and ACH transactions and manual or handwritten checks.

Now that we have shown you how matching transactions works and how you can post a matching transaction with just a few clicks, we will cover how to make any necessary changes to recorded transactions. In the next section, we will cover how to edit banking transactions.

Editing banking transactions

When you first start adding banking transactions to QuickBooks, you will need to review each transaction to ensure it has a proper payee (vendor) or customer and account category assigned to it. As you begin to repeat transactions, QuickBooks will remember how a transaction was recorded previously, and it will automatically assign the payee (vendor) and account category for expenses. Be sure to verify everything is correct before recording the transaction in QuickBooks.

Follow these steps to edit banking transactions in the Banking Center:

1. From the left menu bar, select **Banking**, as indicated in *Figure 10.5*:

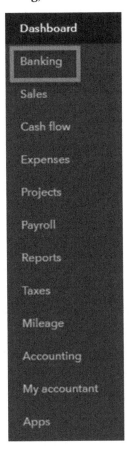

Figure 10.5: Navigating to the Banking Center

2. Click on the **For review** tab, as indicated in *Figure 10.6*:

Figure 10.6: The For review tab in the Banking Center

3. Click anywhere within the edit banking transaction window to make any necessary changes, as indicated in *Figure 10.7*:

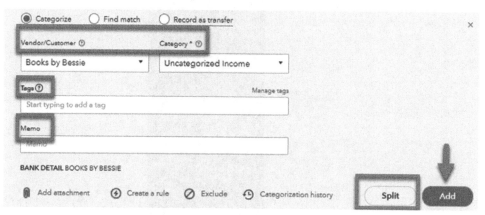

Figure 10.7: Editing a transaction in the Banking Center

You will find the following information in the edit banking transaction window:

- **Vendor/Customer**: For withdrawals, select the payee (vendor) from the drop-down menu. For deposits, select the customer. If it is a new vendor or customer, you can click **Add new** from the drop-down menu and add them here.

- **Category**: From the drop-down menu, select the category (account) that best describes the transaction you are recording (that is, Fuel, Office Supplies, or something else).

- **Tags**: Use tags to earmark or flag specific types of income or expenses you choose to keep tabs on.

- **Customer/project**: If when recording an expense, you need to bill to a customer, select the customer from the drop-down menu so that this transaction is earmarked as a billable expense.

- **Memo**: The bank details will generally appear in this field. This could be the name of the merchant.

- **Split transaction**: To the left of the **Add** button is a split transaction button. A split transaction allows you to assign more than one category (account) to a transaction. For example, let's say you purchased an office chair that cost $300. The total bill was for $325, which includes a shipping charge. You can split this bill by putting the $300 into office expenses and the $25 into shipping/freight expenses.

- **Add**: Once all fields are complete, click on the **Add** button to record this transaction in the check or credit card register in QuickBooks.

 Watch this Intuit video tutorial for a recap of how to categorize banking transactions: `https://quickbooks.intuit.com/learn-support/en-us/bank-transactions/adding-transactions-from-your-bank-credit-card/00/344865`.

As discussed, QuickBooks will automatically recall the vendor or customer and category (account) that was previously used.

If you realize that a transaction that you previously accepted and moved over to the **Categorized** tab needs to be adjusted, you can easily edit this transaction as follows:

1. Click on the **Categorized** tab, locate the transaction, and click on the **Undo** option in the far-right column, as indicated in *Figure 10.8*:

	DATE ▼	DESCRIPTION	AMOUNT	ASSIGNED TO	RULE	ACTION
☐	07/24/2020	CHECK # 5755	-$1,225.00	Added to: Expense: Owner's Pay & Person:		Undo
☐	07/23/2020	QuikTrip	-$30.15	Added to: Expense: Car & Truck:Gas 07/23		Undo

Figure 10.8: Editing a transaction previously accepted in the Banking Center

2. The transaction will appear in the **For review** tab as follows:

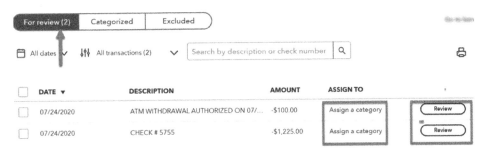

Figure 10.9: The For review tab in the Banking Center

3. You can **Assign a category** (account) by clicking on the link indicated in the preceding screenshot, or click the **Review** button to edit other fields in the transaction.

Pro Tip: Next to the **Categorized** tab is the **Excluded** tab. This tab is used to handle transactions you do not want posted in QuickBooks. For example, if a duplicate transaction was downloaded into QuickBooks (which does happen), you would only want to post one of the transactions that were downloaded. Since you are not able to delete downloaded transactions, you simply mark it as excluded and it will move from the **For review** tab to the **Excluded** tab.

Now that we have shown you how to modify banking transactions and utilize the auto-recall feature, we will introduce you to bank rules in the next section. Using bank rules is the best way to ensure the accuracy of transactions recorded. We will discuss how to create and use bank rules in the next section.

QBCU 4.2.2

Understanding bank rules

Bank rules are a list of conditions that must be met in order for QuickBooks to automatically assign a payee, account (category), class, and a location to download banking transactions to. Bank rules will apply only to bank or credit card transactions in the **For review** tab of the Banking Center. Since most businesses have the same transactions that take place month after month, using bank rules can save you time you would have spent reviewing transactions in the Banking Center before they can be recorded in QuickBooks.

Follow these steps to create a bank rule:

1. Click on **Banking** and select **Rules**.

2. Click on the **Rules** tab, as indicated in *Figure 10.10*:

Figure 10.10: Navigating to bank rules

3. Click on the **New rule** button, as indicated in *Figure 10.11*:

Figure 10.11: Creating a new bank rule

4. The following screen will appear:

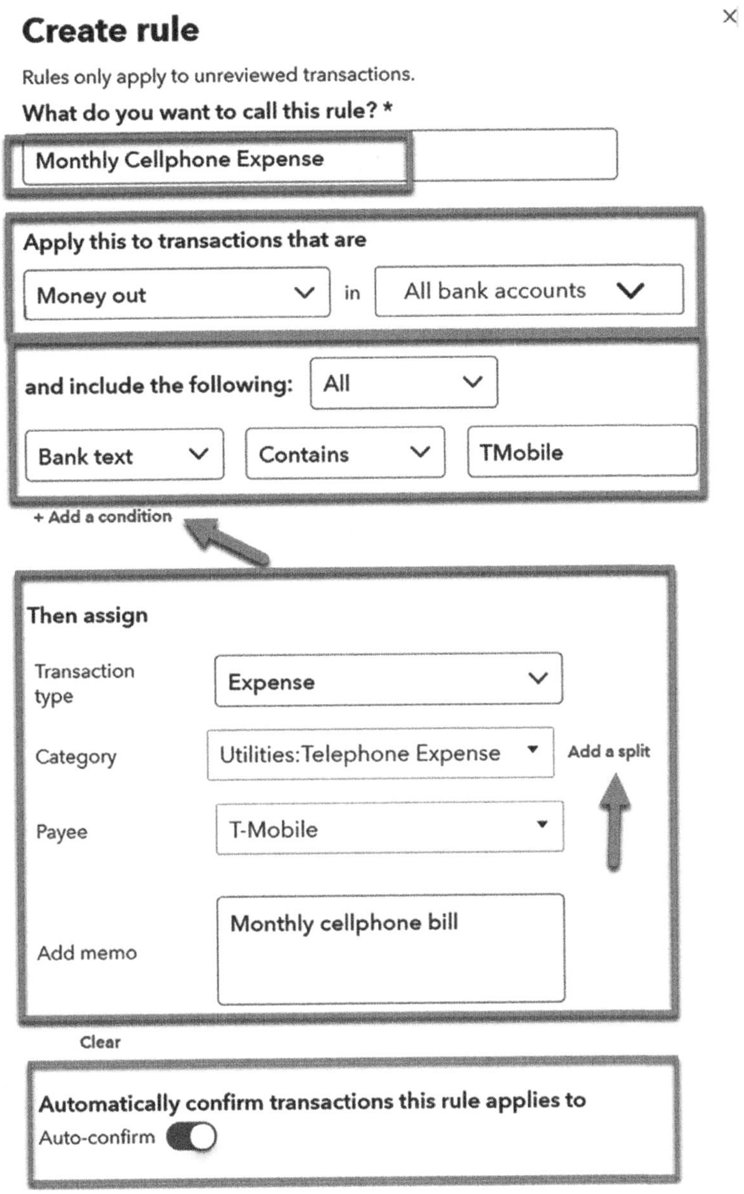

Create rule ✕

Rules only apply to unreviewed transactions.

What do you want to call this rule? *

Monthly Cellphone Expense

Apply this to transactions that are

Money out ⌄   in   All bank accounts ⌄

and include the following: All ⌄

Bank text ⌄   Contains ⌄   TMobile

+ Add a condition

Then assign

Transaction type   Expense ⌄

Category   Utilities:Telephone Expense ▾   Add a split

Payee   T-Mobile ▾

Add memo   Monthly cellphone bill

Clear

Automatically confirm transactions this rule applies to

Auto-confirm 🔘

Figure 10.12: Completing the fields required to create a new bank rule

The following is a brief explanation of the fields to complete for a new bank rule:

- **What do you want to call this rule?**: The first field allows you to assign a name to the rule. In our example, we are using `Monthly Cellphone Expense`.

- **Apply this to transactions that are**: You can apply rules based on Money out or Money in, and choose to apply this to **All** bank accounts or a specific bank account. If you have multiple accounts, you can set up rules that are specific to a bank account even when a vendor is paid using multiple bank accounts.

- **Conditions**: You can create several conditions based on the **Bank text, Description**, or **Amount**. In our example, we have selected **Bank text**.

- **Contains, Doesn't contain, Is exactly**: In the next field, you can select whether the transaction contains, doesn't contain, or is exactly the information that you enter into the next field.

- **Text box**: This field contains text that will appear either in the bank text or description field when the transaction is downloaded into QuickBooks. If you selected the amount as part of your criteria, then you will enter an amount in this field. In our text box, we have entered `T-Mobile`, which is the name of the payee.

- You can click the **Add a condition** link to add multiple conditions. Based on the conditions you have set, QuickBooks will automatically assign a category to the transaction using the information in the next section.

- **Transaction type**: From the drop-down menu, select the type of transaction for which you are creating this rule. In our example, this is an **Expense**.

- **Payee**: From the drop-down menu, select the payee for this rule. In our example, the payee is **T-Mobile**.

- **Category**: From the drop-down menu, select the category (account) that best describes the purchase. In our example, we have selected **Utilities: Telephone Expense**.

- **Add a split**: If the transaction should be split between two or more accounts (categories), you can click the **Add a split** link and indicate the accounts that should be used.

- **Memo**: This field is optional, but can be used to provide additional details about the transaction. In our example, we have used **Monthly cellphone bill**.

Now that you have a better idea of how bank rules work and how to create them, we will show you how to apply these bank rules to banking transactions in the next section.

How do you want to apply this rule? QBCU 4.2.1

At the bottom of this page is the option to **Automatically confirm transactions this rule applies to.** By selecting this auto-confirmation option, QuickBooks will automatically assign the category (account) based on your selections at the top of the page and will automatically record the transaction in QuickBooks without you needing to review it first. If you would prefer to review all transactions before they are recorded, turn this feature off.

> **Pro Tip**: We recommend that you review all banking transactions before they are recorded in QuickBooks. After reviewing transactions for the first couple of months, once you are comfortable they are being categorized correctly, you can always change the bank rules to **Auto-categorize and auto-add** later on.

If set up properly, bank rules can automatically categorize and record 80% or more of your bank and credit card transactions. If you have a lot of transactions coming through, this will save you hours of time, which you can spend on other aspects of your business.

> **Pro Tip**: You can sort the transactions by column. It can be beneficial to sort by description or payee, to group similar transactions and categorize them in a batch.

Start with one bank rule to see how it works, and then add more as you get comfortable with using them. Using bank rules will also help to expedite the reconciliation of bank and credit card accounts. We will discuss this in more detail in the following section.

Reconciling accounts

Reconciling is the process of making sure your QuickBooks records agree with your bank and credit card statements. At a minimum, reconciling should take place on a monthly basis, if not more often. One of the benefits of using cloud-based accounting software such as QBO is that your banking information is downloaded on a daily basis. This means that you could reconcile as often as weekly, or even daily. There is no need to wait until the bank statement arrives at the end of the month to reconcile your accounts.

Follow these steps to reconcile a bank or credit card account:

1.   From the gear icon, select **Reconcile,** as indicated in *Figure 10.13*:

TOOLS

Order checks ☐

Import data

Import desktop data

Export data

Reconcile

Budgeting

Audit log

SmartLook

Resolution center

Figure 10.13: Navigating to Reconcile in QBO

2.   The start reconciliation window will appear, as indicated in *Figure 10.14*:

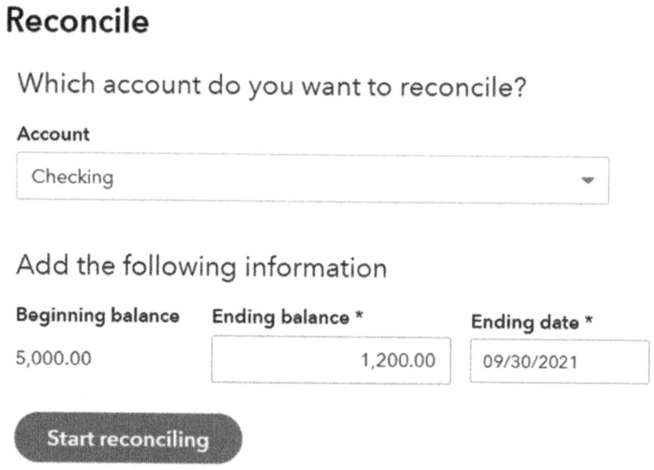

Reconcile

Which account do you want to reconcile?

Account

Checking ▾

Add the following information

Beginning balance   **Ending balance ***   **Ending date ***

5,000.00   1,200.00   09/30/2021

Start reconciling

Figure 10.14: Initial reconciliation window

If a transaction that was previously reconciled has been changed, Quick-Books will include a message on this screen. Be sure to follow the onscreen instructions to troubleshoot the out of balance. This issue must be addressed before proceeding with the current reconciliation.

The fields that need to be completed in the reconciliation window shown in the preceding screenshot are as follows:

- **Account**: From the drop-down menu, select the bank or credit card account you want to reconcile.

- **Beginning balance**: This field will automatically be populated with the ending balance of the previous month. If you have never reconciled the account before, the balance in this field will be the opening balance entered when you created the account in QuickBooks.

- **Ending balance**: Enter the ending balance of the bank or credit card statement you are reconciling.

- **Ending date**: Enter the ending date on the bank or credit card statement you are reconciling. In general, it will be the last day of the month (for example, **09/30/2021**).

Click the **Start reconciling** button once all fields have been completed.

3. On the next screen, the following information will appear. The following is a snapshot of the header information when reconciling accounts:

Figure 10.15: Header information in the reconciliation window

A brief description of the information found in the header window is as follows:

- **STATEMENT ENDING BALANCE**: This field will automatically be populated with the statement ending balance entered on the preceding start reconciliation screen.

- **CLEARED BALANCE**: This field will summarize all the transactions that have cleared on your bank or credit card statement.

- **BEGINNING BALANCE**: This field will automatically be populated from the prior month's reconciliation. If you have not reconciled this account previously, it will display the beginning balance entered when the account was created in QuickBooks.

- **PAYMENTS**: This field will summarize all of the payments/withdrawals that have cleared on your bank or credit card statement.

- **DEPOSITS**: This field will summarize all of the deposits that have cleared on your bank or credit card statement.

- **DIFFERENCE**: The difference between the statement ending balance and the cleared balance will appear in this field. The goal is to reach a difference of zero. Zero indicates all items that have cleared your bank or credit card statement have been recorded in QuickBooks.

 Pro Tip: If you are having trouble reconciling to a difference of zero, compare the deposit total in the header window to the deposit total on your bank statement. If it matches, then you know there is an issue with withdrawals. If it doesn't match, then you know there is an issue with deposits. Do the same comparison on the withdrawal side. You could be out of balance with both, or with just one transaction type.

4. Once your difference equals zero, you can click the **Finish now** button to generate the bank reconciliation reports. Click on the drop-down arrow next to the **Save for later** button as indicated in *Figure 10.16*:

Figure 10.16: The Finish now button

 Pro Tip: Do not click the **Finish now** button if you don't have a difference of zero. Instead, click the **Save for later** option. You can always come back and resume the reconciliation from where you left off.

5. The following is a snapshot of the detailed bank and credit card information that appears after the header information:

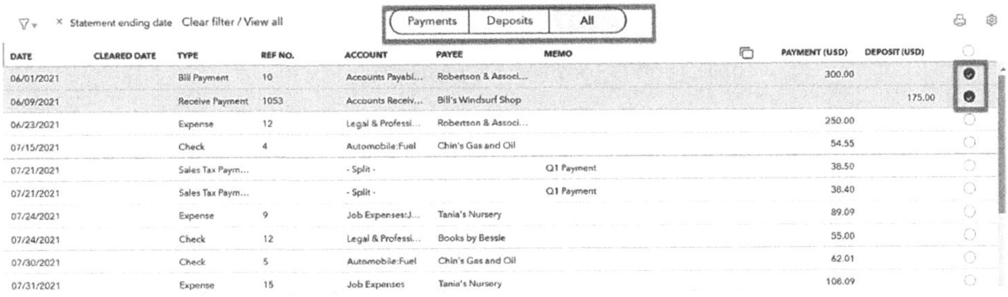

× Statement ending date Clear filter / View all

Payments | Deposits | All

DATE	CLEARED DATE	TYPE	REF NO.	ACCOUNT	PAYEE	MEMO	PAYMENT (USD)	DEPOSIT (USD)
06/01/2021		Bill Payment	10	Accounts Payabl...	Robertson & Associ...		300.00	
06/09/2021		Receive Payment	1053	Accounts Receiv...	Bill's Windsurf Shop			175.00
06/23/2021		Expense	12	Legal & Professi...	Robertson & Associ...		250.00	
07/15/2021		Check	4	Automobile:Fuel	Chin's Gas and Oil		54.55	
07/21/2021		Sales Tax Paym...		- Split -		Q1 Payment	38.50	
07/21/2021		Sales Tax Paym...		- Split -		Q1 Payment	38.40	
07/24/2021		Expense	9	Job Expenses:J...	Tania's Nursery		89.09	
07/24/2021		Check	12	Legal & Professi...	Books by Bessie		55.00	
07/30/2021		Check	5	Automobile:Fuel	Chin's Gas and Oil		62.01	
07/31/2021		Expense	15	Job Expenses	Tania's Nursery		106.09	

Figure 10.17: Bank and credit card details listed in the reconciliation window

The following is a brief explanation of the detailed reconciliation window shown in the preceding screenshot:

- **Transaction type**: At the top of the screen, there are three tabs: **Payments**, **Deposits**, and **All**. You can click on one of the first two tabs to filter by a specific transaction type, or you can select **All**.
- **Transaction details**: The date, transaction type, reference number, category (account), payee, memo, and amount of each transaction that has been recorded in QuickBooks are listed in the details section.

If a transaction appears on your bank or credit card account, you need to put a checkmark in the radio button (located in the far right column) to mark it as cleared in QuickBooks. Each time you mark a transaction as cleared, it will be included in the cleared balance in the header section shown previously. As discussed, after marking all items that have cleared your bank or credit card statement, you should have a difference of zero. If you do not, you are either missing a transaction in QuickBooks or you may have marked a transaction as cleared that does not appear on your statement.

6. After successfully reconciling accounts, be sure to save the summary and detailed bank reconciliation reports. They will be made available after you complete the bank reconciliation. Bank reconciliation reports are one of several reports that auditors will request during an audit, so it is very important to save these reports to your computer. If you forget to save the reports, you can always access them from within the Banking Center.

For a step-by-step recap of how to reconcile an account, watch this Intuit video tutorial: `https://quickbooks.intuit.com/learn-support/en-us/banking-topics/reconcile-an-account-in-quickbooks-online/00/186470`.

After reconciling an account, you may discover that you need to edit a transaction that was previously reconciled. Be sure that you don't change the amount, otherwise your account will be out of balance. However, you can edit the category (account) and description fields easily:

1. Navigate to the chart of accounts and click on the **View register** link next to the bank account, as indicated in *Figure 10.18*:

NAME	TYPE ▲	DETAIL TYPE	QUICKBOOKS BALANCE	BANK BALANCE	ACTION
Business Checking	Bank	Checking	15,980.00		View register ▼
Business Savings	Bank	Savings	8,309.00		View register ▼

Figure 10.18: Editing a transaction that was previously reconciled

2. Make the necessary edits and save your changes.

As discussed, reconciling your accounts will help to ensure you haven't accidentally omitted recording any transactions. Plus, it will help you to ensure that your books agree with your financial institution's records. It's important to reconcile all of your bank and credit card accounts on a monthly basis (or more frequently, if possible), in order to catch errors made by the bank or to identify fraudulent transactions.

Summary

In this chapter, we have discussed how to manage downloaded bank and credit card transactions. You have learned how to match downloaded transactions with transactions previously recorded in QuickBooks. You now know how to make changes to transactions so that the correct payee and category (account) are recorded. You have also learned how to create bank rules in order to reduce the number of transactions you need to review in the Banking Center, which will save you time. Finally, you know the importance of reconciling bank and credit card accounts on a frequent basis to ensure your records are in sync with your financial institution.

We have met our goal of giving you the knowledge to successfully manage your downloaded bank and credit card transactions. Having this knowledge will help you to save the time you would normally have spent manually entering bank and credit card transactions into QuickBooks.

Reconciling your accounts will also help you to become familiar with how much money you are spending, as well as what you are spending it on. Remember, having the ability to control your expenses will help to improve your bottom line.

In the next chapter, we will show you how to generate reports in QuickBooks. There are a number of preset reports in QuickBooks, which means you never have to create a report from scratch. You will learn how to customize existing reports and export them to Excel/PDF or send them as attachments via email.

Join our book's Discord space

Join the book's Discord workspace for a monthly *Ask me Anything* session with the author:
`https://packt.link/QuickBooks`

Section 3: Generating Reports in QuickBooks Online

11

Report Center Overview

Now that you know how to enter income and expenses into QuickBooks, it's time to learn how to generate reports to gain insight into the overall health of your business. In this chapter, we will show you how to navigate through the report center and give you an overview of the reports available. In addition, we'll show you how to customize reports to meet your business needs. We will also cover how to share reports with your accountant and business stakeholders.

Understanding how to run reports will help you to gain insight into all aspects of your business. Having access to your income, expenses, and other key performance indicators will help you to make good business decisions. **QBCU 5.1.1**

The following topics will be covered in this chapter:

- Navigating the report center
- Reports available in the report center
- Customizing reports
- Exporting reports
- Sending reports via email

By the end of this chapter, you will be able to navigate the report center and know which reports you have access to and how to customize reports to meet your needs. You will also be able to export reports to Excel or PDF format and email reports to stakeholders.

 The US edition of QBO was used to create this book. If you are using a version that is outside of the United States, results may differ.

QBCU 5.1.1

Navigating the report center

In this section, we will cover how the report center is organized so that you can easily locate a report. The report center includes several pre-built reports that will give you both summary and detailed information about various aspects of your business. It is organized into three main sections: **Standard**, **Custom reports**, and **Management reports**. The majority of the reports are located in the **Standard** reports section.

1. To access the report center, click on **Reports** located on the left menu bar as indicated here:

Figure 11.1: Navigating to the report center

2. Click on the **Standard** tab as indicated below:

Figure 11.2: Selecting Standard reports

Standard reports are categorized into the following nine reporting groups:

- **Favorites**: You can mark your most frequently used reports as favorites and they will be listed in the **Favorites** group. To add a report to your **Favorites** list, simply click the star icon located to the right of each report.

- **Business Overview**: The **Business Overview** group includes reports that provide insight into the overall health of your business. You will find both a detailed and a summarized overview of profit and loss, the balance sheet, and a statement of cash flow reports in this group.

- **Who owes you**: Money owed to you by your customers is also known as **accounts receivable (A/R)**. In this group, you will find reports to help you to stay on top of your A/R balances. The A/R aging detail and summary, open invoices, and collections reports can be found in this group. In *Chapter 13, Customer Sales Reports in QuickBooks Online*, we will show you how to generate these reports.

- **Sales and customers**: The **Sales and customers** group includes detailed and summary reports that will give you insight into who your top customers are and what products and services they are buying. Income by customer, products and services lists, and sales by customer are just a few of the reports you will find in this group.

- **What you owe**: Money you owe to others is also known as **accounts payable (A/P)**. In this group, you will find reports to help you to stay on top of your A/P balances. A/P aging, bill payment list, and unpaid bills are just a few of the reports you will find in this group. In *Chapter 14, Vendor and Expenses Reports*, we show you how to run the A/P aging report and several other reports in this group.

- **Expenses and vendors**: The **Expenses and vendors** group includes reports that will give you insight into who and what you are spending your money on. Some examples of reports you will find in this group are check detail, expenses by vendor, and open purchase orders.

- **Sales tax**: The sales tax group includes reports that provide details on the sales tax your business has collected. Some examples of reports found here are the sales tax liability report and the sales tax detail report.

- **Employees**: If you have added employees to QuickBooks, this group includes reports that will provide you with employee information. Employee contact list and time activities are a couple of reports that you will find in this group. If you manage payroll in QuickBooks, head over to the **Payroll** reports group for more detailed payroll reports.

- **For my accountant**: Reports that assist your accountant in preparing your taxes can be found in the **For my accountant** reports group. You will find profit and loss, balance sheet reports, and a list of the chart of accounts, along with many other reports in this group.

- **Payroll**: If you have the payroll feature turned on, you will have access to several detailed and summary payroll reports by employee, location, and class.

3. Click on the **Custom reports** tab located next to **Standard**, as indicated below:

Figure 11.3: Selecting Custom reports

Custom reports will include any report you have customized and saved. We will discuss how to customize reports later on.

4. Click on the **Management reports** tab located next to **Custom reports**, as indicated below:

Figure 11.4: Selecting Management reports

Management reports are the third group of reports, and they include professional report packages that you can download and customize with items such as a cover page and a table of contents. These reports can be used when presenting financial statements to a board of directors or a financial institution when seeking financing. The number of reports you can access depends on your **QuickBooks Online (QBO)** subscription level.

Now that you understand how to navigate the report center as well as the variety of reports you can run, we will cover what reports are available to you based on your QuickBooks Online subscription in the following section.

Reports available in the report center

In *Chapter 1, Getting Started with QuickBooks Online*, we discussed the four subscription levels you can purchase for QBO: Simple Start, Essentials, Plus, and Advanced. Depending on the subscription level you have purchased, you could have access to anywhere between 20 and 100 or more reports. Simple Start includes more than 20 reports, Essentials includes more than 40 reports, Plus includes more than 65 reports, and Advanced includes more than 100 reports.

The following is a breakdown of some of the reports you will find in each QBO subscription.

QBO Simple Start includes more than 20 reports, some of which are listed here:

Profit & Loss	Sales by Customer
Balance Sheet	Sales by Product/Services
Statement of Cash Flows	Transaction List by Vendor
Customer Balance Summary	Check Detail
A/R Aging Summary	Payroll Reports (if payroll is on)
Taxable Sales	Customized Reports
Transaction List by Date	Product/Service List
Reconciliation Reports	Deposit Detail

Figure 11.5: A list of reports included in the QBO Simple Start plan

In addition to the reports included in Simple Start, QBO Essentials includes 40 plus reports, including the following:

A/P Aging	Profit & Loss Detail
Bill Payment List	Sales by Customer Detail
Complany Snapshot	Terms Listing
Customer Balance Detail	Trial Balance
Expenses by Vendor	Unbilled Charges
General Ledger	Unpaid Bills
Income by Customer Summary	Vendor Balance

Figure 11.6: A list of reports included in the QBO Essentials plan

QBCU
1.1.1

In addition to the reports included in Simple Start and Essentials, QBO Plus has more than 65 reports, including the following:

Budget Overview	Purchases by Product/Service
Budget vs. Actuals	Purchases by Location/Class
Class Listing	Sales by Location or Class
Profit & Loss by Class	Time Activities by Customer
Profit & Loss by Location	Time Activities by Employee
Open Purchase Orders	Transaction Detail by Account

Figure 11.7: A list of reports included in the QBO Plus plan

In addition to the reports included in Simple Start, Essentials, and Plus, QBO Advanced has more than 100 reports. It also includes a smart reporting tool called Fathom. Smart reporting takes the data from your QuickBooks file and puts it into easy-to-understand reports that will give you insights into profitability, cash flow, and other key performance indicators (KPIs).

Now that you have a better idea of all the reports you have access to with your QBO subscription, you are ready to learn how to customize the reports. In the next section, we will show you how to customize reports to meet your business requirements.

Customizing reports

As discussed, you don't have to create a report from scratch in QuickBooks Online; you can customize an existing report to get the data that you need. You can save any changes you make to a report so you don't have to recreate it each time.

The following are the steps you need to customize a report:

1. Click on **Reports** on the left menu bar to navigate to the report center, as indicated here:

Figure 11.8: Navigating to the report center

2. Select the report you want to customize. In this case, we will customize the **Profit and Loss** report, as indicated:

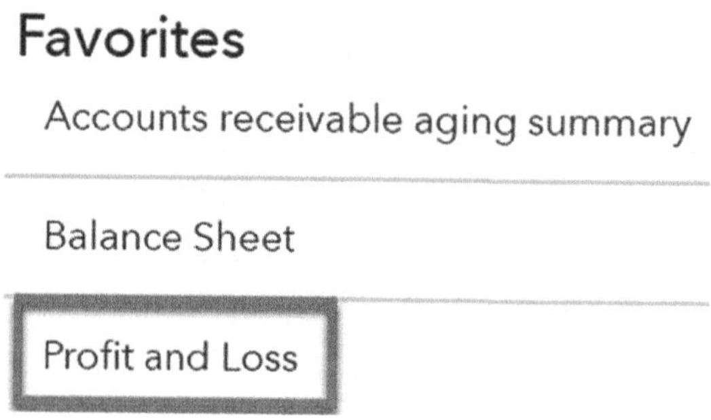

Favorites

Accounts receivable aging summary

Balance Sheet

Profit and Loss

Figure 11.9: Running the Profit and Loss report

3. Click the **Customize** button located in the upper-right corner:

Customize

Figure 11.10: Customizing a report

4. The following customization window will appear:

Customize report

▶ General

▶ Rows/Columns

▶ Filter

▶ Header/Footer

Figure 11.11: Options available to customize the report

As indicated in the preceding screenshot, there are four primary areas you can customize:

- General
- Rows/Columns
- Filter
- Header/Footer

We will cover these areas in detail in the following sections

General report customizations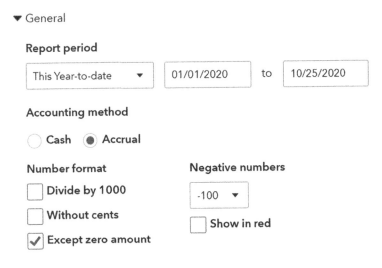

In **General** report customizations, you can select the **Report period, Accounting method**, and how you would like numbers formatted on any report:

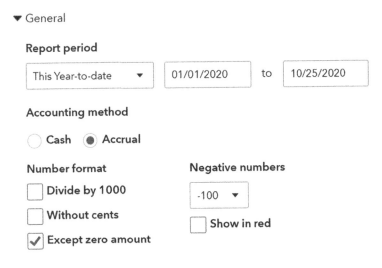

Figure 11.12: General report customizations

The following is a brief explanation of what's included in general report customizations:

- **Report period**: Select the period you would like to see in the report. You can do this by selecting the preset time frames from the drop-down menu or entering the dates directly in the fields.

- **Accounting method**: You can select the accounting method you would like to see the report in (**Cash** or **Accrual**). Reports will automatically default to the accounting method chosen when you set up your QuickBooks account. However, you can change this directly on the report. To change the default accounting method, go to **Company preferences** and select the **Accounting** tab.

- **Number format**: You can format numbers by dividing them by 1,000, removing the cents, and not showing anything with a zero amount.

- **Negative numbers**: From the drop-down menu, you can choose to show negative numbers in one of three ways. The negative sign can be in front of the number or behind the number, or the negative numbers can be in parentheses, for example, -100, 100-, or (100).

Now that you are familiar with general report customizations, we will discuss how to customize rows and columns next.

Row and column report customization

Rows/Columns report customization includes formatting columns, comparing the current data to a previous period, and comparing the number of columns and rows to the grand total on the report:

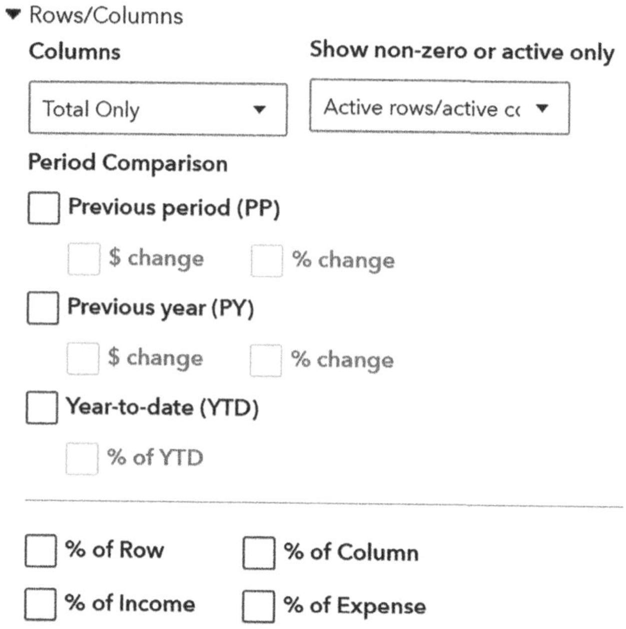

▼ Rows/Columns

Columns   **Show non-zero or active only**

| Total Only ▼ | | Active rows/active cc ▼ |

Period Comparison

☐ **Previous period (PP)**

   ☐ $ change   ☐ % change

☐ **Previous year (PY)**

   ☐ $ change   ☐ % change

☐ **Year-to-date (YTD)**

   ☐ % of YTD

☐ **% of Row**   ☐ **% of Column**

☐ **% of Income**   ☐ **% of Expense**

Figure 11.13: Rows/Columns report customizations

The following is a brief explanation of what's included in **Rows/Columns** report customizations:

- **Columns**: Displays column information by showing totals only, by period (days, weeks, month), or by customers, vendors, or employees.

- **Show non-zero or active only**: Choose to only show non-zero data or all active data (with and without zeros). This option is recommended to keep your reports clean and concise.

- **Period Comparison**: This allows you to see how the current period compares to a previous period, year, or year-to-date. This change can be shown in both a percentage format, dollar amount, or both.

- **% of Row** or **% of Column**: Select these to see the percentage of each item listed on the report compared to other items on the same row or column of the report.

- **% of Income** or **% of Expense**: Select **% of Income** and the program will calculate the percentage of each item listed on the report that makes up the total income reported. A similar calculation is done when you select **% of Expense**, but using the total expenses reported.

For more tips and info on adding columns to reports, watch this Intuit video tutorial: `https://quickbooks.intuit.com/learn-support/en-us/customize-reports/how-to-add-columns-to-reports-comparing-customers-time-periods/00/344896`.

Next, let's discuss the various ways to filter reports.

Using filters to customize reports

To customize reports for specific data, you can filter reports by **Distribution Account**, **Customer**, **Vendor**, **Employee**, and **Product/Service**. To filter a report, put a checkmark in the box to the left of the filter and make your selection from the drop-down menu, as follows:

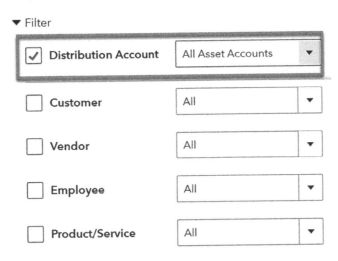

Figure 11.14: Using filters to customize reports

The following is a brief explanation of what's included in filtering reports:

- **Distribution Account**: Click on the drop-down arrow to select the account types you would like to filter on. Some of the options are: all accounts, all balance sheet accounts, all asset accounts, and more.
- **Customer**: Click on the drop-down arrow to select specific customers to filter on, or to select all customers.
- **Vendor**: Click the drop-down arrow to select specific vendors to filter on, or to select all vendors.

- **Employee:** Click on the drop-down arrow to select specific employees to filter on, or all employees.

- **Product/Service:** Click on the drop-down arrow to select specific products and services, multiple products and services, or all products and services.

 For additional tips on how to filter reports, watch this Intuit video tutorial: https://quickbooks.intuit.com/learn-support/en-us/run-reports/ how-to-filter-reports-customers-vendors-products/00/344824.

Next, let's talk a bit about the headers and footers.

Header and footer report customization

You can also customize the header and footer information that appears on reports. This can be useful if you have filtered a report in such a way that the current title is no longer applicable.

To customize the header, you can add a logo, update/change the name of the company that appears on the report, and change the title of the report. You can also choose to have the dates displayed on the report or remove them.

The following is a screenshot of the **Header** information that can be customized on reports:

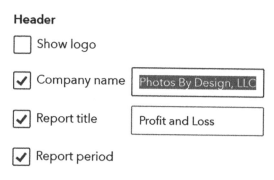

Figure 11.15: Header report customizations

To customize the footer, you can choose whether or not to display the date when the report was prepared, the time the report was prepared, and the report basis.

The following is a snapshot of the **Footer** information that can be customized on reports:

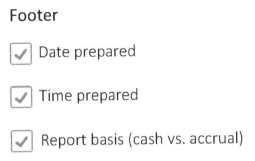

Figure 11.16: Footer customization options

Saving a customized report

After customizing a report, you can save your changes so they will remain each time you run the report. When you run a report, click the **Save customization** button located in the upper-right corner of the screen, as shown below:

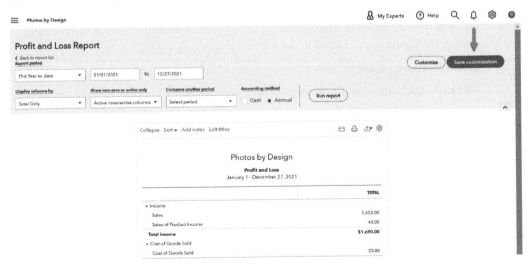

Figure 11.17: Saving your custom report

Below is the window that appears, along with a brief explanation of each field:

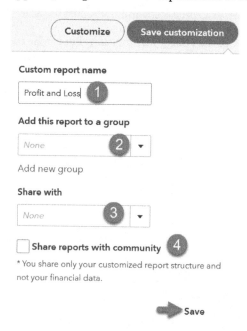

Figure 11.18: Save customization settings

- **Custom report name (1):** The default report name will appear in this field. You can customize the name of the report by adding your business name, for example, **Profit and Loss – Photos by Design**.

- **Add this report to a group (2):** Report groups are used to run multiple reports at once. For example, if you typically run the same five reports when closing the books, you can put all five reports in a group and generate them at the same time. Click **Add new group** directly below the field to create a group.

- **Share with (3):** This field allows you to share the report with other users within your company. Click the drop-down arrow and select specific users or **All**.

- **Share reports with community (4):** You can share the custom reports you create with other business owners of the QuickBooks community. Just click the box shown in the image above and follow the onscreen instructions.

Now that you know how to customize reports to fit your business needs, you are ready to learn how to share reports. You can export reports to Excel, PDF, a printer, or email them directly from QuickBooks.

You have several options to choose from when it comes to exporting your QuickBooks data. Like most programs, you can print a hard copy of any report. If you need to manipulate the data or add additional information, exporting the data to Excel might be a good option. If you need to share your data with your accountant, a board member, or anyone who does not have access to QuickBooks, you can save any report as a PDF document and email the report. Finally, you can email a report directly from QuickBooks.

When you select the email option, you can send it to multiple people and copy in anyone that you need to. When sending a report via email, the report will be attached as a PDF document.

Exporting reports

In this section, we will cover how to export reports to Excel and PDF. In the next section, we will show you the step-by-step process of emailing reports directly from QuickBooks.

When you run a report in QuickBooks, the export data menu will automatically appear in the upper-right corner, as indicated here:

Collapse Sort ▾ Add notes Edit titles

Photos by Design, LLC
PROFIT AND LOSS
January 1 - October 25, 2020

	TOTAL
▾ Income	
Photography Services	22,970.01
Total Income	**$22,970.01**
GROSS PROFIT	**$22,970.01**
▾ Expenses	
Bank and Credit Card Fees	-27.72
▾ Car & Truck	
Gas	30.15
Total Car & Truck	**30.15**
Cellphone Expense	300.00
Charitable Contributions	636.00
Continuing Education and Training	100.00
Contractors	500.00
Job Supplies	1,000.00
Meals & Entertainment	228.46
Miscellaneous Expense	487.41
Office Expense	171.00
Office Supplies & Software	477.05
Supplies	389.42
Utilities	240.00
Total Expenses	**$4,531.77**
NET OPERATING INCOME	**$18,438.24**
NET INCOME	**$18,438.24**

Figure 11.19: Multiple ways to export a report from QBO

The following is a brief explanation of each icon:

- **Envelope**: Click on the envelope icon if you want to email a report directly from QuickBooks.
- **Printer**: The printer icon is used if you would like to print a hard copy of a report.
- **Paper**: The icon that resembles a sheet of paper with an arrow going through it is used to export reports to Excel or PDF.

We will discuss exporting reports to Excel first.

Exporting reports to Excel

As discussed in the previous section, if you need the ability to manipulate the data on a report or add additional columns and rows, you can export reports to Excel.

Follow these steps to export a report to Excel:

1. Navigate to the reports center by clicking on **Reports** on the left menu bar, as follows:

Figure 11.20: Navigating to Reports

2. Select the reporting group that includes the report you wish to export, as follows:

Figure 11.21: Selecting a reporting group

3.   Choose the report you wish to export, as follows:

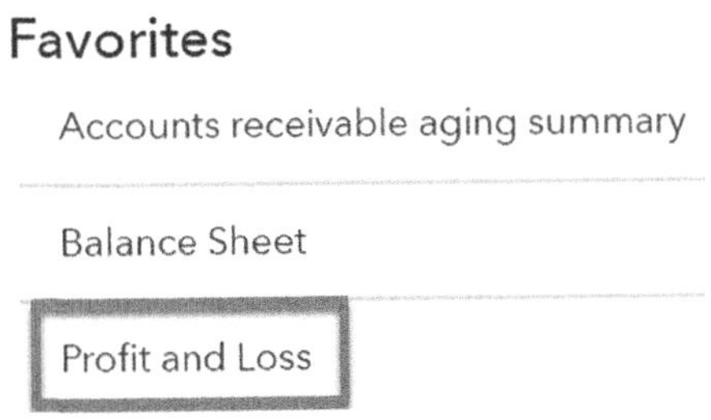

Favorites

Accounts receivable aging summary

Balance Sheet

Profit and Loss

Figure 11.22: Selecting a report to export

4.   The report will appear on your screen:

Collapse   Sort ▼   Add notes   Edit titles   ✉ 🖶 ↗▼ ⚙

Photos by Design, LLC

PROFIT AND LOSS
January 1 - October 25, 2020

	TOTAL
▼ Income	
Photography Services	22,970.01
Total Income	**$22,970.01**
GROSS PROFIT	**$22,970.01**
▼ Expenses	
Bank and Credit Card Fees	-27.72
▼ Car & Truck	
Gas	30.15
Total Car & Truck	**30.15**
Cellphone Expense	300.00
Charitable Contributions	636.00
Continuing Education and Training	100.00
Contractors	500.00
Job Supplies	1,000.00
Meals & Entertainment	228.46
Miscellaneous Expense	487.41
Office Expense	171.00
Office Supplies & Software	477.05
Supplies	389.42
Utilities	240.00
Total Expenses	**$4,531.77**
NET OPERATING INCOME	**$18,438.24**
NET INCOME	**$18,438.24**

Figure 11.23: Sample Profit and Loss report

Click on the icon that resembles a sheet of paper with an arrow going through it, as shown below:

Figure 11.24: Clicking on the Export button

5.   Choose **Export to Excel**, as follows:

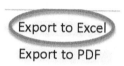

Figure 11.25: Selecting Export to Excel

6.   Your report should appear in Excel, as follows:

Photos by Design, LLC		
Profit and Loss		
January 1 - October 25, 2020		
		Total
Income		
Photography Services		22,970.01
Total Income	$	22,970.01
Gross Profit	$	22,970.01
Expenses		
Bank and Credit Card Fees		-27.72
Car & Truck		
Gas		30.15
Total Car & Truck	$	30.15
Cellphone Expense		300.00
Charitable Contributions		636.00
Continuing Education and Training		100.00
Contractors		500.00
Job Supplies		1,000.00
Meals & Entertainment		228.46
Miscellaneous Expense		487.41
Office Expense		171.00
Office Supplies & Software		477.05
Supplies		389.42
Utilities		240.00
Total Expenses	$	4,531.77
Net Operating Income	$	18,438.24
Net Income	$	18,438.24

Figure 11.26: Profit and Loss report exported to Excel

At this point, you can save the report to your computer and make any necessary changes.

 If the report is not immediately displayed on your screen, look at the very bottom of the screen and there should be an Excel icon. Click on it to display the report in Excel. After exporting a report, any changes you make in QBO will *not* update the report that was exported.

If you need to send reports to anyone outside of the company, I recommend you export the reports to PDF instead of Excel.

Exporting reports to PDF

If you need to share reports with your accountant, members of your board of directors, or a financial institution, exporting the reports to a PDF file is a great option. The initial steps in exporting reports to PDF are identical to those for exporting reports to Excel (in the previous section).

1. Click on **Reports** on the left menu bar, make sure you have selected the right reporting group, and choose the report you wish to export. Once the report appears, click on the icon that resembles a sheet of paper with an arrow going through it.

2. Click on **Export to PDF** as indicated here:

Figure 11.27: Exporting a report to PDF

3. The PDF report will appear on your screen, as indicated here:

PDF	1 / 1		↻ ± 🖶

Photos by Design, LLC

PROFIT AND LOSS

January 1 - October 25, 2020

	TOTAL
Income	
Photography Services	22,970.01
Total Income	**$22,970.01**
GROSS PROFIT	**$22,970.01**
Expenses	
Bank and Credit Card Fees	-27.72
Car & Truck	
Gas	30.15
Total Car & Truck	**30.15**
Cellphone Expense	300.00
Charitable Contributions	636.00
Continuing Education and Training	100.00
Contractors	500.00
Job Supplies	1,000.00
Meals & Entertainment	228.46
Miscellaneous Expense	487.41
Office Expense	171.00
Office Supplies & Software	477.05
Supplies	389.42
Utilities	240.00
Total Expenses	**$4,531.77**
NET OPERATING INCOME	**$18,438.24**

Figure 11.28: Profit and Loss report exported to PDF

You can save the report to your computer by clicking on the arrow pointing down in the upper-right corner or you can print a hard copy of the report by clicking on the print button as shown below:

Figure 11.29: Printing a hard copy of the report

That wraps up three of the four primary ways you can export your data out of QuickBooks so that you can share it with your business stakeholders. In the next section, we will cover one final way to share reports: by sending them via email directly from QuickBooks.

Sending reports via email

Sending reports via email involves the same steps required to export reports to Excel and PDF format.

1. Click on **Reports** on the left menu bar, make sure you have selected the right reporting group, and choose the report you wish to send.

2. Once the report has appeared, click on the icon that resembles an envelope, as follows:

Figure 11.30: Clicking the Email report icon

3. Click on the **Email** option, as follows:

Photos by Design, LLC

PROFIT AND LOSS

January 1 - October 25, 2020

	TOTAL
Income	
Photography Services	22,970.01
Total Income	**$22,970.01**
GROSS PROFIT	**$22,970.01**
Expenses	
Bank and Credit Card Fees	-27.72
Car & Truck	
Gas	30.15
Total Car & Truck	**30.15**
Cellphone Expense	300.00
Charitable Contributions	636.00
Continuing Education and Training	100.00
Contractors	500.00
Job Supplies	1,000.00
Meals & Entertainment	228.46
Miscellaneous Expense	487.41
Office Expense	171.00
Office Supplies & Software	477.05
Supplies	389.42
Utilities	240.00
Total Expenses	**$4,531.77**
NET OPERATING INCOME	**$18,438.24**
NET INCOME	**$18,438.24**

Email | Save as PDF | Print

Figure 11.31: Selecting the Email report option

4. The following window will appear:

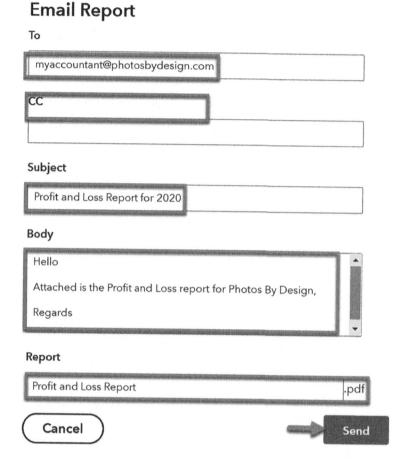

Email Report

To

myaccountant@photosbydesign.com

CC

Subject

Profit and Loss Report for 2020

Body

Hello

Attached is the Profit and Loss report for Photos By Design,

Regards

Report

Profit and Loss Report   .pdf

Cancel   Send

Figure 11.32: Completing the required fields to email the report directly from QBO

The following is a brief description of the fields that need to be completed:

- **To:** Enter the email address of each recipient in this field. You can enter multiple email addresses by putting a comma (,) in-between each one.
- **CC:** Enter the email address for each recipient that needs to receive a carbon copy of the report. To enter multiple email addresses, put a comma (,) in-between each email address.
- **Subject:** This field will automatically be populated with the name of the report. You can make changes to this field.

- **Body:** This field will automatically be populated with a standard message. You can customize the email message to fit your needs.
- **Report:** The report you are emailing will be attached as a PDF document.

After completing all the fields, click the **Send** button to email the report.

 For an overview of how to best use the report center to generate the reports needed for your business, watch this Intuit video tutorial: `https://quickbooks.intuit.com/learn-support/en-us/run-reports/how-to-use-reports-center-categories-insights-information/00/344862`.

Emailing reports can be an easy and secure way to share data with your accountant and stakeholders in your business. The reports are attached in PDF format so they cannot be manipulated.

Summary

As promised, we have introduced you to the report center and covered all of the different types of reports available at your fingertips. You have learned how to run reports, edit the data on reports, and save your changes. We have shown you how to share your data by printing a hard copy, exporting the information to Excel, saving to PDF format, and emailing directly from QuickBooks. This will help you to safely and securely share information on a need-to-know basis instead of giving access to your company data.

In the next chapter, we will dive deeper into business overview reports. As discussed at the beginning of this chapter, business overview reports give you insight into the overall health of your business. The profit and loss statement, balance sheet report, statement of cash flows, and the budgeting/forecasting tools available are included in business overview reports.

Join our book's Discord space

Join the book's Discord workspace for a monthly *Ask me Anything* session with the author: `https://packt.link/QuickBooks`

12
Business Overview Reports

In *Chapter 11, Report Center Overview*, we explained how to navigate the Report Center, the reports that are available based on your **QuickBooks Online (QBO)** subscription level, and how to customize reports to meet your business needs. In this chapter, we will discuss the three primary reports that provide a good overview of your business: profit and loss statements, balance sheet reports, and statements of cash flows. We will explain what information is included in each report, how to customize it, and how to generate the report. In addition, we will show you how to create a budget from scratch so that you can keep track of your income and expenses in relation to the set budget for the year. This information will go a long way in helping you make decisions about your business. Finally, we will introduce you to the Cash Flow planner and the Audit Log report.

By the end of this chapter, you will have a better understanding of what information you will find on the profit and loss statement, balance sheet, and statement of cash flow reports. In addition, you will know how to generate each report as well as create an income and expense budget from scratch.

The following topics will be covered in this chapter:

- Understanding profit and loss statements
- Generating balance sheet reports
- Understanding the statement of cash flows
- Creating a budget
- Using the Cash Flow planner
- Generating the Audit Log report

The US edition of QBO was used to create this book. If you are using a version that is outside the United States, the results may differ.

QBCU
5.1.1 # Understanding profit and loss statements

In this section, we will show you how to customize and generate a profit and loss statement. The **profit and loss statement**, also referred to as the **income statement**, shows you how profitable a business is for a period of time. This report summarizes all the income and expenses that have been incurred by a business for a specific period of time. The difference between income and expenses is shown on the report as either net profit (income exceeds expenses) or net loss (expenses exceed income). Like most reports, you can customize the profit and loss statement to meet your business needs.

Follow these steps to generate and customize a profit and loss statement:

1. Navigate to **Reports** in the left menu bar, as shown in *Figure 12.1*:

Figure 12.1: Navigating to the Report Center from the left menu bar

2. Scroll down to the **Business Overview** section and select **Profit and Loss**, as shown in *Figure 12.2*:

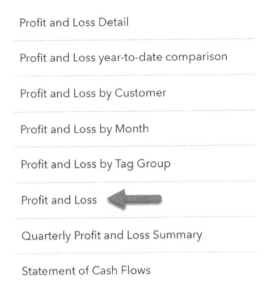

Figure 12.2: Selecting the Profit and Loss report

As you can see, there are several different types of profit and loss reports that you can run in QuickBooks Online: the **Profit and Loss Detail** report, the **Profit and Loss year-to-date comparison**, **Profit and Loss by customer**, **Profit and Loss by Month**, **Profit and Loss by Tag Group**, and the **Quarterly Profit and Loss Summary** are preset custom reports.

3. You can customize the date range, columns to display, and accounting period, as shown in *Figure 12.3*:

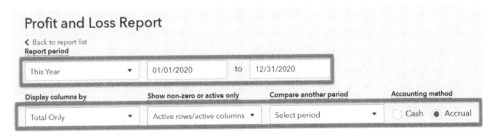

Figure 12.3: Choosing the report's parameters

Brief descriptions of the basic customization options for a profit and loss report are as follows:

- **Report period**: From the drop-down menu, you can choose a preset time period (such as this year) and the from/to date fields will be populated automatically for you. The other option is to type directly into the from/to date fields.

- **Display columns by**: There are a number of options you can choose from when it comes to how to display columns. From the drop-down, you can select days, weeks, months, quarters, years, customers, vendors, employees, and products or services.

- **Show non-zero or active only**: This field allows you to determine whether you want columns and rows to be displayed for all active accounts, regardless of whether they have activity or a zero amount. You can also choose non-zero, which means only accounts that have an amount will show up on the report.

- **Compare another period**: As we discussed in *Chapter 11, Report Center Overview*, you can compare your data to a previous period by making a selection from the drop-down.

- **Accounting method**: As we discussed in *Chapter 11*, you can choose the accounting method you would like to run the report for, cash or accrual. You can learn more about the cash and accrual methods in *Chapter 1, Getting Started with QuickBooks Online*.

Additional customizations can be made by using number formatting, selecting rows/columns, using filters, and editing header and footer information. Refer to *Chapter 11* for step-by-step instructions on how to customize reports in QuickBooks Online.

4. The following is a snapshot of a sample profit and loss report that has been generated in QuickBooks Online:

Photos by Design, LLC

PROFIT AND LOSS

January - December 2020

	TOTAL
Income	
Photography Services	22,970.01
Total Income	$22,970.01
GROSS PROFIT	$22,970.01
Expenses	
Bank and Credit Card Fees	-27.72
Car & Truck	
Gas	30.15
Total Car & Truck	30.15
Cellphone Expense	550.00
Charitable Contributions	636.00
Continuing Education and Training	100.00
Contractors	500.00
Job Supplies	1,000.00
Meals & Entertainment	228.46
Miscellaneous Expense	487.41
Office Expense	171.00
Office Supplies & Software	477.05
Supplies	389.42
Utilities	320.00
Total Expenses	$4,861.77
NET OPERATING INCOME	$18,108.24
NET INCOME	$18,108.24

Figure 12.4: Sample Profit and Loss report

In this profit and loss report, **Photos by Design, LLC** has a total income of **$22,970.01** and expenses totaling **$4,861.77**, which yields a net profit of **$18,108.24** for the period January 1 to December 31, 2020. If an income or expense account has a negative balance, it is a good idea to click and check the individual transactions to see if an item has been categorized to the wrong account. You can drill down to the detailed transactions by clicking on an amount in the report.

Pro Tip: Watch this step-by-step Intuit video tutorial, which recaps how to run a profit and loss statement: `https://www.youtube.com/watch?v=nSGeKUO4HHE&f eature=youtu.be`.

Now that you understand the information you will find on a profit and loss statement, as well as how to generate a customized profit and loss statement, we will cover the balance sheet report next. We will show you how to customize a balance sheet report to meet your specific business requirements.

QBCU
5.1.1

Generating balance sheet reports

A balance sheet report summarizes the assets, liabilities, and owner's equity for a business at any point in time. This report allows you to assess the **liquidity** (access to cash or assets that can be quickly turned into cash) of a business, which is important to potential investors and creditors. As with most reports, you can customize the balance sheet report to meet your business needs. We will show you how to generate the report and customize it in this section.

Follow these steps to generate and customize a balance sheet report:

1. Navigate to **Reports** in the left menu bar, as shown in *Figure 12.5*:

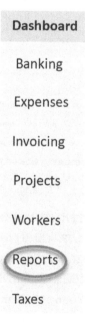

Figure 12.5: Navigating to the Report Center from the left menu bar

2. Scroll down to the business overview section and select **Balance Sheet**, as shown in *Figure 12.6*:

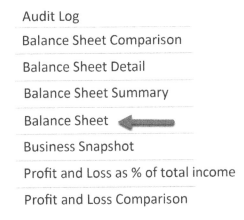

Figure 12.6: Choosing the Balance Sheet report

As you can see, there are several different types of balance sheet reports you can run in QuickBooks Online. The **Balance Sheet Comparison** report, the **Balance Sheet Detail** report, and the **Balance Sheet Summary** report are preset custom reports.

3. You can customize the date range, columns to display, and accounting period, as shown in *Figure 12.7*:

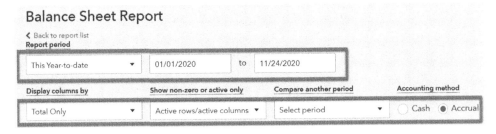

Figure 12.7: Selecting the parameters for the balance sheet report

A brief description of the basic customization options for a balance sheet report is as follows:

- **Report period**: From the drop-down menu, you can choose a preset time period (such as this year) and the from/to date fields will be populated automatically for you. The other option is to type directly into the from/to date fields.

- **Display columns by:** There are a number of options you can choose from when it comes to how to display columns. From the drop-down, you can select days, weeks, months, quarters, years, customers, vendors, employees, and products or services.

- **Show non-zero or active only:** This field allows you to determine whether you want columns and rows to be displayed for all active accounts, regardless of whether they have activity or a zero amount. You can also choose non-zero, which means only accounts that have an amount will show up on the report.

- **Compare another period:** As we discussed in *Chapter 11, Report Center Overview*, you can compare your data to a previous period by making a selection from the drop-down.

- **Accounting method:** As we discussed in *Chapter 11*, you can choose the accounting method you would like to run the report for, cash or accrual. You can learn more about the cash and accrual methods in *Chapter 1, Getting Started with QuickBooks Online*.

Additional customizations can be made by using number formatting, selecting rows/columns, using filters, and editing header and footer information. Refer to *Chapter 11* for step-by-step instructions on how to customize reports in QuickBooks Online.

4. The following is a snapshot of a sample balance sheet report that has been generated in QuickBooks Online:

Photos by Design, LLC

BALANCE SHEET

As of December 31, 2020

	TOTAL
ASSETS	
Current Assets	
Bank Accounts	
Business Checking	15,980.00
Business Savings	8,309.00
WFB Checking	2,464.92
WFB Savings	2,095.00
Total Bank Accounts	$28,848.92
Accounts Receivable	
Accounts Receivable (A/R)	4,350.00
Total Accounts Receivable	$4,350.00
Other Current Assets	
Inventory Asset	225.00
Total Other Current Assets	$225.00
Total Current Assets	$33,423.92
Fixed Assets	
Camera	6,000.00
Total Fixed Assets	$6,000.00
TOTAL ASSETS	$39,423.92
LIABILITIES AND EQUITY	
Liabilities	
Current Liabilities	
Accounts Payable	
Accounts Payable (A/P)	150.00
Total Accounts Payable	$150.00
Credit Cards	
Visa Credit Card	1,200.00
Total Credit Cards	$1,200.00
Total Current Liabilities	$1,350.00
Total Liabilities	$1,350.00
Equity	
Opening Balance Equity	22,315.09
Owner's Investment	90.01
Owner's Pay & Personal Expenses	-2,439.42
Retained Earnings	
Net Income	18,108.24
Total Equity	$38,073.92
TOTAL LIABILITIES AND EQUITY	$39,423.92

Figure 12.8: Sample Balance Sheet report

In this balance sheet report, **Photos by Design, LLC** has total assets of **$39,423.92**, liabilities totaling **$1,350.00**, and total equity of **$38,073.92** for the period January 1 to December 31, 2020.

Now that you understand the information you will find on a balance sheet report, as well as how to generate a customized balance sheet, we will cover the statement of cash flows next. We will show you how to customize the statement of cash flows, which gives you insight into the cash flow of a business.

 Pro Tip: When examining your balance sheet, you should have backup documentation that supports the numbers. This includes bank statements and reconciliations, A/R aging reports, A/P aging reports, credit card statements, and loan payment coupons, to name a few.

QBCU
5.1.1

Understanding the statement of cash flows

The statement of cash flows is a detailed report that shows the cash coming in and going out of your business over a period of time. It groups cash flow into three categories: operating, investing, and financing activities. **Operating** activities include items that are part of the day-to-day business operations, such as cash due from customers (accounts receivable) or money due to vendors (accounts payable). **Investing** activities include the purchase of assets for the business, such as a computer. **Financing** activities include money coming in from a business loan or line of credit.

Similar to the profit and loss and balance sheet reports, you can customize the statement of cash flows to meet your business needs. We will show you how to generate the report and customize it in this section.

Follow these steps to customize and generate a statement of cash flows report:

1. Navigate to **Reports** in the left menu bar, as shown in *Figure 12.9*:

Figure 12.9: Navigate to the Report Center from the left navigation bar

2. Scroll down to the **Business Overview** section and select **Statement of Cash Flows**, as shown in *Figure 12.10*:

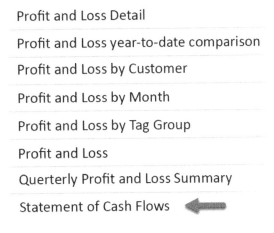

Figure 12.10: Selecting Statement of Cash Flows

3. You can customize the date range and columns to display, as shown in *Figure 12.11*:

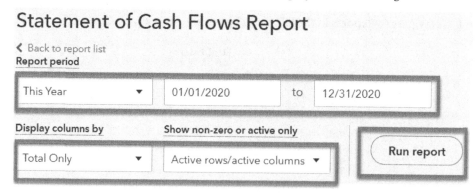

Figure 12.11: Choosing the parameters of the Statement of Cash Flows Report

Brief descriptions of the basic customization options for a statement of cash flows report are as follows:

- **Report period**: From the drop-down menu, you can choose a preset time period (such as this year) and the from/to date fields will be populated automatically for you. The other option is to type directly into the from/to date fields.

- **Display columns by**: There are a number of options you can choose from when it comes to how to display columns. From the drop-down, you can select days, weeks, months, quarters, years, customers, vendors, employees, and products or services.

- **Show non-zero or active only**: This field allows you to determine whether you want columns and rows to be displayed for all active accounts, regardless of whether they have activity or a zero amount. You can also choose non-zero, which means only accounts that have an amount will show up on the report.

4. After making your selections, click the **Run report** button.

5. A statement of cash flows similar to the following will appear on your screen:

Photos by Design, LLC

STATEMENT OF CASH FLOWS

January - December 2020

	TOTAL
OPERATING ACTIVITIES	
Net Income	18,108.24
Adjustments to reconcile Net Income to Net Cash provided by operations:	
Accounts Receivable (A/R)	-4,350.00
Inventory Asset	-225.00
Accounts Payable (A/P)	150.00
Visa Credit Card	1,200.00
Total Adjustments to reconcile Net Income to Net Cash provided by operations:	-3,225.00
Net cash provided by operating activities	$14,883.24
INVESTING ACTIVITIES	
Camera	-6,000.00
Net cash provided by investing activities	$ -6,000.00
FINANCING ACTIVITIES	
Opening Balance Equity	22,315.09
Owner's Investment	90.01
Owner's Pay & Personal Expenses	-2,439.42
Net cash provided by financing activities	$19,965.68
NET CASH INCREASE FOR PERIOD	$28,848.92
CASH AT END OF PERIOD	$28,848.92

Figure 12.12: Sample Statement of Cash Flows

In this Statement of Cash Flows report, **Photos by Design, LLC** has a net cash inflow of **$14,883.24** from **operating activities**, a net cash outflow of **$6,000.00** from **investing activities**, and a net cash inflow of **$19,965.68** from **financing activities** for the period January 1 to December 31, 2020.

Pro Tip: Financial statements should be reviewed on a monthly basis at a minimum after all bank and credit card accounts have been reconciled. This will allow you to identify any issues so that you can correct them before filing your tax returns.

Now that you understand the information you will find on a statement of cash flows, as well as how to generate a customized report, we will show you how to create a budget from scratch.

Creating a budget

After you've been in business for a year or two, you may want to take advantage of tools that will help you strategize and plan for the future. You can create a budget in QuickBooks Online from scratch or use existing data from the previous year. When you create a budget, you can keep track of your actual income and expenses to see whether you are coming in over or under budget.

QuickBooks allows you to create budgets for all income and expense accounts. You can also create a budget for specific customers. We will show you how to create a budget from scratch in this section.

Follow these steps to create a budget:

1.   Click on the gear icon and select **Budgeting**, as shown in the following screenshot:

TOOLS

Order checks ↗

Import data

Import desktop data

Export data

Reconcile

Budgeting

Audit log

SmartLook

Resolution center

Figure 12.13: Navigating to Budgeting from the TOOLS menu

2. The following screen will appear:

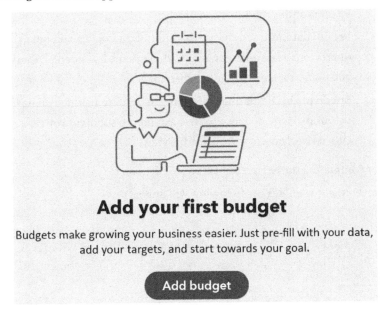

Add your first budget

Budgets make growing your business easier. Just pre-fill with your data,
add your targets, and start towards your goal.

Add budget

Figure 12.14: The Add budget button

Click on the **Add budget** button.

3. On the next screen, you will need to complete the header information for the new budget:

New Budget

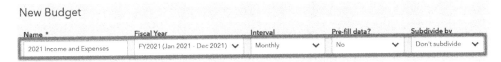

Figure 12.15: Choosing the parameters of the budget

Brief explanations of the information included in the header screen are as follows:

*   **Name**: Type the name of the budget into this field. This will generally include the fiscal year, along with a brief description.

*   **Fiscal Year**: Select the fiscal year the budget is for (for example, **FY 2021 (Jan 2021 – Dec 2021)**).

- **Interval:** Select the interval you would like to use from the drop-down. You can select monthly, quarterly, or yearly.

- **Pre-fill data:** You can choose to import data from QuickBooks for the current year or previous year (and then make adjustments if needed). Otherwise, choose **No** if you prefer to manually enter the budget.

- **Subdivide by:** If this budget is going to be for a customer, choose a customer from the drop-down. You also have the ability to subdivide by class, if you use classes. Otherwise, leave it as **Don't subdivide**.

4. After completing the header information, click **Next**.

5. A screen that resembles the following will appear:

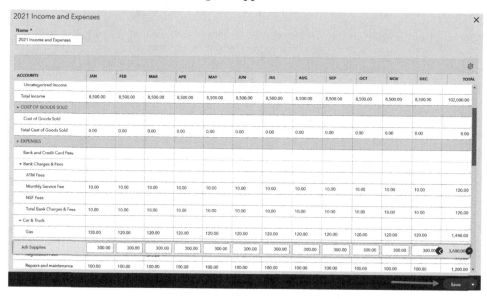

Figure 12.16: Complete budget template

Enter an amount in each cell and press *Tab*. If the budgeted amount for each month is the same, enter the amount in the **JAN** column and then click the blue arrow that appears to copy that figure to all the remaining months (**FEB** to **DEC**). Be sure to repeat this step until you have completed all the income and expense items.

QuickBooks will automatically total each month, along with each income and expense item. Be sure to click the **Save** button located in the bottom-right corner to save your work.

Pro Tip: For certain entities, such as non-profits that need to use up a certain budgeted amount each year, you can put the total budgeted amount in the first month of the fiscal year. Then, your profit and loss budget versus actuals report will show the amount you have remaining in each line item as the year progresses.

6. After saving your budget, click on the **X** in the upper-right corner of the screen, and the following screen will appear:

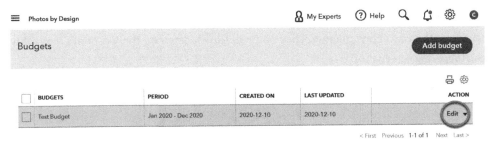

Figure 12.17: Editing an existing budget

This screen will show a list of budgets that have been created. In addition, you can access your budget reports by clicking on the **Edit** button. There are two reports that you can run to review and manage your budget: a budget overview report and a budget versus actuals report.

A brief description of the information you will find on both reports is as follows:

- **Budget overview report**: After entering your budget, you can run this report to review the budget to ensure that it is accurate. If changes are required, you can go back into the budget template to make the necessary changes. Like most reports in QBO, you can export the budget overview report to Excel or PDF. You can also email the budget overview report directly from QuickBooks.

- **Budget versus actuals report**: The budget versus actuals report includes side-by-side columns, one for the budgeted amount and one for the actuals as of a specific time period. The difference between the budget and the actuals will appear in a variance column. This information can help you determine the areas where you are within your budget or over budget, so that you can make any necessary adjustments.

Like the budget overview report, you can export the budget versus actuals report to Excel or PDF, plus, you can email the report directly from QuickBooks.

You now know how to create a budget from scratch for income and expenses, as well as how to generate the budget overview report and the budget versus actuals report.

Using the Cash Flow planner

One of the challenges many small businesses face is staying on top of their cash flow. Within QuickBooks Online, you can access the new Cash Flow planner. This planner will allow you to create real or hypothetical scenarios without affecting your QuickBooks data.

To access the Cash Flow planner, click on **Cash flow** located on the left menu bar, as shown in the following screenshot:

Figure 12.18: Navigating to the Cash flow center

The Cash flow center will appear as shown below:

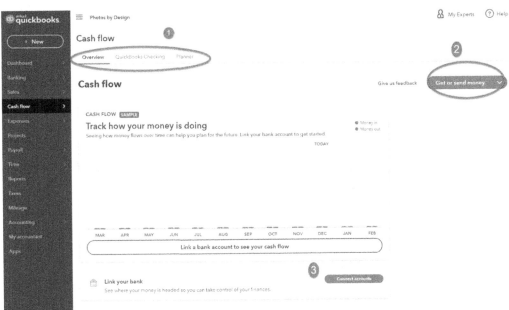

Figure 12.19: Cash flow center window

Here is a brief explanation of how this tool works:

- The cash flow tool has three tabs **(1)**: **Overview** (shown in the preceding screenshot), **QuickBooks Checking**, and **Planner**. On the **Overview** tab, you will have a cash flow graph that shows all 12 months of your fiscal year. You can also link accounts and get or send money, which we will discuss below. The **QuickBooks Checking** tab allows you to apply for a checking account with QuickBooks. The **Planner** tab allows you to create real or hypothetical scenarios without affecting your actual QuickBooks data.

- **Get or send money (2)**: Click the drop-down arrow and you will see an option to pay a bill or invoice a customer directly from this screen. Once you have saved the transaction, you can return to this screen to see the impact on your cash flow.

- **Connect accounts (3)**: As discussed in *Chapter 5, Customizing QuickBooks for Your Business*, you can connect accounts to QuickBooks so transactions will automatically be imported. As you can see, you can also connect accounts within the Cash flow center.

- **Expected money in (4):** In this section, you will see a dollar amount listed for invoices overdue or due soon. In our example, **$21.90** is the total expected money in.

- **Expected money out:** In this section (not shown), you will see a dollar amount listed for bills or expenses that are overdue or due soon.

To get the most out of the Cash Flow planner, be sure to connect all of your business debit and credit card accounts. In addition, add any real or hypothetical scenarios to get an idea of how your cash flow will be impacted. Best of all, you don't have to worry about it affecting your actual QuickBooks data.

QBCU 5.3.1

Generating the Audit Log report

The Audit Log report shows you everything that has happened in your company file so you can keep track of who has been in QuickBooks and what they have been doing. It shows you the date a change was made, the user who made the change, what the change (event) was, and the history if there is more than one change that was made.

Follow the steps below to generate the Audit Log report:

1. Navigate to **Reports** in the left menu bar, as shown in *Figure 12.20*:

Figure 12.20: Navigating to the Report Center from the left navigation bar

2. Scroll down to the **Business overview** section and select **Audit Log**, as shown in *Figure 12.21*:

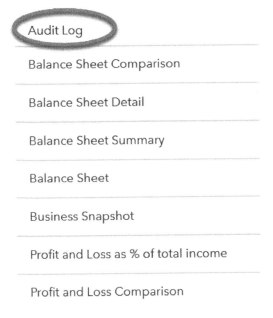

Figure 12.21: Clicking on Audit Log in the Business overview group

3.   The Audit Log report will appear:

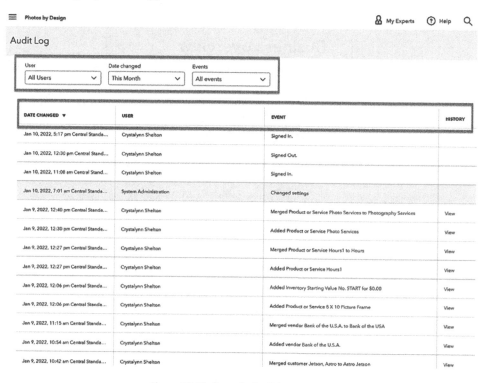

Figure 12.22: Sample Audit Log report

At the top of the report, there are three fields you can use to filter the report by **User**, **Date changed**, and **Events**.

This report will come in handy if there is ever a question as to who changed what in your data file. Unlike most reports in QuickBooks, the only option for exporting this information is by clicking the print button in the upper-right corner to print a hard copy. Email and exporting this report to Excel or PDF is not available.

Summary

As discussed in *Chapter 11, Report Center Overview*, once you have customized the reports you plan to use on a regular basis, it is a good idea to memorize them and/or create a group of memorized reports that will appear in your **Custom reports** tab. In this chapter, we explained the information you can find on the three primary financial reports: profit and loss statements, balance sheet reports, and statements of cash flows.

We also showed you how to customize the reports and generate them. In addition, we showed you how to create a budget from scratch and run budget reports. Finally, we touched on what you can do with the QuickBooks Cash Flow planner, and showed you how to generate the Audit Log report to view the history of changes to your company file.

In the next chapter, we will show you what reports are available in QBO to help you stay on top of customers and sales.

Join our book's Discord space

Join the book's Discord workspace for a monthly *Ask me Anything* session with the author: `https://packt.link/QuickBooks`

13

QBCU
5.1.2

Customer Sales Reports in QuickBooks Online

In the previous chapter, we covered how to customize and generate key business overview reports, which gave you insight into your entire business. In this chapter, we will focus on reports that provide you with insight into your customers and sales. There are four primary reports we will discuss in this chapter: accounts receivable (A/R) aging reports, open invoices reports, sales by customer reports, and sales by product/services reports. In each section, we will discuss the information you will find on each report, how to customize the reports, and how to generate each report.

Reviewing these reports on a consistent basis will let you know who owes you money, who your best customer is, and which products and services are selling the most. Having access to this information will help you to make informed business decisions.

The following topics will be covered in this chapter:

- Generating an accounts receivable aging report
- Generating an open invoices report
- Generating a sales by client report
- Generating a sales by product/service report

 The US edition of QBO was used to create this book. If you are using a version that is outside the United States, the results may differ.

Generating an accounts receivable aging report

The **accounts receivable aging report**, also referred to as the **A/R aging report**, categorizes unpaid customer invoices into groups based on the number of days they are past due. In general, there are five main categories (**current, 1-30 days, 31-60 days, 61-90 days,** and **91 and over**). QuickBooks calculates the number of days they are past due based on the invoice date. Business owners should review this report on a weekly basis and use it to follow up on invoices that are past their due date.

Follow these steps to generate an A/R aging report:

1. Navigate to **Reports** from the left menu bar, as indicated in *Figure 13.1*:

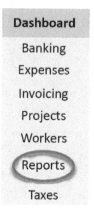

Figure 13.1: Navigating to the Report center

2. Scroll down to the **Who owes you** section and select **Accounts receivable aging summary,** as indicated in *Figure 13.2*:

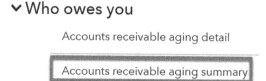

Figure 13.2: Selecting the Accounts receivable aging summary report

Notice that there is an **Accounts receivable aging summary** report and an **Accounts receivable aging detail** report. The detailed report includes information about each outstanding invoice for all customers. This includes the invoice number, invoice date, due date, and invoice amount.

The A/R summary report only includes one total for each customer for each of the applicable categories (for example, current, 1-30 days, and 31-60 days). However, you can drill down to the detail simply by clicking on a dollar amount in the report.

3. You can customize the reporting period, columns, aging method, days per aging period, and the number of periods for the A/R aging report, as indicated in *Figure 13.3*:

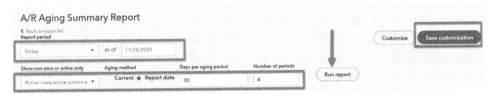

Figure 13.3: Choosing the parameters for the A/R aging summary report

The basic customization features available for the A/R aging report are:

- **Report period**: Customize the data range as needed by selecting the reporting period from the drop-down menu. You can choose from 28 options, including the following: today, this week, this month, this quarter, or this year. You can also enter a specific date range by selecting **Custom** from the drop-down menu.

- **Show non-zero or active only**: From the drop-down menu, you can choose to display non-zero only, which means only accounts that have activity will show up on the report. You can also choose to show all active accounts with zero activity.

- **Aging method**: You can select **Current**, which will calculate the age of the invoices as of today's date, or **Report date**, which will use the report period to calculate the number of days an invoice is past its due date.

- **Days per aging period**: You can determine the number of days per aging period. In our example, we have 30 days per aging period: 1-30, 31-60, 61-90, and 91 and over.

- **Number of periods**: You can determine the number of periods for your report. For example, in the A/R aging summary report that we will run next, there are four periods: 1-30, 31-60, 61-90, and 91 and over.

4. After making your selections, you can click the **Save customization** button and enter a name for this report. Next time you want to run this report, simply click on **Custom reports** and click on the report you wish to run.

5. Click the **Run report** button to generate an accounts receivable aging summary report, similar to the one shown in *Figure 13.4*:

Photos by Design, LLC

A/R AGING SUMMARY

As of November 28, 2020

	CURRENT	1 - 30	31 - 60	61 - 90	91 AND OVER	TOTAL
Barney Rubble			2,500.00			$2,500.00
Elroy Jetson				-150.00		$ -150.00
WALT DISNEY WORLD			2,000.00			$2,000.00
TOTAL	$0.00	$0.00	$4,500.00	$ -150.00	$0.00	$4,350.00

Figure 13.4: Sample A/R aging summary report

Pro Tip: Credits that appear in the report should be reviewed to determine if the customer has prepaid, overpaid, or if a payment was recorded without an open invoice.

In this sample A/R aging summary report, **Photos by Design** has outstanding invoices totaling **$4,350**. Of that total, **$0** are current, which means all invoices are due or past due. There are no invoices 1-30 days past due, **$4,500.00** is 31-60 days past due, and there is a credit for **-$150.00** that is 61-90 days past due, while no invoices are more than 90 days past due. All of the outstanding invoices are within the 31-60 day category.

To avoid incurring a bad debt or sending a customer to a collection agency (collection agencies will go after customers for outstanding amounts due on your behalf; in return, they collect a percentage of the debt as their fee), I recommend you follow up on past due invoices on a weekly basis.

Generating an open invoices report

The open invoices report is a list of unpaid customer invoices. It is very similar to the accounts receivable aging detail report, but it does not group invoices by the number of days they are past due. However, the open invoices report does include detailed information, such as customer name, invoice date, invoice number, invoice amount, transaction type, and payment terms. Like the A/R aging report, this report can help you to stay on top of the money owed to you. Next, we will walk through how to customize and generate the open invoices report.

Perform the following steps to customize and generate an open invoices report:

1. Navigate to **Reports** from the left menu bar, as indicated in *Figure 13.5*:

Figure 13.5: Navigating to the Reports center

2. Scroll down to the **Who owes you** section and select **Open Invoices**.

3. Customize the report period and the aging method of the open invoices report, as indicated in *Figure 13.6*:

Figure 13.6: Selecting the parameters for the open invoices report

The basic customizations available for an open invoices report are:

- **Report period**: From the drop-down menu, select the date range you would like to run the report for. You can enter a specific date or choose from 28 options, including the following: today, this week, this month, this quarter, or this year.

- **Aging method**: You can choose to calculate the age of the invoices based on the current date (the date you run the report) or based on the report date you entered into the report period.

4. After making your selections, click the **Run report** button to generate the report.

5. An open invoices report should look similar to the one in *Figure 13.7*:

Photos by Design, LLC

OPEN INVOICES

As of November 28, 2020

DATE	TRANSACTION TYPE	NUM	TERMS	DUE DATE	OPEN BALANCE
Barney Rubble					
08/31/2020	Invoice	1005	NET 45	10/15/2020	2,500.00
Total for Barney Rubble					$2,500.00
Elroy Jetson					
09/10/2020	Credit Memo	1010		09/10/2020	-150.00
Total for Elroy Jetson					$ -150.00
WALT DISNEY WORLD					
08/31/2020	Invoice	1007	Net 30	09/30/2020	2,000.00
Total for WALT DISNEY WORLD					$2,000.00
TOTAL					$4,350.00

Figure 13.7: Sample open invoices report

In this sample open invoices report, **Photos by Design, LLC**, has several open invoices outstanding. All customers with open (unpaid) invoices are listed, along with the details of each invoice as of **November 28, 2020**. Open invoices total **$4,350**. This amount should equal the total of the A/R summary and detailed reports if they are generated for the same time period.

Review this report on a weekly basis and use it to follow up with customers whose invoices are becoming due or past due.

Generating a sales by client report

The sales by client report will give a business owner insight into who their best customers are. In addition, you will gain insight into customers who seldom make purchases, which can help you when creating a marketing campaign to increase customer sales. The sales by client summary report includes a list of your customers and the total amount sold during the time period specified. We will show you how to customize and generate this report next.

 In general, you will see the term *customers*, which refers to people who you provide goods and services for. However, during the setup of Photos by Design, we updated the advanced settings to refer to customers as *clients*. Therefore, you will see the word *client* in place of *customer* throughout this section.To learn more about advanced settings, refer to *Chapter 3, Company File Setup*.

Follow these steps to customize and generate a sales by client report:

1. Navigate to **Reports** in the left menu bar, as indicated in *Figure 13.8*:

Figure 13.8: Navigating to the Report center

2. Scroll down to the sales and customer section and select the **Sales by Customer Summary** option, as indicated in *Figure 13.9*:

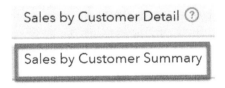

Figure 13.9: Running the sales by client summary report

Similar to the A/R aging report, the sales by customer report also has a sales by customer detail report. The primary difference between the two reports is that the detail report will display specific invoice information, such as the invoice date, invoice number, and invoice amount, while the summary report does not include this level of detail and is more pertinent for a high-level overview.

3. You can customize the report period, columns displayed, non-zero rows, compare the current data to a previous period, and select the accounting method to use for the sales by client summary report, as shown in *Figure 13.10*:

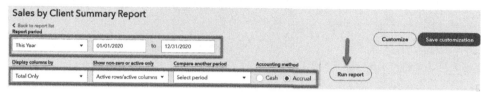

Figure 13.10: Choosing the parameters for the sales by client summary report

The basic customizations available for the sales by customer summary report are:

- **Report period**: Select the time period to run the report for. You can enter a specific date range or choose from 29 options, including the following: this week, this month, this quarter, or this year.

- **Display columns by**: Choose how you want the columns to be displayed. From the drop-down, you can choose from the following: total, days, weeks, months, quarters, years, by customer/client, or by product/service.

- **Show non-zero or active only**: Select this option if you want to display columns and rows for all active accounts or only non-zero accounts.

- **Compare another period**: Compare the current period to a previous period by selecting one from the drop-down. The options available are previous period, previous year, or year to date.

- **Accounting method**: Choose the accounting method to run the report for, cash or accrual. To learn more about cash versus accrual accounting, refer to *Chapter 1, Getting Started with QuickBooks Online.*

You can click the **Save customization** button to save your report selections and follow the onscreen instructions to save the report as a custom report. The next time you want to run the report, click on the **Custom Reports** tab, and all of your custom reports will appear in this tab.

4. After making your selections, click the **Run report** button to generate the report.

5. A sales by customer summary report, similar to the one shown in the following screenshot, should appear:

Photos by Design, LLC

SALES BY CLIENT SUMMARY

January - December 2020

	TOTAL
Barney Rubble	7,396.19
Elroy Jetson	-150.00
FRED FLINTSTONE	2,000.00
George Jetson	2,450.00
PARAMOUNT PICTURES	1,500.00
WALT DISNEY WORLD	3,000.00
WILMA FLINTSTONE	2,500.00
Not Specified	500.00
TOTAL	$19,196.19

Figure 13.11: Sample sales by client summary report

In this sample sales by client summary report, the total sales for the period January 1 to December 31, 2020, is **$19,196.19**.

Generating a sales by product/service report

The sales by product/service report gives a business owner insight into which products and services are selling the most, as well as which products and services are not selling. Similar to the sales by customer report, you can use this information to create a marketing plan that will help you to sell slow-moving products and services.

This information can also help you determine whether you should add new products and services or eliminate an existing product or service. The sales by product/service report includes the quantity sold (if applicable), the total sales amount, the percentage of sales, the average price, the cost of goods sold, and the gross margin of each item sold.

Follow these steps to generate and customize the sales by product/service report:

1. Navigate to **Reports** from the left menu bar, as indicated in *Figure 13.12*:

Figure 13.12: Navigating to the Report center

2. Scroll down to the sales and customer section and select the **Sales by Product/Service Summary** option, as indicated in *Figure 13.13*:

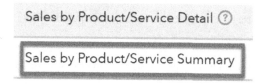

Figure 13.13: Running the Sales by Product/Service Summary report

Similar to the A/R aging report and the sales by customer report, the sales by product/service report includes a detailed version. It will break down each product or service sold, along with the date and amount for each. The summary version is ideal for a high-level overview.

3. Customize the report period, columns displayed, and non-zero rows, and select the accounting method to use for the sales by product/service report:

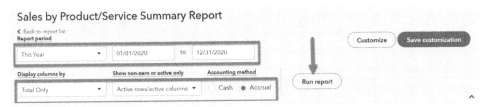

Figure 13.14: Choosing the parameters for the sales by product/service summary report

Here is a brief explanation of the fields to complete in order to generate a sales by product/service report:

- **Report period**: Select the time period to run the report for. You can enter a specific date range or choose from the following: today, this week, this month, this quarter, or this year.

- **Display columns by**: Choose how you want the columns to be displayed. From the drop-down, you can choose from the following: total, days, weeks, months, quarters, years, by the customer, or by the product/service.

- **Show non-zero or active only**: Change this option depending on whether you want to display columns and rows for all active accounts or only non-zero accounts.

- **Accounting method**: Choose the account method to run the report for, cash or accrual. To learn more about cash versus accrual accounting, refer to *Chapter 1, Getting Started with QuickBooks Online.*

As previously, you can click the **Save customization** button to save your report selections and follow the onscreen instructions to save the report as a custom report. The next time you want to run the report, click on the **Custom Reports** tab, and all of your custom reports will appear in this tab.

4. After making your selections, click the **Run report** button to generate the report.

5. A sales by product/service report similar to the one shown in the following screenshot should appear:

Craig's Design and Landscaping Services
SALES BY PRODUCT/SERVICE SUMMARY
January - December 2020

	QUANTITY	AMOUNT	% OF SALES	AVG PRICE	COGS	GROSS MARGIN	GROSS MARGIN %
				TOTAL			
Design							
Design	30.00	2,250.00	21.89 %	75.00			
Fountains							
Concrete	10.00	122.50	1.19 %	12.25			
Pump	4.00	72.75	0.71 %	18.1875	20.00	52.75	72.51 %
Rock Fountain	9.00	2,475.00	24.08 %	275.00	375.00	2,100.00	84.85 %
Total Fountains		2,670.25	25.98 %		395.00		
Lighting	3.00	45.00	0.44 %	15.00			
Rocks	25.00	384.00	3.74 %	15.36			
Services	8.00	503.55	4.90 %	62.94375			
Total Design		5,852.80	56.93 %		395.00		
Landscaping							
Gardening	56.50	1,447.50	14.08 %	25.619469			
Installation	5.00	250.00	2.43 %	50.00			
Maintenance & Repair	1.00	50.00	0.49 %	50.00			
Sod	90.00	2,231.25	21.70 %	24.7916667			
Soil	20.00	200.00	1.95 %	10.00			
Sprinklers							
Sprinkler Heads	25.00	50.00	0.49 %	2.00			
Sprinkler Pipes	37.00	148.00	1.44 %	4.00	10.00	138.00	93.24 %
Total Sprinklers		198.00	1.93 %		10.00		
Trimming	2.00	30.00	0.29 %	15.00			
Total Landscaping		4,406.75	42.87 %		10.00		
Pest Control							
Pest Control	5.00	110.00	1.07 %	22.00			
Total Pest Control		110.00	1.07 %				
Not Specified	-1,397.50	-89.50	-0.87 %	0.0640429			
TOTAL		$10,280.05	100.00 %		$405.00		

Figure 13.15: Sample sales by product/service summary report

In the preceding sales by product/service summary report, total sales for the period January 1 to December 31, 2020, are **$10,280.05**, and the cost of goods sold totals **$405.00**. Design services had the highest sales of **$5,852.80**, or **56.93%** of total sales. Pest control had the lowest sales of **$110.00**, which equates to **1.07%** of overall sales. The sales by product/ service report is the final report that we will cover in this chapter.

 Pro Tip: All reports can be memorized and saved in a group for easy access to use on a regular basis. We showed you how to memorize reports in *Chapter 11, Report Center Overview.*

Summary

All of the objectives for this chapter have been met. Let's recap: we have shown you how to customize and generate four key reports that will give you insight into your customers and sales. The four reports we have covered are accounts receivable (A/R) aging reports, which provide you with the number of days for which customer invoices remain unpaid; open invoices reports, which show all unpaid customer invoices; sales by customer summary reports, which include key sales data for each of your customers; and sales by product/service reports, which include the products and services that are your top sellers. These reports are important in assisting you with staying on top of unpaid customer invoices so that you can get paid faster. It is much easier to maintain a positive cash flow if payments are received on time.

In the next chapter, we will show you how to customize and generate key reports that will give you an insight into your vendors and expenses.

Join our book's Discord space

Join the book's Discord workspace for a monthly *Ask me Anything* session with the author: `https://packt.link/QuickBooks`

14

QBCU
5.1.3

Vendor and Expenses Reports

Having access to reports that will give you detailed insight into what your expenses are, who you are paying, and the amount paid to each vendor will help you to control expenses and maintain a profitable business. There are a number of reports in **QuickBooks Online (QBO)** that will help you understand what you owe to vendor suppliers and other creditors.

We will dive into the information you can expect to find in each report, how to customize the report, and how to generate reports. We will also discuss ways you can use reports to help you manage your expenses and cash flow. I recommend you run these reports and review them on a weekly basis. Having access to this information will help you to manage your cash flow and stay on top of the money that goes out of your business.

In this chapter, we will focus on the following key reports:

- Generating an accounts payable (A/P) aging report
- Generating an unpaid bills report
- Generating an expense by vendor summary report
- Generating a bill payments report

 The US edition of QBO was used to create this book. If you are using a version that is outside of the United States, results may differ.

Generating an accounts payable (A/P) aging report

An accounts payable aging report, also known as an A/P aging report, groups unpaid bills based on the number of days they are outstanding or due. Similar to the A/R aging report that we saw in the previous chapter, there are five main groups: **current, 1-30 days, 31-60 days, 61-90 days**, and **91 days and over**. QuickBooks calculates the age of a bill by using the bill date. To stay on top of bills, business owners should review this report on a weekly basis, and take the necessary steps to pay bills that are nearly due. For bills coming due, you should go ahead and process the payment online with your financial institution or write a check directly from QuickBooks.

Follow these steps to generate an A/P aging report:

1. Navigate to **Reports** from the left menu bar, as indicated in *Figure 14.1*:

Figure 14.1: Navigating to the Report Center

2. Scroll down to the **What you owe** section and select **Accounts payable aging summary**, as indicated in *Figure 14.2*:

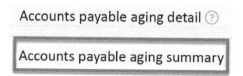

Figure 14.2: Selecting the Accounts payable aging summary report

In addition to the **Accounts payable aging summary** report, there is an **Accounts payable aging detail** report. The detailed report includes information about each bill for the vendor. This includes the bill date, bill number, due date, and amount due. The summary report, on the other hand, includes the open balance for each vendor, grouped by the age of the bill (current, 1-30 days, 31-60 days, 61-90 days, and 91 days and over).

3. Click on the **Customize** button and you can customize the report period, format numbers, columns to display, aging method, days per aging period, and the number of periods for the A/P aging summary report. You can also filter by the vendor and configure other general customizations, as indicated in *Figure 14.3*:

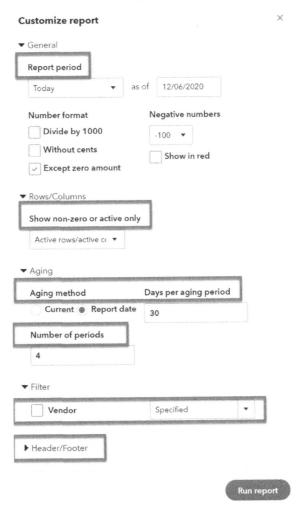

Figure 14.3: Report customization options

The following are brief descriptions of the customizable fields available for an A/P aging summary report:

- **Report period**: You can select preset dates from the drop-down menu, which includes **Today, This week, This month, This quarter,** or **This year.** If you prefer a custom date range, select **Custom** from the dropdown and manually enter the dates.

- **Show non-zero or active only**: Choose to display non-zero only, which means only accounts with activity for the report period specified will be displayed on the report. You can also choose to show active accounts only, which means any account that was made inactive will not be shown on the report.

 You can learn more about how to make accounts inactive in *Chapter 5, Customizing QuickBooks for Your Business.*

- **Aging method**: You can choose an aging method of **Current** or **Report date. Current** will calculate the age of each bill as of today's date, whereas **Report date** will use the report period to calculate the number of days a bill has remained outstanding (unpaid).

- **Days per aging period**: Customize the number of days per aging period or use the standard 30 days per aging period.

- **Number of periods**: Similar to **Days per aging period**, you can also customize the number of periods in which to group bills. In the preceding example, we have chosen four periods (1-30, 31-60, 61-90, and 91 days and over).

- **Filter**: You can filter the A/P aging report for a specific vendor by selecting the vendor from the dropdown.

- **Header/Footer**: You can customize the header information, such as report title, and the footer information, such as date/time prepared.

4. After making your selections, click the **Run report** button.

5. An A/P aging summary report—similar to the following one—will appear:

Photos by Design, LLC

A/P AGING SUMMARY

All Dates

	CURRENT	1 - 30	31 - 60	61 - 90	91 AND OVER	TOTAL
The Phone Company		150.00	150.00			$300.00
TOTAL	$0.00	$150.00	$150.00	$0.00	$0.00	$300.00

Figure 14.4: Sample A/P aging summary report

In this sample A/P aging summary report, Photos by Design's outstanding bills total **$300.00** with **The Phone Company**. Of this amount, **$150** is 1-30 days past due and **$150** is 31-60 days past due. Click on any amount or the **TOTAL** column to see the details of the bill. In order to maintain favorable credit terms with vendor suppliers, the business owner needs to make a payment or make arrangements to pay the past due amount.

Before contacting vendor suppliers, you need to run an unpaid bills report to see the details behind the open balances on this A/P aging summary report. We will show you how to generate an unpaid bills report next.

Generating an unpaid bills report

An unpaid bills report is a list of all bills that have not been paid, as of the date range for the report. It is very similar to an A/P detail report, with the exception that it does not group invoices based on the number of days outstanding. The report includes details such as the vendor's name and a list of all unpaid bills, including amount, due date, number of days past due, and open balance. You can use this report to quickly identify bills that are past due. This will allow you to follow up with vendors, to make payment arrangements for any bills that are past due or coming due.

Follow these steps to generate and customize an unpaid bills report:

1. Navigate to **Reports** from the left menu bar, as indicated in *Figure 14.5*:

Figure 14.5: Navigating to the Reports Center

2. Scroll down to the **What you owe** section and select **Unpaid Bills**, as indicated in *Figure 14.6*:

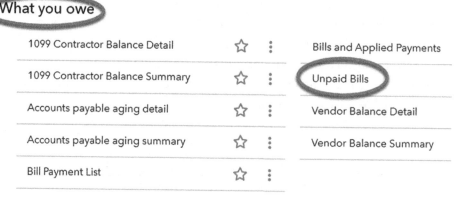

Figure 14.6: Running the unpaid bills report

3. Customize the unpaid bills report by clicking on the **Customize** button and selecting a report period, an aging method, minimum days past due, a filter, and header/footer info, as indicated in *Figure 14.7*:

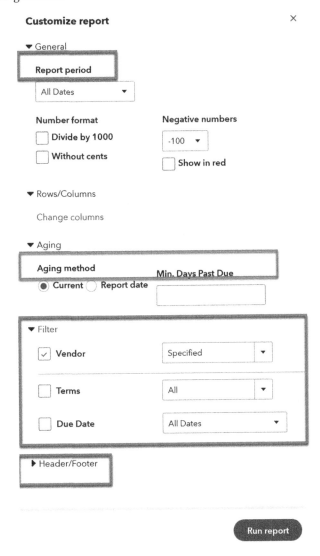

Figure 14.7: Report customization options

The following are brief descriptions of the customizable fields available for an unpaid bills report:

- **Report period**: Select the date range for which to run the report. You can manually enter a date range, or choose from the following: **Today, This Week, This Month, This Quarter**, or **This Year**.

- **Aging method**: The aging method is used to calculate the number of days a bill is past its due date. You can select the **Current** option, which will use today's date, or you can select the **Report date** option. The **Report date** option will use the report period to calculate the number of days the bill remains unpaid.

- **Min. Days Past Due**: If applicable, you can enter a minimum number of days a bill is past due, or you can leave this field blank.

- **Filter**: You can filter the unpaid bills report by selecting a specific vendor, payment terms, and due date of the bill.

- **Header/Footer**: Similar to the A/P aging report, you can customize the report title and the report date and time in the **Header/footer** section.

4. After making your selections, click the **Run report** button to generate the unpaid bills report.

5. An unpaid bills report, similar to the following one, should appear:

Photos by Design, LLC

UNPAID BILLS

All Dates

DATE	TRANSACTION TYPE	NUM	DUE DATE	PAST DUE	AMOUNT	OPEN BALANCE
The Phone Company						
11/01/2020	Bill		11/01/2020	35	150.00	150.00
12/01/2020	Bill		12/01/2020	5	150.00	150.00
Total for The Phone Company					$300.00	$300.00
TOTAL					$300.00	$300.00

Figure 14.8: Sample unpaid bills report

In this sample unpaid bills report, Photos by Design has unpaid bills totaling **$300.00**. As seen in the previous section, the total unpaid amount is due to **The Phone Company**. The oldest bill has been past due for **35** days in the amount of **$150.00**.

This report lists the vendors in alphabetical order and includes the vendor name, contact phone number, bill date, due date, number of days past due, and outstanding amount. To maintain good credit with your vendor suppliers, you should review this report on a weekly basis and contact vendors to make payment arrangements.

To help you stay on top of what you are spending your money on, you need to review the expenses by vendor report. We will show you how to run this report next.

Generating an expenses by vendor summary report

In order to maintain a healthy and positive bottom line, you need to be aware of what your business expenses are. An expenses by vendor summary report provides detailed information about the vendors with whom you are spending your money. This report includes a list of vendors and the total amount you have paid for a specific time period. You can use this report to gauge what your largest expenses are. Plus, you can also use the information on this report to negotiate better pricing with those suppliers from whom you purchase the most.

Follow these steps to generate an expenses by vendor summary report:

1. Navigate to **Reports** from the left menu bar, as indicated in *Figure 14.9*:

Figure 14.9: Navigating to the Report Center

2. Scroll down to the **Expenses and vendors** section and select the **Expenses by Vendor Summary** report, as indicated in *Figure 14.10*:

Figure 14.10: Selecting the Expenses by Vendor Summary report

3. You can customize an expenses by vendor summary report by clicking on the **Customize** button and selecting the reporting period, accounting method, number format, columns to display, and period comparison, as indicated in *Figure 14.11*:

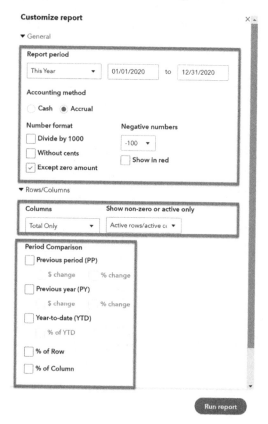

Figure 14.11: Report customization options

The following are brief descriptions of the customizable fields available for an expenses by vendor summary report:

- **Report period**: From the drop-down menu, select a reporting period, or manually enter the date range for which to run the report.

- **Accounting method**: Select the accounting method (**Cash** or **Accrual**) for which you would like to run the report.

- **Number format**: Format numbers by dividing by 1,000, displaying them with or without cents, and making negative numbers red. You have three formatting options for negative numbers: **-100**, **(100)**, or **100-**.

- **Columns**: You can format the report to display information by total only, days, weeks, months, quarters, years, customers, or vendors.

- **Show non-zero or active only**: You can choose to display non-zero only, which means only accounts with activity for the period will show up on the report. You can also show active accounts only, which means any account that was made inactive will not be shown on the report.

 You can learn more about how to make accounts inactive in *Chapter 5, Customizing QuickBooks for Your Business*.

- **Period comparison**: You can compare the current period to a previous period from the drop-down menu.

4. After making your selections, click the **Run report** button to generate the report.

5. An expenses by vendor summary report, similar to the following one, should be displayed:

Photos by Design, LLC

EXPENSES BY VENDOR SUMMARY
January - December 2020

	TOTAL
Photo Supply Co	1,000.00
VCC	636.00
Mobile Phones USA	500.00
Suzy Contractor	500.00
ABC Office Supply	450.00
The Electric Co.	400.00
Supplies	389.42
Contractor	380.00
The Phone Company	300.00
Restaurants	228.46
Office Purchases	171.00
Owner	107.41
Amazon	100.00
Gas Purchases	30.15
Intuit	-0.67
TOTAL	**$5,191.77**

Figure 14.12: Sample expenses by vendor summary report

In the sample expenses by vendor summary report, total expenses for **Photos by Design** are **$5,191.77**. **Photo Supply Co**. received the highest payment of **$1,000**. The report gives business owners insight into who they are spending their money with. As discussed, this can be helpful when it comes to negotiating a better price for goods and services.

To drill down to specific payments made to vendors, you can run a bill payments report. We will show you how to generate this report next.

Pro Tip: The vendor summary report is great for reviewing what you have paid vendors for the year to determine who may be subject to 1099s. You can quickly review the report to see who you have paid $600 or more to, which is the threshold for generating a 1099 form. You can learn more about how to process 1099s in *Chapter 16, Managing 1099 Contractors in QuickBooks Online*.

Generating a bill payments report

A bill payments report includes detailed payment information about the bills you have paid. The report is broken down by the method of payment (for example, cash, credit card, or check). It includes the payment date, check number (if applicable), vendor, and amount paid. If you want to determine the payments made for a specific time period, this report will give you the information you need.

To generate a bill payments report, follow these steps:

1. Navigate to **Reports** from the left menu bar, as indicated in *Figure 14.13*:

Figure 14.13: Navigating to the Report Center

2. Scroll down to the **What you owe** section and select **Bill Payment List**, as indicated in *Figure 14.14*:

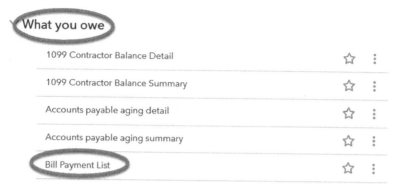

Figure 14.14: Running the bill payment list report

3. On the next screen, you can customize the report period and determine how the report is grouped, as indicated in *Figure 14.15*:

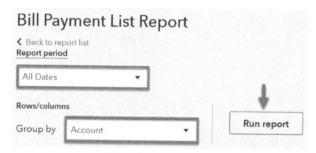

Figure 14.15: Customizing the bill payment list report

The following are brief descriptions of the customizable fields for a bill payments report:

- **Report period**: Select a preset time period, such as today, this week, this month, this quarter, or this year. You can also select **Custom**, and enter a date range.

- **Group by**: When it comes to sorting, you can group the report by account, vendor, day, week, month, quarter, or year.

4. After making your selections, click the **Run report** button to generate the bill payment list report.

5. A bill payment list report, similar to the following one, should be displayed:

Photos By Design, LLC

BILL PAYMENT LIST

All Dates

DATE	NUM	VENDOR	AMOUNT
Checking			
09/12/2019	1	Brosnahan Insurance Agency	-2,000.00
09/13/2019	3	Books by Bessie	-75.00
09/14/2019	6	PG&E	-114.09
08/25/2019	7	Hicks Hardware	-250.00
09/14/2019	45	Tim Philip Masonry	-666.00
06/13/2019	10	Robertson & Associates	-300.00
09/08/2019	11	Hall Properties	-900.00
Total for Checking			**$ -4,305.09**
Mastercard			
09/13/2019	1	Cal Telephone	74.36
09/15/2019	1	Cal Telephone	56.50
09/15/2019	1	Norton Lumber and Building Materials	103.55
Total for Mastercard			**$234.41**

Figure 14.16: Sample bill payment list report

In the sample bill payment list report, **Photos by Design** has paid a total of **-$4,305.09** in checks and **$234.41** via Mastercard. When funds are withdrawn from the checking account, a negative amount reduces the balance in the checking account. This is the reason why the total for checks is **-$4,305.09**. On the other hand, a payment made with a credit card increases the balance due on that card, which is represented by a positive number. This report includes the payment date, check number (or payment reference number), vendor, and amount paid.

You can run this report for any time period, to gain insight into payments made to all vendors. This information can help you to forecast the amount of cash you need available to meet your obligations to vendors.

Pro Tip: Don't forget to memorize reports that you will use on a regular basis. This will save you time reformatting and searching for reports. To learn how to memorize reports, head over to *Chapter 11, Report Center Overview.*

Summary

In this chapter, we have provided you with information about four key reports that will help you to control your business expenses and stay on top of payments to your vendors. Our goal was to introduce you to the A/P aging report, the unpaid bills report, the expenses by vendor report, and the bill payments report. We have accomplished this goal by providing step-by-step instructions on how to customize and generate each of these reports. In addition, we have explained how these reports will help you to stay on top of unpaid bills so that you can maintain a good credit history with your vendors.

In the next chapter, we will show you how to set up and manage your employees and contractors.

Join our book's Discord space

Join the book's Discord workspace for a monthly *Ask me Anything* session with the author: https://packt.link/QuickBooks

Section 4: Managing Employees and Contractors

15
Managing Payroll in QuickBooks Online

Managing payroll is one of the most important aspects of your business. If not done right, it could negatively impact your employees since they may not be paid the right amount. It could also result in interest and penalties if payroll taxes are not filed and paid on time.

There are four main aspects of managing payroll: setting up your employees with the proper deductions and benefit elections, processing payroll by ensuring the hours paid are correct and on time, generating payroll reports to gain an insight into total payroll costs, and filing payroll tax forms and making payments on time. By the end of this chapter, you will be able to set up your employees, pay your employees, generate key payroll reports, file payroll tax forms, and make payroll tax payments. If you do not understand how payroll works, it is highly recommended that you use the full service payroll option offered by Intuit QuickBooks.

In this chapter, we will cover the following topics:

- Setting up payroll
- Running payroll
- Generating payroll reports
- Filing payroll tax forms and payments

 The US edition of QBO was used in this book. If you are using a version that is outside of the US, results may differ.

Setting up payroll

The most important aspect of ensuring an accurate payroll is to set up the payroll properly before you run your first payroll. Setting up a payroll involves gathering information about your employees, such as their names, mailing addresses, and social security numbers. As an employer, you will need a federal tax ID number and a separate bank account for payroll checks and payroll taxes. You will need to determine what benefits you will offer employees, how often you will pay employees (for example, weekly, bi-weekly, or monthly), and the payment method you will use (for example, paper check or direct deposit).

In the following sections, we will provide you with a checklist of information you need to have handy to complete your employer profile and set up employees. First, we will show you how to set up payroll in QBO.

Payroll setup checklist and key documents

As discussed, the key to ensuring the accuracy of payroll checks, payroll tax forms, and payments is to ensure your payroll is set up properly. To set up a payroll, you will need to gather information from your employees. Also, you will need to have certain documents and information handy to complete the employer information section.

The following table shows a summarized checklist of the information required to set up your payroll:

Employee info	Employer info
Hire date	Federal tax ID (FEIN)
Form W-4: Employee withholding info	State employer ID number (if applicable)
Salary or hourly rate	Bank account information
Sick or vacation accrual rate	Employee benefits
Payroll deductions and contributions	Employee travel reimbursement policy
Payment method	Other compensation: bonuses, commissions
Direct deposit authorization (if applicable)	Other deductions: wage garnishment

Table 15.1: Checklist of employee and employer info needed to set up payroll

The following is a brief explanation of the **employee** information required to set up payroll:

- **Hire date:** This is the official start date for an employee. This information will be used to determine benefits eligibility as well as vacation and sick pay.

- **Form W-4**: This is an official form issued by the **Internal Revenue Service (IRS)** to gather employee withholding information, which determines the amount of federal tax withheld from paychecks. You can download this form from IRS.gov and include it in your employee new hire packet.

- **Salary or hourly rate**: This is the agreed-upon salary or hourly rate for an employee.

- **Sick or vacation accrual rate**: The number of hours an employee can earn toward sick or vacation leave.

- **Payroll deductions and contributions**: These are the deductions or contributions for health care, 401(k), or other benefits an employee has agreed to participate in.

- **Payment method**: Most employers will pay their employees in the form of a check or direct deposit. If the employee signs up for a direct deposit, they will need to complete a direct deposit authorization form.

- **Direct deposit authorization**: If an employee would like their paycheck to be electronically deposited into their bank account, this form gives the employer the authority to do so. Employers must keep this form on file along with other payroll information.

 Pro Tip: Employee files are important for all businesses and should comply with all federal, state, and local requirements. When in doubt, seek guidance from a CPA or human resource professional.

The following is a brief explanation of the **employer** information required to set up payroll:

- **Federal employer identification number (FEIN)**: Employers are required to have a federal tax ID number before they can process payroll for employees. This number is used by the IRS to keep track of employee and employer payroll tax payments and filings. If you don't have a FEIN, you can apply for one at IRS.gov.

- **State employer ID number**: If you live in one of the eight states that are subject to income tax, you will need to apply for a state employer identification number. Similar to the FEIN, the state employer ID number is used to keep track of payroll taxes.

- **Bank account information**: As discussed, you need to set up a separate bank account to keep track of payments made to employees in the form of payroll checks or direct deposits. Also, all payroll tax payments made to the IRS or your state need to be made out of this account. Since most payments are made electronically, you will need the routing number of your financial institution and the full account number.

Similar to your business checking account, you will need to add the payroll bank account to your chart of accounts list in QuickBooks. Refer to *Chapter 5, Customizing QuickBooks for Your Business*, where we cover how to add an account to the chart of accounts list.

- **Employee benefits**: Details regarding benefits provided to employees will need to be entered into QuickBooks. This includes the employee and employer portions of health care, 401(k) plans, and sick leave and vacation pay.

- **Employee travel reimbursement policy**: If employees travel on behalf of your business and incur expenses, such as business meals, airfare, and hotel costs, you need to set up your payroll to reimburse employees for these.

 A simpler way to handle employee reimbursements is to process the payments outside of payroll. This would involve setting up an employee as a vendor and writing a check to reimburse them for business expenses paid with personal funds.

- **Other compensation**: If you pay bonuses or commissions, or make other forms of payment to employees, you will need to include this information in your payroll setup.

- **Other deductions**: On occasion, you may receive wage garnishments for employees who owe back taxes or child support. These are court-ordered requests that you cannot ignore. Instead, you must set up the garnishment amount as a deduction for the employee. These requests will typically have an end date that is based on the total outstanding amount. Be sure to set these payments up exactly as they are outlined in the letter. If you don't, you could be subject to penalties as a result.

Now that you have a better understanding of the key documents and information required to properly set up payroll, you are ready to complete the payroll setup.

Setting up payroll in QBO

Setting up payroll in QBO can be done in six easy steps:

1. Click on **Payroll** on the left menu bar to navigate to the Payroll Center, as shown in *Figure 15.1*:

Figure 15.1: Navigating to the Payroll Center

2. Activate the payroll by clicking on the **Get started** button, as shown in *Figure 15.2*:

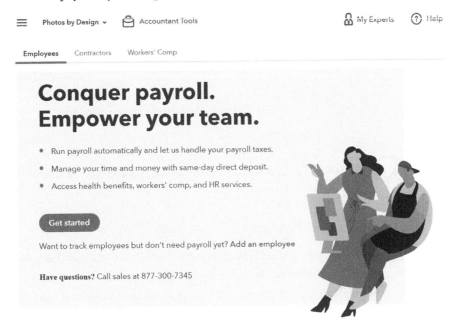

Figure 15.2: Clicking the Get started button to begin setting up payroll

3. On the next screen, you will have the option of selecting a payroll plan, as indicated in *Figure 15.3*:

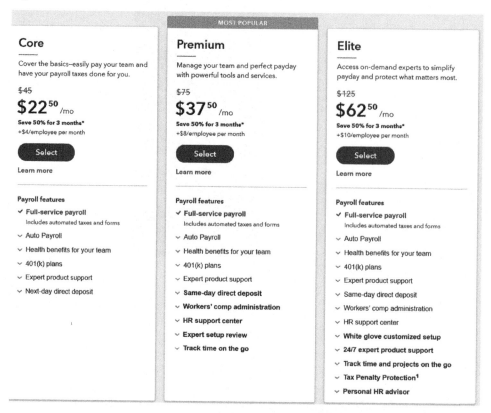

Figure 15.3: Intuit QuickBooks payroll plans

 Note: Pricing is based on the current rates and it is subject to change.

The following is a brief explanation of each QBO payroll plan:

- **Core:** This plan is ideal for employers who prefer to manage their payroll in-house. The subscription fee includes updated payroll tax tables that are used to automatically calculate payroll taxes and payroll checks for you—no manual calculation required! With this plan, you can process payroll checks, electronically make payroll tax payments, and file payroll tax forms. This plan also includes next-day direct deposit.

- **Premium:** This plan includes all of the features outlined in the Core plan plus workers' comp administration, an HR support center, a QuickBooks expert who will review your payroll setup, and the ability to allow employees to track time using their mobile device. When setting up payroll, links will be available for applying for certain state ID numbers that are required.

- **Elite:** This plan is ideal for employers that prefer to outsource their payroll duties. It includes white-glove customized setup, payroll processing, completion of tax forms, and automated payroll tax payments. In addition, Intuit will process all year-end tax forms and filings such as mailing and filing W-2 forms. Unlike the Core and Premium plans, you get the ability to track projects from any mobile device, tax penalty protection, access to a personal HR advisor, and 24/7 product support, which can be beneficial if there is an issue with a payroll or an individual paycheck. Voids and corrections must be made by the payroll service.

QuickBooks Payroll is available in all 50 states and all payroll plans include the following key features:

- Unlimited payroll runs
- Calculated paychecks and taxes
- Automated taxes and forms
- Workforce portal
- Custom user access by setting permission levels
- Garnishment and deductions management
- Payroll reports

It is advised to check local payroll tax filing requirements to confirm that the payroll subscription you have chosen can handle all necessary filings.

4. After selecting the plan you want, the payroll welcome message should appear on your screen, as indicated in *Figure 15.4*:

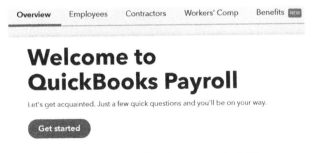

Figure 15.4: Payroll welcome page in QBO

Before you proceed to the next step, you will see a couple of questions pop up on your screen. First, you need to indicate whether you have paid employees this year. If you have, you will need to gather the year-to-date payment information for each employee so that you can enter it into QuickBooks; otherwise, the W-2 forms will be incorrect at the end of the year. Second, you will need to enter the date of your next payroll (in other words, the first payroll you plan to run in QBO).

When you are done, click the **Get started** button.

5. The following screen will appear:

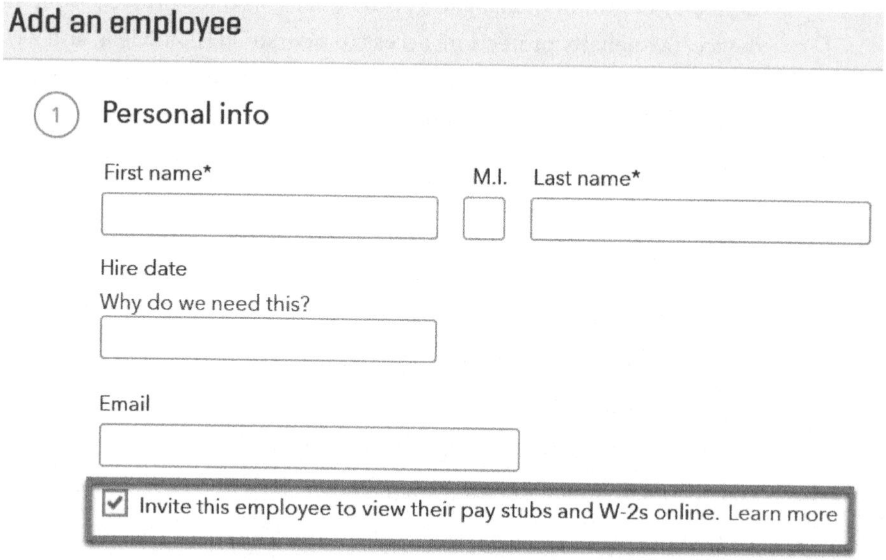

Add an employee

① Personal info

First name*   M.I.   Last name*

Hire date
Why do we need this?

Email

☑ Invite this employee to view their pay stubs and W-2s online. Learn more

Figure 15.5: Adding an employee

To add a new employee, enter their first and last name, hire date, and email address. Check the box under the email address to invite the employee to an online portal where they can view and print their pay stubs and W-2 forms.

6. Complete the employee payroll information, as indicated in *Figure 15.6*:

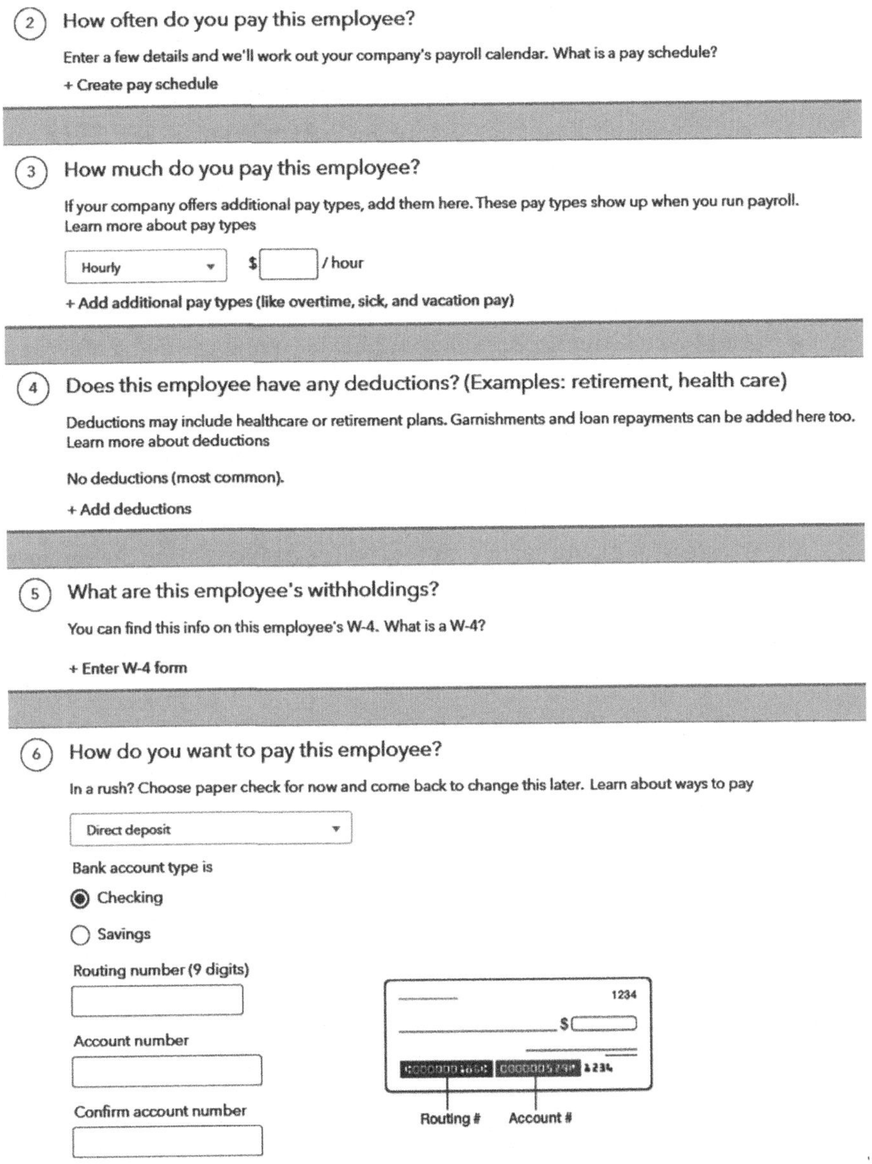

② **How often do you pay this employee?**

Enter a few details and we'll work out your company's payroll calendar. What is a pay schedule?

+ Create pay schedule

③ **How much do you pay this employee?**

If your company offers additional pay types, add them here. These pay types show up when you run payroll. Learn more about pay types

| Hourly ▼ | $ [   ] / hour |

+ Add additional pay types (like overtime, sick, and vacation pay)

④ **Does this employee have any deductions? (Examples: retirement, health care)**

Deductions may include healthcare or retirement plans. Garnishments and loan repayments can be added here too. Learn more about deductions

No deductions (most common).

+ Add deductions

⑤ **What are this employee's withholdings?**

You can find this info on this employee's W-4. What is a W-4?

+ Enter W-4 form

⑥ **How do you want to pay this employee?**

In a rush? Choose paper check for now and come back to change this later. Learn about ways to pay

| Direct deposit ▼ |

Bank account type is

⦿ Checking

◯ Savings

Routing number (9 digits)

[   ]

Account number

[   ]

Confirm account number

[   ]

Routing #   Account #

Figure 15.6: Completing employee information

A brief explanation of the employee information required follows:

- **Create a pay schedule**: Create a pay schedule based on when you pay employees. You can create one pay schedule for all employees (for example, every other Friday) or multiple pay schedules—one for hourly employees and one for salary employees. Click on the **+ Create pay schedule** link in *step 2* (shown in the preceding screenshot) to get started.

- **Employee pay rate**: In *step 3*, set up the hourly rate or annual salary for an employee. You can also set up other payment types, such as overtime, sick leave, and vacation. Click on the **Add additional pay types** link and follow the onscreen prompts.

- **Employee deductions**: Add all applicable employee deductions in *step 4*. This includes health benefits, 401(k) contributions, and wage garnishments. Click the **Add deductions** link to get started.

- **Employee withholdings**: Enter the employee withholding information from the W-4 form completed by the employee. This information will determine the amount of federal and state income tax that will be deducted from the employee's payroll check.

- **Payment method**: From the drop-down box, select **Check** or **Direct deposit** as the payment method. If an employee opts for direct deposit, use the completed direct deposit authorization form discussed previously to complete the routing number and account number of the financial institution.

 Pro Tip: It's a good idea to request a copy of a voided check from employees to verify the bank routing and account number the employee has provided. If the deposit account is not a checking account, employees can request a letter from their financial institution that includes this information.

7. Click the **Next** button to save the information you have entered.

8. After entering the employee information, your screen should resemble the following screenshot:

Figure 15.7: Employee listing in the Payroll center

Within this screen, you can review all employees you have added, their pay rate, and the method of payment for their paycheck. In addition, you can add more employees by clicking the **Add an employee** button located on the right side of the screen.

In this section, we have shown you how to add employees and their tax deductions, tax withholdings, and payment methods. Be sure to complete *steps 1* through *6* for all employees. Once you have set up all of your employees, you are ready to run payroll. The number of payroll schedules created in *step 6* will determine how often you run payroll. If all employees get paid on the same day, you will run the payroll based on the number of times employees are paid (for example, weekly or bi-weekly).

 Watch this Intuit video tutorial, which recaps how to add employees to payroll: https://youtu.be/-qixsS1k3sQ.

In the next section, we will show you how to run your payroll in five easy steps.

Running payroll

After setting up your employees, you are ready to run your first payroll. It's important to run payroll so that your employees are paid on time and to ensure you meet all of your payroll deadlines to the state and local tax authorities.

Running payroll in QBO can be done in six easy steps:

1. Click on **Workers** on the left menu bar to navigate to the Payroll Center:

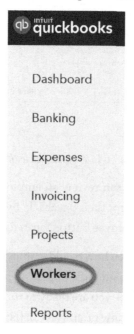

Figure 15.8: Clicking on Workers to navigate to the Payroll Center

2. Click the **Let's go** button as indicated to create paychecks for employees:

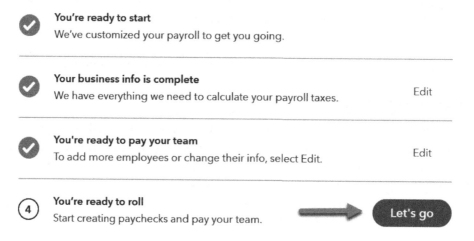

Figure 15.9: Clicking the Let's go button to run payroll

3. On the next screen, you will select employees and enter the payroll hours, as indicated in *Figure 15.10*:

Figure 15.10: Selecting employees to run payroll for

A brief explanation of the payroll processing screen follows:

- **Bank account**: From the drop-down menu, select the payroll bank account you created in the previous section on setting up your payroll. Once you select the account, the current balance will appear to the right of the account name.

- **Pay period**: The **Pay period** field will automatically be populated based on the payment schedule you created in the previous section on setting up the payroll.

- **Pay date**: This field will automatically be populated based on the payroll schedule you created.

- **TOTAL PAY**: The grand total of the payroll (including wages and taxes) will appear in the upper right-hand corner of the screen.

- **EMPLOYEE**: Select all employees or specific employees to pay by putting the green checkmark in the box to the left of the employee column.

- **PAY METHOD**: A symbol representing the payment method (direct deposit or paper check) will appear in this field.

- **SALARY**: For salaried employees, the salary amount for the pay period will automatically appear in this field.

- **REGULAR PAY HRS**: For hourly employees, you will need to enter the number of hours worked for the pay period.

- **MEMO**: Enter in this field any additional information that you want to document regarding the payment.

- **TOTAL PAY**: This column includes the total gross pay for each employee.

4. Click the **Next** button to save the information.

5. After entering the payroll hours, you can review the total payroll cost on the next screen:

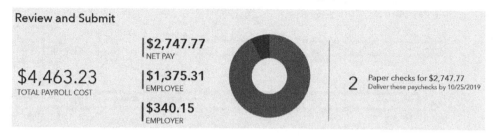

Figure 15.11: Reviewing payroll details and submitting

The preceding screenshot provides a high-level overview of the current payroll being processed. As you can see, the total payroll cost is **$4,463.23**. This comprises **$340.15** in employer payroll taxes, employee payroll taxes of **$1,375.31**, and net pay of **$2,747.77** for two employees. Paper checks will be issued to these employees on **10/25/2019**.

Click the **Next** button to save the information.

6. On the next screen, you will submit payroll for processing, as indicated in *Figure 15.12*:

Pay period: 10/17/2019 to 10/23/2019   **Pay date:** 10/25/2019

EMPLOYEE	PAY METHOD	TOTAL HOURS	TOTAL PAY	EMPLOYEE TAXES	NET PAY
BR Rubble, Barney	Paper check	40.00	$2,200.00	$747.03	$1,452.97
BR Rubble, Betty	Paper check	40.00	$1,923.08	$628.28	$1,294.80
	TOTALS:	**80.00**	**$4,123.08**	**$1,375.31**	**$2,747.77**

Back	Preview payroll details	Submit payroll ▾

Figure 15.12: Clicking the Submit payroll button to process payroll

Here, you can do a final review of each employee's payroll check. Once you are satisfied, click the **Submit payroll** button as indicated to process the payroll checks. If employees have opted for direct deposit, they will be able to view their paystubs by logging in to the employee portal you invited them to during the setup process. If employees elected to receive a paper check, you will follow the onscreen prompts to print payroll checks.

Watch this Intuit video tutorial, which recaps how to run payroll: `https://youtu.be/dH2HPSIRDTQ`.

Now that you have learned how to properly set up employees and run payroll, it's time to learn how to generate payroll reports. QuickBooks includes several summaries and detailed reports that will give you insight into total employee costs and employer costs.

Generating payroll reports

By now, you know that QBO includes a library of preset reports that provide business owners with an insight into every aspect of their business. There are several summaries and detailed reports you can generate to gain insight into your payroll costs, payroll deductions and contributions, vacation and sick leave, and payroll taxes. These reports will help you to complete payroll tax forms and make payroll tax payments to the appropriate state and federal tax authorities.

Follow these steps to generate payroll reports:

1. Click on **Reports** on the left navigation bar, as indicated in *Figure 15.13*:

Figure 15.13: Navigating to the Reports Center

2. Scroll down to the **Payroll** section and you will see several reports, as indicated in *Figure 15.14*:

Employee Details	☆	Payroll Tax Payments	☆
Employee Directory	☆	Payroll Tax and Wage Summary	☆
Multiple Worksites	☆	Recent/Edited Time Activities	☆
Paycheck List	☆	Retirement Plans	☆
Payroll Billing Summary	☆	Time Activities by Employee Detail	☆
Payroll Deductions/Contributions	☆	Total Pay	☆
Payroll Details	☆	Total Payroll Cost	☆
Payroll Summary by Employee	☆ ⋮	Vacation and Sick Leave	☆
Payroll Summary	☆	Workers' Compensation	☆
Payroll Tax Liability	☆		

Figure 15.14: Payroll reports available in QBO

3. The following is a brief description of the information you will find on five key payroll reports:

    - **Paycheck List**: This report includes a list of paychecks that have been issued. You can use this report to edit check numbers, print pay stubs, and more.

    - **Payroll Deductions/Contributions**: This report details payroll deductions by employee as well as employer contributions made for each pay period.

    - **Payroll Summary by Employee**: This is a comprehensive report that includes wages, deductions, and taxes totaled by the employee or payroll period.

    - **Total Payroll Cost**: This report includes all costs associated with paying employees, such as total pay, net pay, deductions, and taxes.

    - **Vacation and Sick Leave**: This report details the total vacation and sick pay that has been used as well as the remaining balance left.

4. To generate a report, simply click on the report and select the pay period you would like to see data for. Similar to other QBO reports, you can save payroll reports as PDF files or export them to Excel. Refer to *Chapter 11, Report Center Overview*, for step-by-step instructions on how this works.

One of the key benefits of generating reports is that the information you need to file payroll tax forms and make payroll tax payments is included. In the next section, we will discuss your options for filing and making payroll tax payments.

Filing payroll tax forms and payments

Employers are required to file payroll tax forms and make payroll tax payments at both the federal and state level. The due dates will vary by employer and are generally based on the dollar amount of the payroll and other factors specific to your business. The IRS.gov website (http://IRS.gov) is the best resource for finding out what the federal requirements are. At the state level, you should contact the **Employment Development Department (EDD)** to learn what the requirements are for your state. As discussed in the *Setting up payroll* section, you will need to obtain a state employer ID number. Once you do so, you should receive information about filing and paying state payroll taxes, if applicable.

There are a few key reports that you should generate to assist you with completing payroll tax forms:

- **Payroll Tax Liability**: This report provides you with the details of how much payroll tax you are required to pay and how much you have already paid to state and federal tax authorities.

- **Payroll Tax Payments**: This report provides you with the details of all tax payments you have made.

- **Payroll Tax and Wage Summary**: This report shows total and taxable wages that are subject to federal and province/region/state withholding.

 Pro Tip: If you sign up for the payroll QuickBooks Elite plan, Intuit will file all of your tax forms and submit all payroll tax payments for you. However, if you sign up for the Core or Premium plans, you will be responsible for filing all paperwork and making all payroll tax payments before the due date.

As discussed, it's important to file all payroll tax forms and mail payroll tax payments before they are due. Otherwise, you could be subject to hefty penalties and fines if you do not. Contact the IRS to get information about federal forms and due dates, and contact the EDD in your state for information regarding the state forms and due dates.

Summary

We have met our goal for this chapter of showing you how to manage your payroll from start to finish. To recap, you now know what information is required to set up employees and how to set them up. We covered how to enter the hours for each pay period and submit payroll for processing. You know what payroll reports are available so that you can gain insight into your total payroll costs, and finally, we discussed the importance of filing payroll tax forms and submitting payroll tax payments on time. You are now equipped to add employees, run your payroll, run payroll reports, and use this information to file your payroll tax returns. Be sure to consult with a CPA, HR professional, or a payroll expert to ensure payroll is set up properly. Otherwise, you run the risk of encountering errors, which could result in steep penalties.

In the next chapter, we will cover how to manage 1099 contractors. While these folks are not employees, you will need to set them up in QuickBooks to properly track payments for reporting purposes.

Join our book's Discord space

Join the book's Discord workspace for a monthly *Ask me Anything* session with the author: https://packt.link/QuickBooks

16

QBCU
3.1.4

Managing 1099 Contractors in QuickBooks Online

If you hire an individual to perform services for your business and they are not an employee, they are considered an independent contractor (also known as a **1099 contractor**). Payments to 1099 contractors must be tracked so that you can report this information to the **Internal Revenue Service (IRS)** at the end of the year. To ensure that payments are tracked properly, you will need to set up contractors in QuickBooks; add an account to post all payments to; pay contractors with a paper check, electronic fund transfer (EFT), or debit/credit card; and provide a 1099 form to all the contractors who meet the threshold at the end of the year. If the total payments to a contractor equal $600 or more, you must issue a 1099 form and report this information to the IRS. Failure to track and report payments to 1099 contractors could lead to penalties and fines.

In this chapter, we will show you how to set up 1099 contractors, how to make payments to 1099 contractors, and what to do at the end of the year to report payments to independent contractors.

 Pro Tip: Be sure to visit www.irs.gov to learn about any changes made to 1099 forms each year.

In this chapter, we will cover the following topics:

- Setting up 1099 contractors
- Tracking and paying 1099 contractors
- 1099 year-end reporting

Let's get started with setting up 1099 contractors in QuickBooks Online.

 The US edition of QBO was used to create this book. If you are using a version that is outside of the United States, results may differ.

Setting up 1099 contractors

It's important to set up 1099 contractors correctly in QuickBooks to ensure payments are tracked for 1099 reporting purposes. In QuickBooks, contractors are set up as vendors, which is anyone that you pay who is not an employee. To learn more about how to set up vendors, refer to *Chapter 6, Managing Customer, Vendor, and Products and Services Lists*. To ensure that the information you enter is accurate, request a W9 form from all of your contractors. This form will include the contractor's name or the name of their company, their federal tax ID number or social security number, their business entity (for example, sole proprietor, partnership, or corporation), and their mailing address.

 Pro Tip: It is best practice to obtain a completed W9 form from each vendor before you make your first payment to them. Having this information is important because you will need it to create a 1099 form, if applicable.

Follow these steps to set up a 1099 contractor in QuickBooks:

1.   Navigate to the **Expenses** tab, as shown in *Figure 16.1*:

Figure 16.1: Navigating to Expenses

2. A screen similar to the one shown in the following screenshot will appear. Ensure that you are on the **Vendors** tab:

Figure 16.2: Clicking on Expenses and then Vendors

3. Select **New vendor**, as shown in *Figure 16.3*:

Figure 16.3: Clicking the New vendor button

4. The following screen will appear for the new vendor:

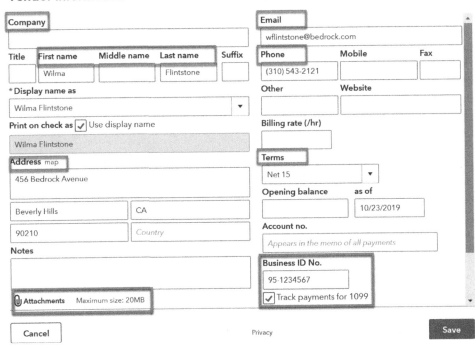

Figure 16.4: Completing the Vendor Information form to set up a 1099 contractor

At a minimum, you should complete the fields specified in the preceding screenshot. It is also a good idea to attach the completed W9 form to the vendor record. You can do this by clicking on **Attachments**, which is located at the bottom of the screen, above the **Cancel** button.

 Pro Tip: To ensure that payments to a contractor are marked for 1099 reporting, be sure to put the checkmark in the box that appears below the **Business ID No.** field. If you forget to do this, payments will not be tracked for 1099 reporting.

Repeat *steps 1* through *4* for each 1099 contractor you pay throughout the year. Once you have added all of your contractors to QuickBooks, you are ready to make payments. We will discuss how to track and pay 1099 contractors next.

Tracking and paying 1099 contractors

The simplest way to keep track of payments to 1099 vendors is to create an account called **Contractor expenses**. This account should be added to your chart of accounts list and used to post all 1099 payments. For more information on adding accounts to the chart of accounts, refer to *Chapter 5, Customizing QuickBooks for Your Business*.

You can pay 1099 contractors the same way you do other vendors. You can write a check, send a wire transfer, or use your debit/credit card to make payments to contractors. Refer to *Chapter 9, Recording Expenses in QuickBooks Online*, to learn more about how to pay contractors.

 Pro Tip: Beginning with the 2011 tax year, the IRS requires you to exclude from Form 1099-MISC payments made to a 1099 vendor via debit card, credit card, or gift card. Payments made through third-party payment networks such as PayPal should also be excluded. Instead, these payments are reported by the card issuers and third-party networks on Form 1099-K.

Now that you know how to add independent contractors to QuickBooks, set up an account to track payments, and make payments, it's time to discuss what you will do with this information.

1099 year-end reporting

1099 year-end reporting consists of printing and mailing 1099 forms to contractors who meet the $600 threshold and reporting this information to the IRS by January 31 of each year.

This date is subject to change, so be sure to visit IRS.gov each year to confirm the due date. Similar to a W2 form for an employee, the 1099 form includes the amount you have paid to a contractor within the calendar year. This form is used by independent contractors to report their earnings for the year on their tax returns. Failure to provide this information to the IRS and the contractors could result in fines and penalties.

When you are ready to generate 1099 forms, the process to do this is very simple. First, you review the accuracy of your information and the basic contact information for each contractor. Then, you review the payments that have been flagged as 1099 payments. If this information is correct, you can have Intuit process your 1099 forms electronically for a fee. Another option is to manually print and mail the 1099 forms yourself.

Follow these steps to learn how to do 1099 reporting:

1. Navigate to the **Expenses** tab, as shown in *Figure 16.5*:

Figure 16.5: Navigating to Expenses

2. From the **Vendors** tab, click on the **Prepare 1099s** button, as shown in *Figure 16.6*:

Figure 16.6: Clicking the Prepare 1099s button

3.   If this is your first time preparing 1099s, the following screen will appear:

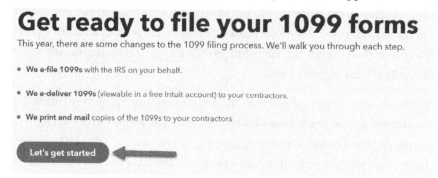

Figure 16.7: Clicking Let's get started to file your 1099 forms

Click the **Let's get started** button.

4.   On the next screen, you can review your company information and make any necessary corrections:

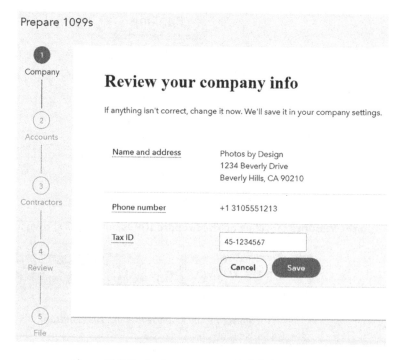

Figure 16.8: Reviewing your company info for accuracy

Click the **Save** button when you are done.

5. Click **Next** at the bottom of the screen and select the box and the account you have categorized 1099 payments to, as shown in *Figure 16.9*:

Categorize payments to contractors

Select the type of payments you made or the expenses you recorded. Then select the expense accounts used for these payments. Not sure which categories to choose?

See which expense accounts you used

Common payment types

☑ Non-employee compensation (most common) Box 1 1099-NEC

    [Contractors ▾]

☐ Rents Box 1 1099-MISC

Direct sales

☐ Direct Sales - NEC Box 2 1099-NEC

☐ Direct Sales - MISC Box 7 1099-MISC

Other payment types

☐ Royalties Box 2 1099-MISC

☐ Other Income Box 3 1099-MISC

☐ Medical Payments Box 6 1099-MISC

☐ Substitute Payments in lieu of dividends or interest Box 8 1099-MISC

☐ Crop Insurance Proceeds Box 9 1099-MISC

☐ Gross Proceds Paid to an Attorney Box 10 1099-MISC

Figure 16.9: Categorizing payments to contractors

Pro Tip: In general, you will select **Box 1, Nonemployee Compensation** on the 1099 forms you generate for the contractors you have paid. In the dropdown below this box, select the account these payments were posted to. To learn more about which box to select, refer to the IRS instructions for Form 1099. You can find this information at IRS.gov.

6. On the next screen, review your contractors' information to ensure that it is accurate:

Review your contractors' info

Make sure your contractors' details are correct. To see which contractors meet the 1099 threshold, click **Next**.
Need to add anyone?

                      [Add from Vendor list]

CONTRACTOR NAME	ADDRESS	TAX ID	EMAIL	ACTION
Fred Flintstone	456 Bedrock Avenue Beverly Hills CA 90210	95-6789543	flintstone@bedrock.com	Edit
Wilma Flintstone	456 Bedrock Avenue Beverly Hills CA 90210	95-1234567	wflintstone@bedrock.com	Edit

Figure 16.10: Reviewing contractors' info for accuracy

Note that you cannot print 1099 forms if the mailing address and tax ID (or social security number) are missing. You must obtain this information prior to printing 1099 forms.

7. A list of contractors that meet the 1099 threshold will be displayed on the next screen:

Check that the payments add up

Only those contractors you paid above the threshold (usually $600) get a 1099.
IMPORTANT: Credit card payments to contractors should be **excluded.** Why?
Need to add or edit payments?

▽ ▼ 2018 | 1099 contractors that meet threshold   Print Information Sheet   ⚙

CONTRACTOR	BOX 7	TOTAL	EXCLUDED	ALL PAYMENTS
Fred Flintstone	$1,200.00	$1,200.00		$1,200.00
Wilma Flintstone	$600.00	$600.00		$600.00

Figure 16.11: Reviewing 1099 payments for accuracy

In order to meet the 1099 threshold, contractors must receive payments totaling $600 or more within the calendar year. If a contractor was paid less than $600, you are not required to issue a 1099 form and the contractor will not show up in the preceding list.

8. On the next screen, select the 1099 plan that works best for you:

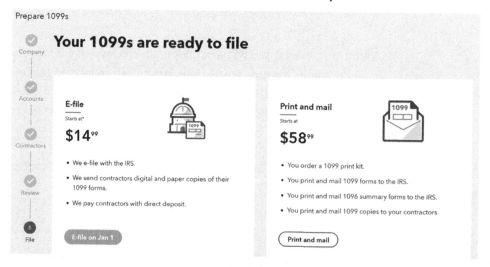

Figure 16.12: Choosing the method you wish to use to file 1099 forms

The two 1099 plans available are:

- **E-file**: This plan starts at $14.99 and is a full-service plan. Intuit will e-file 1099 forms, print and mail copies of the 1099 forms to your contractors, and give contractors access to view their 1099 forms online.

 Pro Tip: This is the most efficient way to process your 1099 forms. They will be sent to vendors as well as the IRS. You will also have a copy to keep on file for your records. While printing and mailing is an option, it is recommended to file electronically if possible.

- **Print and mail**: This plan starts at $58.99 and is ideal for business owners that prefer to process their 1099 forms in-house. Intuit will mail you a 1099 kit that will include blank 1099 forms you can print on. You are responsible for mailing all 1099 forms to your contractors and sending copies to the IRS before the deadline.

To select a plan, just click the button at the bottom of the plan you want to choose and follow the onscreen prompts to complete filing your 1099 forms.

Summary

In this chapter, we discussed how to set up 1099 contractors in QuickBooks, how to track payments that have been made to 1099 contractors, the various ways you can pay 1099 contractors, and how to report and file 1099 forms at the end of the year. If you hire individuals such as an attorney or a bookkeeper to provide services to your business, you now know how to set them up in QuickBooks and track payments that are made to them throughout the year. You also know that the threshold for reporting 1099 payments is $600 in payments within a calendar year. Finally, we have shown you how to sign up for the 1099 service provided by Intuit so that you can print and mail 1099 forms.

1099 reporting is just one of many tasks that must be performed at the end of the year. In the next chapter, we will discuss other tasks that must be completed so that we can close the books for the year.

Join our book's Discord space

Join the book's Discord workspace for a monthly *Ask me Anything* session with the author:
`https://packt.link/QuickBooks`

Section 5: Closing the Books and Handling Special Transactions

17
Closing the Books in QuickBooks Online

After you have entered all of your business transactions into QuickBooks for the year, you will need to finalize your financial statements so that you can hand them off to your accountant to file your taxes. To ensure you have recorded all business transactions for the financial period, we have included a checklist that you can follow to close your books. Closing your books will ensure that no additional transactions are entered into QuickBooks once you have finalized your financial statements. If you have a bookkeeper or an accountant who manages your books, they should ensure that all of the steps have been completed. In this chapter, we will cover each item on the checklist. This includes reconciling all bank and credit card accounts, making year-end accrual adjustments (if applicable), recording fixed asset purchases made throughout the year, recording depreciation, taking a physical inventory, adjusting retained earnings, and preparing financial statements.

 Pro Tip: Adding your tax preparer or CPA as a user will allow them to access your QuickBooks data. They will be able to run reports and review the items needed to prepare your tax return. Later on in this chapter, we will show you how to give your accoutant access to your data.

The chapter objectives are summarized as follows:

- Reviewing a checklist for closing your books
- Recording journal entries
- Giving your accountant access to your data

By the end of this chapter, you will know all of the tasks you need to complete in order to close your books for the year. While most small businesses close their books annually, if you close your books on a monthly or a quarterly basis, you will still need to follow the steps outlined in this chapter. In the following section, we will cover the details of the checklist.

 The US edition of QBO was used to create this book. If you are using a version that is outside the United States, the results may differ.

Reviewing a checklist for closing your books

As discussed, there are several steps you will need to take in order to close your books for the financial period. How often you close your books (for example, monthly, quarterly, or annually) will determine how often you need to complete these steps. Remember the importance of closing your books, as this will ensure that all transactions for the financial period have been recorded and that your financial statements are accurate, which is important because your accountant will use them to file your business tax return.

The following is a checklist of the steps you need to complete in order to close your books. You should complete them in the order presented:

1. Reconciling all bank and credit card accounts

2. Making year-end accrual adjustments

3. Reviewing new fixed asset purchases and adding them to the chart of accounts

4. Making depreciation journal entries

5. Taking physical inventory and reconciling this with your books

6. Adjusting retained earnings for owner/partner distributions

7. Setting a closing date and password

8. Preparing key financial reports

We will discuss each of these eight steps in detail, starting with reconciling all bank and credit card accounts.

Reconciling all bank and credit card accounts

In *Chapter 10, Reconciling Downloaded Bank and Credit Card Transactions*, you learned how to reconcile your bank and credit card accounts. It's important for you to reconcile these accounts before closing the books so that you can ensure that all income and expenses for the period have been recorded in QuickBooks.

This will ensure that your financial statements are accurate and that you don't miss out on any tax deductions.

Making year-end accrual adjustments

If you are on the **accrual** basis of accounting, you need to make sure that all income and expenses that have been incurred for the period are recorded. As discussed in *Chapter 1, Getting Started with QuickBooks Online*, accrual basis accounting means that you recognize income when services have been rendered, regardless of when payment is received. The same concept is applied to expenses. For example, if you made a purchase in December but have not yet received the bill for it, you will need to record an adjusting journal entry before you close the books in order to record the purchase. We will discuss journal entries in more detail later in this chapter.

Pro Tip: Record all accounts receivable for the end of the period, which means invoice all customers for work performed. Similarly, be sure to record all accounts payable (vendor bills) for any expenses incurred in the period.

Reviewing new fixed asset purchases and adding them to the chart of accounts

If you purchased any fixed assets during the year, you should add these to QuickBooks. Fixed assets are subject to depreciation, which is a tax-deductible expense. Tax-deductible expenses can reduce your tax bill, so you want to make sure that you take all of the deductions to which you are entitled. If you have not recorded new fixed asset purchases, then you will not have depreciation expenses recorded, which means you will miss out on what could be a significant tax deduction. It's also important to conduct a physical check to ensure that all of the assets on the books still exist and have not been disposed of.

To add fixed assets to QuickBooks, you will need to have the following information on hand:

- Date of purchase
- Purchase price
- Type of asset
- Make and model (if applicable)
- Year

Pro Tip: Your tax preparer should have a detailed list of fixed assets that have been reported on previous tax returns. It is a good idea to review this list annually to ensure it includes new purchases and/or disposal of assets.

Follow these steps to add a fixed asset to QuickBooks:

1. From the left menu bar, click on **Accounting**, as indicated in *Figure 17.1*:

Figure 17.1: Navigating to Accounting

2. Select the chart of accounts and then click the **New** button, as indicated in *Figure 17.2*:

Figure 17.2: Clicking the New button

3. For a new fixed asset, complete the fields as shown in *Figure 17.3*:

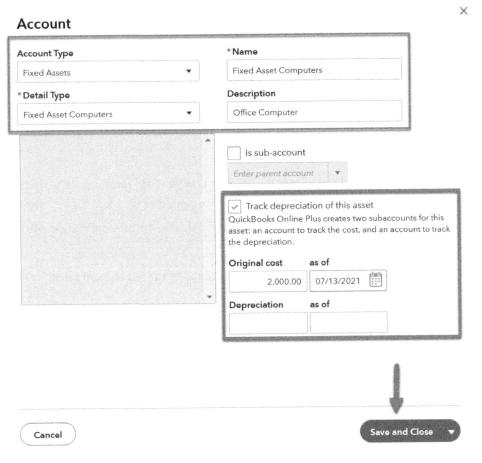

Figure 17.3: Clicking the Save and Close button to save the fixed asset

The following is a brief explanation of the fields that need to be completed for a new fixed asset:

- **Account Type**: From the drop-down menu, select **Fixed Assets**.
- **Detail Type**: From the drop-down menu, select the type of fixed asset account you need to add. The options include the following: buildings, computers, copiers, furniture, tools, equipment, telephone, software, furniture and fixtures, and vehicles.
- **Name**: Type the name of the fixed asset in this field.
- **Description**: Type a more detailed description of the fixed asset in this field.

- **Track depreciation of this asset**: By putting a checkmark in this box, you are indicating that the asset is depreciable. When saving this fixed asset, QuickBooks will automatically create an account to track the cost of the asset, and another account to track depreciation.

 If you don't want a separate depreciation account for each asset, leave this field blank.

- **Original cost**: Enter the amount that you paid for the asset in this field. This information will be used to calculate depreciation.
- **as of**: Enter the date of purchase in this field. This information will be used later on to calculate depreciation.

4. Click the **Save and Close** button to add the asset to your chart of accounts list.

Be sure to complete *steps 1* through *4* for each fixed asset you have purchased during the accounting period. If you have a large number of fixed assets, it is not recommended to have a separate accumulated depreciation account for each one.

Making depreciation journal entries

Depreciation is the reduction in value of an asset due to wear and tear after it has been in service for a period of time. To reflect the reduced value, you must record the depreciation expense on your books. Depreciation is also a tax-deductible expense, which can help to reduce your overall tax liability. After adding fixed assets to QuickBooks, you need to record depreciation expenses for the period. Unfortunately, QuickBooks does not compute depreciation for you. Therefore, you will need to calculate depreciation manually, or have your accountant do this for you. In the *Recording journal entries* section of this chapter, we will show you how to record journal entries in QuickBooks.

Taking physical inventory and reconciling this with your books

Reconciling inventory involves making sure that the product you have on your shelf matches what your books reflect as on-hand inventory. You should take a physical inventory count at least once a year, if not more often. After taking a physical count, any discrepancies between the books and the physical count should be recorded in QuickBooks as inventory adjustments. After recording these inventory adjustments, your books and your warehouse will be in sync.

Follow these steps to record inventory adjustments in QuickBooks:

1. Click on the **+ New** button and select **Inventory qty adjustment** in the **Other** column, as indicated in *Figure 17.4*:

Other

Bank deposit

Transfer

Journal entry

Statement

Inventory qty
adjustment

Figure 17.4: Choosing Inventory qty adjustment

2. Complete the fields for the inventory adjustment, as indicated in *Figure 17.5*:

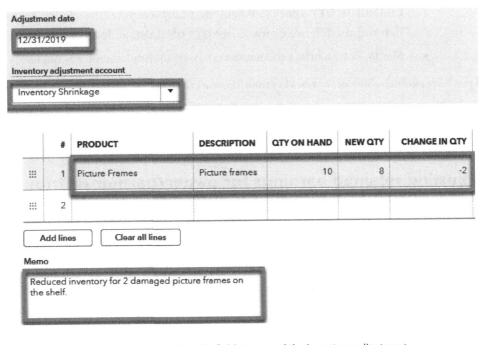

Adjustment date

12/31/2019

Inventory adjustment account

Inventory Shrinkage ▼

	#	PRODUCT	DESCRIPTION	QTY ON HAND	NEW QTY	CHANGE IN QTY
⁞⁞⁞	1	Picture Frames	Picture frames	10	8	-2
⁞⁞⁞	2					

| Add lines | Clear all lines |

Memo

Reduced inventory for 2 damaged picture frames on the shelf.

Figure 17.5: Completing the fields to record the inventory adjustment

The following is a brief explanation of the fields that need to be completed in order to record an inventory adjustment:

- **Adjustment date:** Enter the effective date of the adjustment. This date should be on or before the last day of the closing period. For example, if you close your books annually, this date should be as of 12/31/xx if you are on a calendar year.

- **Inventory adjustment account: Inventory Shrinkage** is the default account that will appear in this field. However, you can click the drop-down arrow and select a different account, or add a new one.

- **PRODUCT:** From the drop-down menu, select the item for which you are making an adjustment.

- **DESCRIPTION:** This field will automatically be populated based on the description in QuickBooks. You can also enter a description directly in this field.

- **QTY ON HAND:** This field will automatically be populated with what you currently have recorded in QuickBooks. This field cannot be adjusted.

- **NEW QTY:** Enter the quantity, based on the physical count that was taken in this field.

- **CHANGE IN QTY:** QuickBooks automatically computes the adjustment required by taking the difference between the **QTY ON HAND** and **NEW QTY** values entered.

- **Memo:** Enter a brief explanation as to why the adjustment was made.

If you have extensive inventory tracking requirements that go beyond what's available in Quick-Books Online, visit the Intuit App center, where there are over 700 add-on programs that integrate seamlessly with QBO. In *Chapter 18, Handling Special Transactions in QuickBooks Online*, we show you how to navigate the QuickBooks app center.

Adjusting retained earnings for owner/partner distributions

Retained earnings are the cumulative amount of your income and expenses for the prior period. This amount will post to the retained earnings account after the end of your fiscal/calendar year has been closed. QuickBooks will automatically make this entry for you. Depending on the type of organization (Corporation, Partnership, LLC, Sole Proprietorship, or Non-Profit), you may need to move this balance to other equity accounts. To distribute profits to the owners, you will need to create a journal entry to an equity account entitled *owner's draw* or *owner distributions* and offset it with retained earnings. We will show you how to create journal entries next.

Recording journal entries

A journal entry is used to adjust your books for transactions that have not been recorded throughout the accounting period. Depreciation expense for fixed assets, income and expense accruals, and adjustments to retained earnings are three examples we have discussed in this chapter.

Follow these steps to record a journal entry in QuickBooks:

1. Click the **+ New** button and select **Journal entry**, as indicated in *Figure 17.6*:

Figure 17.6: Selecting Journal entry below the Other column

2. A screen similar to the one shown in the following screenshot will appear:

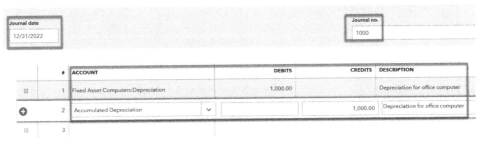

Figure 17.7: Journal Entry template

The following is a brief explanation of the fields that need to be completed in order to record a journal entry:

- **Journal date:** Enter the effective date of the journal in this field.

- **Journal no.:** QuickBooks will automatically populate this field with the next available journal number. If this is the first journal entry you have recorded, you can enter a starting number (such as 1000), and QuickBooks will increment each journal entry number thereafter.

- **ACCOUNT**: Select the account from the drop-down menu.

- **DEBITS**: Enter the debit amount in this field.

- **CREDITS**: Enter the credit amount in this field.

- **DESCRIPTION**: Type a detailed description of the purpose of the journal entry in this field. Adding a detailed description is recommended; it is helpful when referring to a journal entry and explaining why the entry was made.

Be sure to record all journal entries prior to generating financial statements. If you give your CPA or accountant access to your data, they can record all of the necessary journal entries and then generate the financial reports required to file your tax returns.

Setting a closing date and password

In an effort to maintain the integrity of your data, you should set a closing date and password after you have entered all transactions for the closing period. By setting a closing date, users will receive a warning message if they attempt to enter transactions that affect the closing period. For example, if you set a closing date of 12/31/22, users will receive a warning message if they attempt to enter any transactions dated 12/31/22 or prior.

Follow these steps to set a closing date and password in QBO:

1. Click on the gear icon and then select **Account and Settings** in the **Your Company** column, as indicated in *Figure 17.8*:

Figure 17.8: Selecting Account and Settings in the Your Company column

2. Click on the **Advanced** tab, as indicated in *Figure 17.9*:

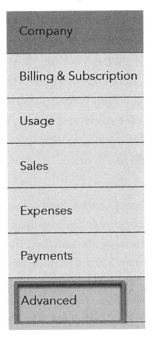

Figure 17.9: Clicking the Advanced option

3. The **Accounting** preferences are located at the very top of the next screen, as indicated in *Figure 17.10*:

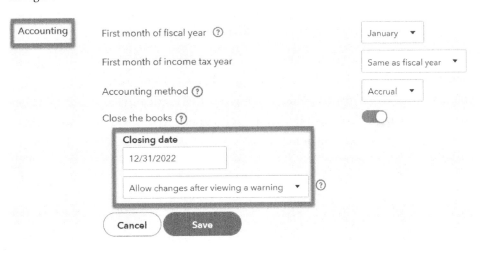

Figure 17.10: Reviewing Accounting preferences

QBCU 1.2.2 In the **Close the books** section, you can enter the closing date (that is, **12/31/22**), which will give users a warning if they attempt to enter transactions dated on the closing date or prior to that date. There are two types of warning messages. The first warning message is **Allow changes after viewing a warning**. This message will allow users to proceed with entering the transaction after they close out of the warning message. The second warning message is **Allow changes after viewing a warning and entering a password**. This message requires users to enter a password in order to proceed with entering transactions. To choose this option, select it from the drop-down field as shown in *Figure 17.10* and enter the password you would like to use.

 Pro Tip: Since QuickBooks does not have a formal closing process, this is highly recommended to keep users from making changes to years where tax returns have already been filed. Don't give the closing password to anyone who is not authorized to enter transactions after the closing date.

Preparing key financial reports

After you have completed the first seven steps in the closing checklist, you are ready to prepare financial statements. There are three primary financial statements you will need to prepare:

- The trial balance
- The balance sheet
- The income statement (profit and loss)

In *Chapter 12, Business Overview Reports*, you learned what the balance sheet and income statement reports are, how to interpret the data, and how to generate these reports in QuickBooks. Your accountant, or **certified public accountant (CPA)**, will also request a trial balance report. A trial balance report lists all of the debits and credits recorded in QuickBooks for the period. If everything has been recorded properly, debits will always equal credits on this report.

Follow these steps to run a trial balance report in QuickBooks:

1. Navigate to **Reports**, as indicated in *Figure 17.11*:

intuit quickbooks
Dashboard
Banking
Expenses
Invoicing
Projects
Workers
Reports

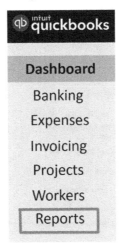

Figure 17.11: Clicking Reports to navigate to the Reports Center

2. In the **For my accountant** section, click on **Trial Balance**, as indicated in *Figure 17.12*:

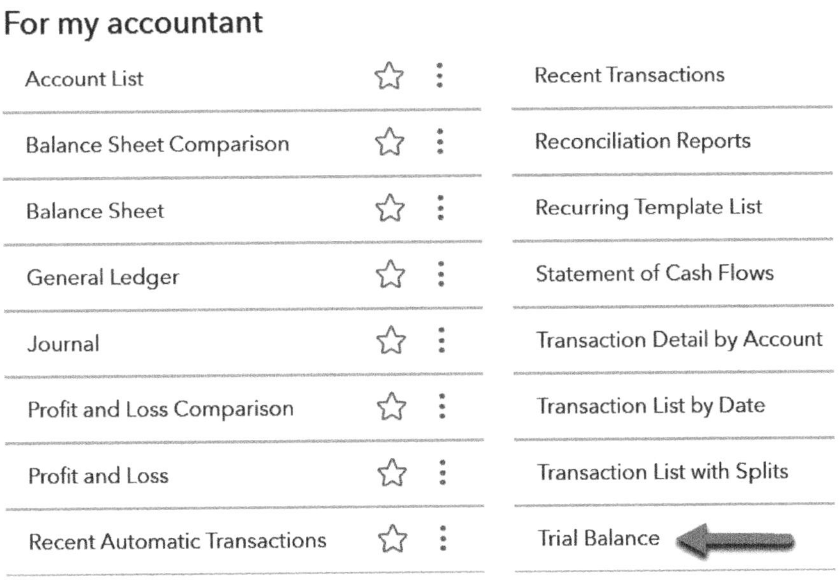

For my accountant
Account List
Balance Sheet Comparison
Balance Sheet
General Ledger
Journal
Profit and Loss Comparison
Profit and Loss
Recent Automatic Transactions
Recent Transactions
Reconciliation Reports
Recurring Template List
Statement of Cash Flows
Transaction Detail by Account
Transaction List by Date
Transaction List with Splits
Trial Balance

Figure 17.12: Running the Trial Balance report

3. The trial balance report will appear. Click the **Customize** button to see the following options:

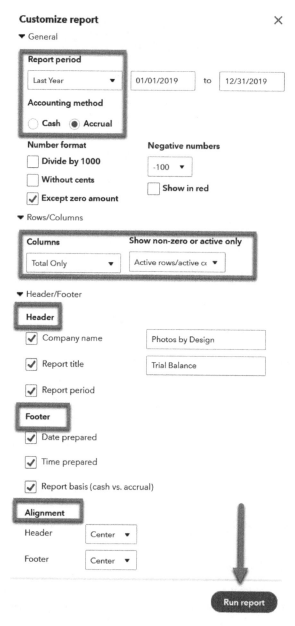

Figure 17.13: Reviewing the report customization options

There are a number of options available to customize the trial balance report. The following is a brief description of some of the information that can be customized:

- **Report period**: You can select a preset report period such as **Last Year** from the drop-down menu, or type a specific date range in the fields to the right of the preset field.

- **Accounting method**: As previously introduced in this book, you can choose the accounting method you want to be applied to the report, cash or accrual.

- **Number format**: There are a variety of options for formatting the numbers on a report. Omitting the cents and excluding accounts with a zero balance are just a couple of the options shown in the preceding screenshot.

- **Rows/columns**: Choose which rows/columns are visible on the report.

- **Header**: You can edit the company name and the title of the report in the header section.

- **Footer**: You can choose to show the date/time when the report was prepared.

- **Alignment**: You can decide how to best align the information that appears in the header and footer sections of the report.

4. When you are done with your customizations, click the **Run report** button.

5. A report similar to the one in the following screenshot will appear:

Photos By Design, LLC

TRIAL BALANCE
As of December 31, 2019

	DEBIT	CREDIT
Business Checking	4,730.00	
Accounts Receivable (A/R)	5,350.00	
Inventory Asset	150.00	
Accounts Payable (A/P)		5,400.00
Bank of the U.S.A		1,200.00
Opening Balance Equity		4,450.00
Retained Earnings	1,800.00	
Photography Services		275.00
Sales		6,800.00
Car & Truck	45.00	
Meals & Entertainment	80.00	
Office Supplies & Software	450.00	
Rent & Lease	5,400.00	
Utilities:Telephone Expense	120.00	
TOTAL	**$18,125.00**	**$18,125.00**

Figure 17.14: Sample Trial Balance report

As discussed, the total debits column should always equal the total credits column, as it does in the preceding report. If it does not, you will need to look into any discrepancies. The good news is, 99.99% of the time, this report will balance because QuickBooks does not allow you to post one-sided journals, which means that for every debit, there is always an offsetting credit to keep things in balance. If you do have a trial balance that does not balance, you should calculate the difference between the debits and credits, and then look for that amount on the report. Most likely, there is an amount in one of the columns (debit or credit) that does not appear in the other column.

To summarize, you will need to review three key financial reports before closing your books: the balance sheet, the income statement (profit and loss), and the trial balance report. If you have a CPA or an accountant who reviews your financials and prepares your tax return, you can give that person access to your books so that they can run these reports without having to bother you. We will discuss giving your accountant access to your data next.

 Pro Tip: Always review the information on your reports one last time before sharing them with any third party outside of your organization. You can set these reports up in memorized groups and send them instead of running them individually. Refer to *Chapter 11, Report Center Overview*, for more information on this.

Giving your accountant access to your data

If you have an accountant or tax preparer to whom you need to grant access to your data, you can create a secure user ID and password for them. All you need to do is request their email address so that you can send them an invitation to access your data.

Follow these steps to invite an accountant to access your QuickBooks data:

1. Click on the gear icon and select **Manage Users** in the **Your Company** column, as indicated in *Figure 17.15*:

Your Company

Account and Settings

Manage Users

Custom Form Styles

Chart of Accounts

QuickBooks Labs

Figure 17.15: Selecting Manage Users from the Your Company column

2. On the **Manage users** page, click on **Accounting firms**, as indicated in *Figure 17.16*:

Manage users
Users 1
Accounting firms 1

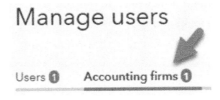

Figure 17.16: Clicking on Accounting firms

3. Click on the **Invite** button, as indicated in *Figure 17.17*, to invite your accountant to access your QuickBooks data:

Invite

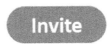

Figure 17.17: Clicking the Invite button

4. Enter the name and email address of your accountant, as indicated in *Figure 17.18*:

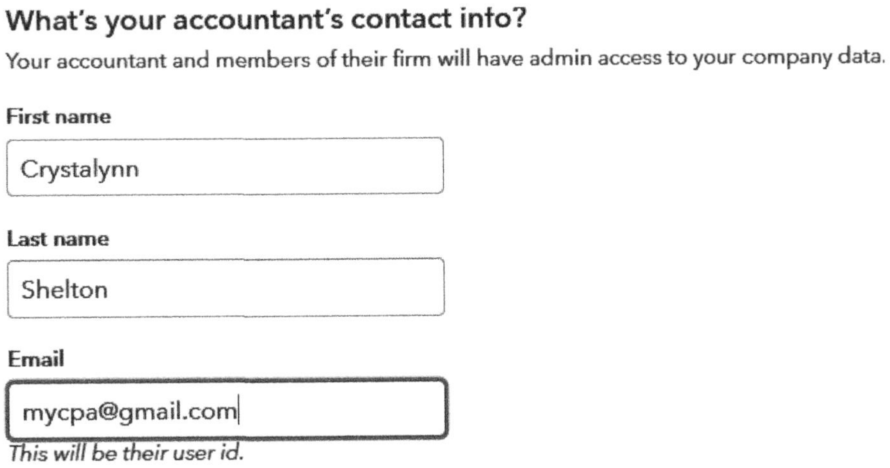

What's your accountant's contact info?
Your accountant and members of their firm will have admin access to your company data.
First name
Crystalynn
Last name
Shelton
Email
mycpa@gmail.com
This will be their user id.

Figure 17.18: Completing the fields for the accountant invite

5. Once you have entered your accountant's contact information, click the **Send** button. Your accountant will receive an email, inviting them to access your QBO account. They will need to accept the invitation and create a secure password. Their user ID will be the email address that you entered in the form (shown in the preceding screenshot).

Once you have given your accountant access to your books, they can simply log in to QuickBooks in order to get the information they need to prepare your taxes. This is highly recommended if your accountant will be making any year-end adjustments. You can add/remove permissions access as needed if you prefer them only to have access at tax time.

Summary

In this chapter, you have learned about the key tasks that need to be completed to close your books for the accounting period. As discussed, you need to reconcile all bank and credit card accounts, record year-end accrual adjustments (if you are on the accrual basis of accounting), add fixed asset purchases, record depreciation expenses, take a physical inventory and make the necessary adjustments, adjust retained earnings for distributions made to the business owners, set a closing date and password, and prepare key financial statements. You can perform these tasks yourself, or you can give your accountant access to your QuickBooks data to take care of this for you.

This chapter is the last one that covers the QuickBooks features most small businesses will use. In the next chapter, we will cover some additional topics, such as adding apps to QBO, managing credit card payments, and recording bad debt expenses.

Join our book's Discord space

Join the book's Discord workspace for a monthly *Ask me Anything* session with the author: https://packt.link/QuickBooks

18

Handling Special Transactions in QuickBooks Online

So far, we have covered the most common transactions for which small businesses use Quick-Books. However, there are a few more topics that we would like to share with you. While some of these may not apply to your business when you are starting out, it's a good idea to be aware that they exist.

First, we will start by using apps in QBO. Apps are a great way to help you streamline day-to-day business tasks that can be time-consuming. Next, we will show you how to record credit card payments from customers. This is an excellent way to get paid faster. Third, we will show you how to create professional-looking sales templates. If you have several expenses that you pay weekly, monthly, or quarterly, you should set them up as recurring transactions. We will also cover how to create and manage recurring transactions in this chapter. If you have a business loan or line of credit, you need to keep track of payments and overall outstanding balances in QuickBooks. Petty cash is often used for small purchases such as stamps or lunch for the office. Due to this, we will show you how to keep track of petty cash. While you always hope it doesn't happen to you, there may come a time when you need to record a bad debt, so we will show you how to properly record bad debt expense. Finally, we will show you how to record delayed charges. Delayed charges are used to keep track of the services you have provided to customers that you will invoice at a later date.

In this chapter, we will cover the following topics:

- Using apps in QuickBooks Online

- Managing credit card payments
- Customizing sales templates
- Setting up business loans and lines of credit
- Managing petty cash
- Recording bad debt expense
- Tracking delayed charges and credits

We will begin by learning how to search for apps in the QuickBooks app store and locate apps that are ideal for your business.

 The US edition of QBO was used to create this book. If you are using a version that is outside of the United States, results may differ.

**QBCU
1.6.1
1.6.3**

Using apps in QuickBooks Online

There are many benefits and a few risks of extending functionality through apps. Some of the **benefits** of using apps in QBO are:

- The ability to expand the functionality of the software so you can have what you need to run all aspects of your business.
- Access to more than 700 apps that integrate seamlessly with QBO, allowing you to manage your inventory, accept online payments, pay your bills, and manage your eCommerce transactions.
- The companies featured in the QuickBooks app store have gone through an extensive vetting process and were approved by Intuit to create apps that will help you simplify tasks, streamline data entry, and sync with QuickBooks.

A couple of the **risks** involved with using apps are:

- The apps are not free, which means the fees charged to use the app will be in addition to what you pay for your monthly QBO subscription, so be sure to do a cost/benefit analysis to ensure you can take on the additional cost.
- You will need to give permission for your data in QBO to be shared with any company whose app you wish to use. You can be confident that your data is secure, since that is also a requirement to become a partner with Intuit.

The app store is organized into categories based on app functionality. Customer reviews are included, along with short video demonstrations to show you how the app works and customer service information if you have additional questions. In this section, we will provide you with an overview of the app center, show you how to find apps that are relevant to your business needs, and show you how to add apps to QuickBooks Online.

 Pro Tip: Because of the large number of apps that are available, ProAdvisors and accountants are not well versed in all apps. Therefore, you will need to reach out to the technical support team for the app that you choose for assistance with setup, implementation, and training needs.

Overview of the QuickBooks App Center QBCU 1.6.2

The layout of the App Center is very simple. You can easily search for apps, see a list of the apps you have added, and check out apps that have been recommended based on the type of business you have. Let's take a look at the layout of the app center:

1. On the left menu bar, click on **Apps** to navigate to the App Center, as follows:

Figure 18.1: Navigating to the QuickBooks App Center

2. The App Center will be displayed, as shown in *Figure 18.2*:

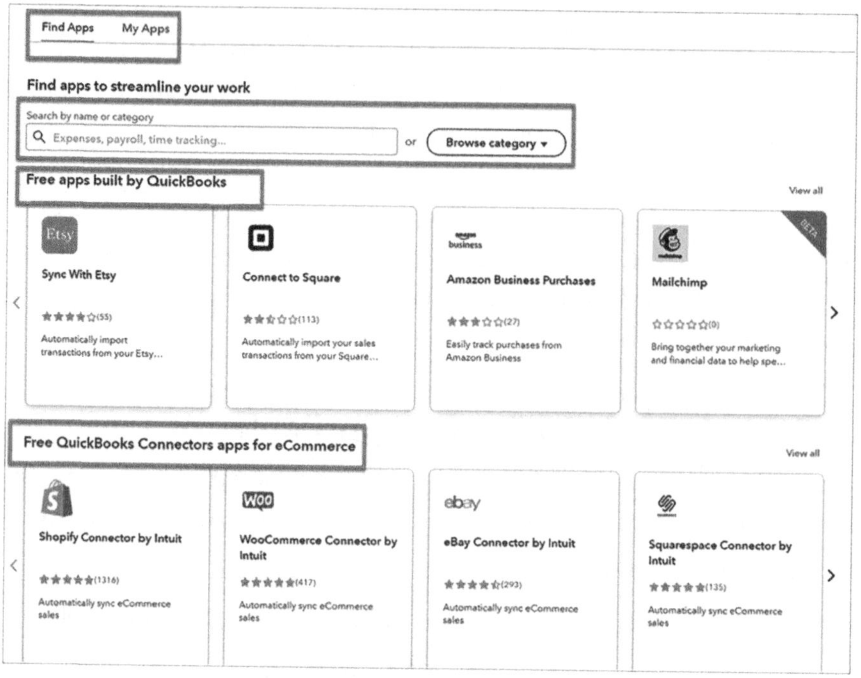

Figure 18.2: QuickBooks App Center

The five key areas of the QuickBooks App Center featured in the preceding screenshot are as follows:

- **Find Apps**: If you are looking for an app, you want to make sure that you are on this tab. You can search for apps in two ways, by typing in the name of the app or browsing by category.

- **My Apps**: Click on this tab if you want to see which apps are currently connected to your QuickBooks data.

- **Search options**: If you know the name of the app you are searching for, you can simply type the name of the app into the search box shown in the preceding screenshot. However, if you don't know the name of the app and simply want to search by category, you can do so by clicking on the **Browse category** button. A few of the categories you can search by include get paid, manage workers, make payments, manage customers, manage projects, and many more.

- **Free apps built by QuickBooks**: In this section, you will find apps that were created by QuickBooks.

- **Free QuickBooks Connectors apps for eCommerce**: This section will feature apps that are ideal for eCommerce businesses. Shopify, WooCommerce, eBay, and Squarespace are just a few of the eCommerce apps that integrate with QuickBooks.

If you're not sure which app to choose, I recommend that you schedule a live demo with the app company so that you can see how the app works and get your questions answered. Many companies offer a trial period of 14 days or more so that you can try the app before you buy it. Like QBO, there are no contracts, so you can cancel your subscription at any time. Let's now walk through an example of how to find apps for your business.

Finding apps for your business [QBCU 1.6.2]

As we mentioned previously, there are more than 700 apps in the QuickBooks App Center. While it can be overwhelming at first, you should focus on the needs of your business. There is a lot of information in the center about each app, which will save you the time you would have normally spent doing research. Let's take a look at an app to see what kind of information you can expect to find here.

Scroll down to the **Most Popular** category and click on the **Bill.com** app. You will be greeted with the following screen:

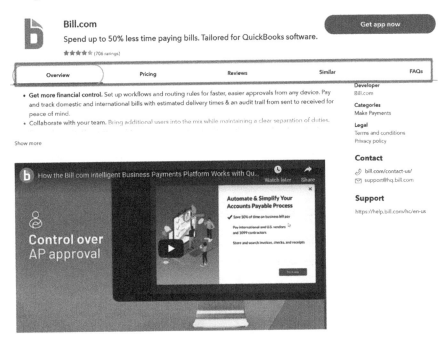

Figure 18.3: The app profile for the Bill.com app

The following is a brief description of the information you will find in the app profile:

- **Overview**: The **Overview** tab includes a list of the key benefits the app has, how the app works with QuickBooks Online, and additional details. Like Bill.com, most apps will include a short video to demonstrate how the app works, along with additional screenshots of the user interface.

- **Pricing**: Unfortunately, these apps are not free. Pricing will vary and is usually subscription-based, like QuickBooks Online. However, you will be billed by the third-party company (in this case, Bill.com), not QuickBooks. The good news is that most apps will offer a free trial period of at least 14 days.

- **Reviews**: Like most products, you will see a rating of the app based on customer reviews. Click on the link to see what customers are saying about the app. The more reviews an app has, the better the chance of getting a broad perspective.

- **Similar**: The **Similar** tab shows a list of apps that have similar functionality to the one you are looking at.

- **FAQs**: A list of the most frequently asked questions and answers can be found on this tab.

Once you have decided which app(s) to go with, it's easy to get started. Simply click on the **Get app now** button located on each app profile. Follow the onscreen instructions to complete the app's setup.

 Pro Tip: Reaching out to an industry-specific professional organization is a great way to find out the most popular apps used for your industry. This may help narrow down your search for the right fit.

There are several apps that allow you to accept credit card payments from customers. If you sign up for one of these apps, it will make managing credit card payments that much easier in QuickBooks. Next, we will explain how to manage credit card payments.

Managing credit card payments

QBCU 2.3.4

In addition to traditional payments such as cash and checks, you should accept credit cards as another form of payment. While there are fees associated with accepting credit card payments, there are several benefits. First, you can get paid faster with a credit card than waiting to receive a check in the mail.

Second, if you sign up for a QuickBooks Payments account (`https://quickbooks.intuit.com/payments/?sc=seq_intuit_pay_click_ft`), you can email customers their invoice, which includes a payment link. They can click on the link, enter their payment information, and pay their invoice in a matter of minutes, which is much faster than waiting to receive a check in the mail. Best of all, QuickBooks will mark the invoice as paid, which automatically reduces your accounts receivable balance. As we discussed in *Chapter 8, Recording Sales Transactions in QuickBooks Online*, you can send your customers payment reminder emails, which will include a copy of the open invoices, along with a payment link.

QBCU
2.3.4

If you decide to go with a third-party processor, you can manually record these payments in Quick-Books. In this section, we will show you how to record credit card payments that have been received from customers via QuickBooks Payments and a third-party credit card processing company.

Before you can perform the steps, you will need to have an active QuickBooks Payments account that is connected to your QBO account. Visit QuickBooks Payments (`https://quickbooks.intuit.com/payments/?sc=seq_intuit_pay_click_ft`) to learn more about how this works. If you are using a third-party processor, you may be able to connect your account to QuickBooks. Contact your credit card processor to find out if they are compatible with QuickBooks Online.

Follow these steps to record a credit card sale:

1. Click on the **+ New** button and select **Sales receipt** from the **Customers** column, as shown in *Figure 18.4*:

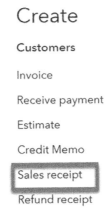

Figure 18.4: Navigating to Sales receipt

2. Fill in the fields in the sales receipt form, as shown in *Figure 18.5*:

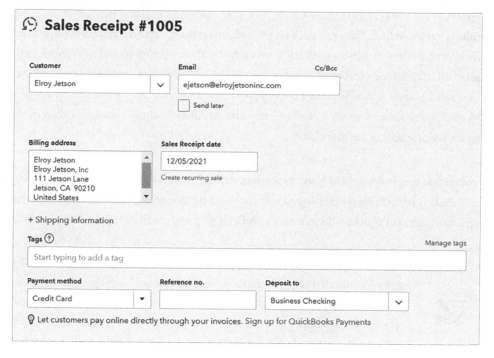

Figure 18.5: Completing the sales receipt form

After selecting the customer from the drop-down menu, the email and billing address fields will automatically be populated with the information you have on file.

3. Next, select a payment method from the drop-down menu. When you select **Credit Card** as the payment method and you have a QuickBooks Payments account, you will see an option to enter credit card details directly below the **Payment method** field.

4. The following screen will appear so that you can enter the required credit card information, as shown in *Figure 18.6*:

Figure 18.6: Completing the Credit Card payment information

In the preceding screenshot, the credit card number has been removed for security reasons. Be sure to complete all of the necessary fields and click the **Use this info** button to save the information.

> **Pro Tip**: After entering the customer's credit card information, QuickBooks will keep this information on file. You won't have to enter it again unless your customer would like to use a different payment method or the credit card expires.

5. This will take you back to the sales receipt form, where you can fill in the details of the services provided and the amount. When you click the **Save** button, the credit card payment will be processed and an email with the sales receipt attached will be sent to the customer.

> **Pro Tip:** If you don't have a QuickBooks Payments account, you can still enter the credit card information and save it. However, you will need to process the credit card payment outside of QuickBooks using your third-party merchant company. When the payment is deposited into your bank account, you will need to match it up with the sales receipt in the online banking center. To learn more about matching transactions, read *Chapter 10, Reconciling Downloaded Bank and Credit Card Transactions.*

You now know the benefits of accepting credit card payments from customers and how to manage these payments in QuickBooks. You can impress your customers further by creating invoices, estimates, and sales receipts that include your company logo and branding style. We will show you how to customize sales templates next.

**QBCU
2.3.1**

Customizing sales templates

QuickBooks allows you to create custom sales forms to match your brand and style. Taking the time to customize sales templates will allow you to create professional-looking forms so your customers can easily see what they owe and make payments online in just a few minutes. You can customize invoices, estimates, and sales receipt templates. Follow these steps to learn how to customize these sales templates:

1. Click on the gear icon and select **Custom Form Styles** from the **Your Company** column, as shown in *Figure 18.7*:

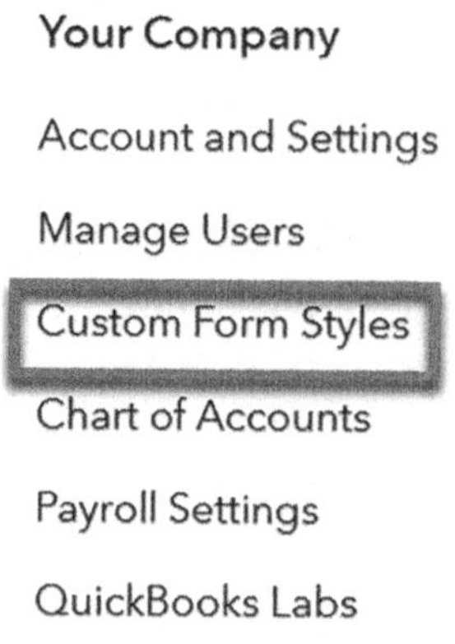

Your Company

Account and Settings

Manage Users

Custom Form Styles

Chart of Accounts

Payroll Settings

QuickBooks Labs

Figure 18.7: Navigating to Custom Form Styles

2. Click on the **New style** button and select a sales template to customize:

Figure 18.8: Clicking the New style button

3. The following window will display three areas you can customize for sales templates:

Figure 18.9: Three customization options for sales templates

The following is a brief explanation of the information you can customize in each of these areas:

- **Design**: The **Design** section allows you to create your template style and format. You will select a template design, add your company logo, add your brand colors, and choose the font size and style.

- **Content**: For **Content**, you can select what information you would like to appear on the sales template, including your basic contact information, such as business telephone number and mailing address. You can also add your website and email address to the form. In the billing section, you can determine how much detail you would like to include in the sales form. For example, an invoice should include a list of each product or service you are billing the customer for.

- **Emails**: QuickBooks allows you to email a sales form directly to customers. In this section, you can decide whether you want any details of the form to be included in the body of the email. Also, you can choose to have a PDF document attached to the email.

4. After completing each section, click the **Done** button at the bottom of the screen to save your changes. A preview of your customized sales form should appear, as shown in *Figure 18.10*:

Photos By Design, LLC

P.O. Box 1915
Burbank, CA 91507
US
crystalynnshelton@att.net
www.photosbydesign

Invoice

BILL TO
Smith Co.
123 Main Street
City, CA 12345

INVOICE# 12345
DATE 01/12/2016
DUE DATE 02/12/2016
TERMS Net 30

ACTIVITY	DESCRIPTION	QTY	RATE	AMOUNT
Item name	Description of the item	2	225.00	450.00
Item name	Description of the item	1	225.00	225.00

SUBTOTAL		675.00
TOTAL		$675.00
BALANCE DUE		**$675.00**

Figure 18.10: Sample custom invoice for Photos by Design, LLC

You can create an unlimited number of templates for various types of sales and customers. It is easy to make changes to them anytime. The best part is that you don't have to create any templates from scratch.

Now that you know how easy it is to customize sales templates, you can use one of these templates to create a recurring transaction. We will show you how to create and manage recurring transactions next.

Setting up business loans and lines of credit

If you take out a business loan or line of credit, you need to track the payments that have been made, as well as the outstanding balance owed in QuickBooks. This will ensure that your financial statements include the money that is owed to all creditors. If this information is not included in QuickBooks, it will not show up on your financial statements. If this information is not reported in your financial statements, you will have inaccurate reports and you could miss out on legitimate tax deductions.

In this section, we will cover how to set up a business loan or line of credit, how to track payments, and how to stay on top of the outstanding balances owed.

Adding a business loan or line of credit to the chart of accounts

The first step to properly tracking loans and lines of credit in QuickBooks is to set them up on the chart of accounts. We will do this next. Follow these steps:

1. Navigate to **Accounting** and select **Chart of Accounts**, as shown in *Figure 18.11*:

Figure 18.11: Navigating to Accounting

2. Click on the **New** button located to the left of **Run Report**, as shown in *Figure 18.12*:

Figure 18.12: Clicking the New button

3. Fill in the fields, shown in the following screenshot, to add a new business loan or line of credit account:

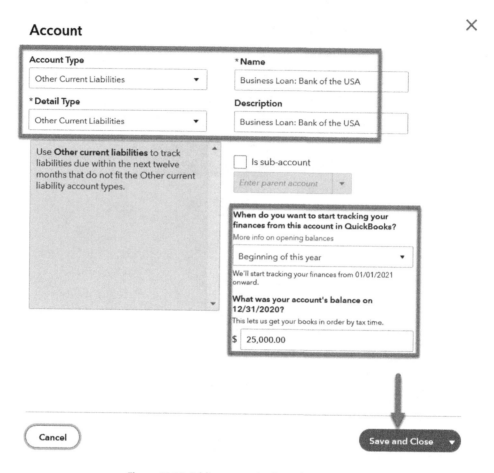

Figure 18.13: Adding a new business loan account

A brief description of the fields in the preceding screenshot is as follows:

- **Account Type**: Business loans and lines of credit generally fall into one of two account types: current liabilities or long-term liabilities. Current liabilities have a term of less than one year, while long-term liabilities have a term greater than one year. Select either **Current Liabilities** or **Long-term Liabilities** from the drop-down menu.

- **Detail Type:** Based on your selection regarding the account type, you will see a list of options in this field. As you can see, both the line of credit and loan payable are listed. Select the detail type that best describes the account you are setting up.

- **Name:** In this field, enter the name of the account. This will generally include the type of liability (loan or line of credit) and the name of the financial institution (**Business Loan: Bank of the USA**, in our case).

- **Description:** In this field, you can simply copy and paste the name or include a more detailed description, such as the account number of the loan or line of credit.

- **When do you want to start tracking your finances from this account in Quick-Books?:** Select the time period that best describes when you will start tracking payments for this account in QuickBooks.

- **What was your account's balance on 12/31/2020?:** Depending on your selection in the preceding field, QuickBooks will require you to enter the balance of this account as of the date you indicated you want to start tracking the payments for this account.

 Pro Tip: Another way to record a beginning balance for a line of credit (or loan) is by categorizing the transaction to the loan account (created above) when you receive the funds in your bank account.

4. Click the **Save and Close** button to add the loan or line of credit account to your chart of accounts list.

If you haven't done so already, you will need to repeat these steps to add an interest paid or interest expense account to the chart of accounts list. You will track the interest portion of your payments in this account. Now, we'll cover how to make payments on a loan or line of credit.

Making payments on a loan or line of credit

In general, you can make payments on a loan or line of credit in the same manner that you pay other creditors. You can write a check or have the funds automatically deducted from your bank account. Here, we will walk through how to record a payment.

Follow these steps to make payments on a loan or line of credit:

1.   Click on the **+ New** button and then select **Check** in the **Vendors** column, as shown in
     Figure 18.14:

Figure 18.14: Navigating to Check

2.   Fill in the fields for the loan payment:

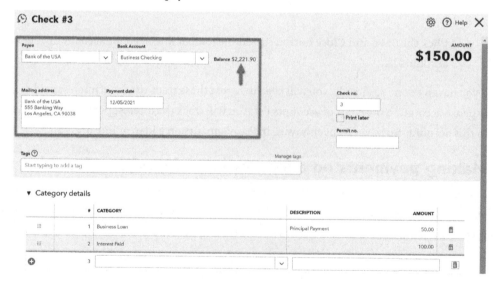

Figure 18.15: Completing the check form to record payment for loan

A brief description of the fields you need to complete in order to record a payment for a loan or line of credit is as follows:

- **Payee**: From the drop-down menu, select the payee. If you haven't added the payee to QuickBooks, you can do so here by selecting **Add new** from the drop-down menu.

- **Bank Account**: If you have more than one bank account, you need to select the bank account that you want to write the check from in the drop-down menu. When you select the bank account, the current balance will appear to the right of the field, as indicated in the preceding screenshot.

- **Mailing address**: This field will automatically be populated with the address on file for the payee you've selected. If you don't have an address on file, you can type the information directly into this field. However, it's best to go to the vendor profile and add the address information there. If you type it in this field, the address will not be saved to the payee's profile.

- **Payment date**: Enter the check date or the date the payment was deducted from your bank account.

- **CATEGORY**: In this field, you need to select accounts that are affected by this payment. In general, that will be the loan payable account (principal) and an interest expense account. The portion of the payment that applies to the principal amount should be allocated to the loan payable account. The portion of the payment that applies to the interest should be allocated to the interest paid account.

- **DESCRIPTION**: Type a brief description of what the payment is for in this field.

- **AMOUNT**: Enter the amount you wish to pay in this field.

 Pro Tip: In order to accurately record the proper amounts for the principal and interest accounts, you may need to refer to your loan statement to see how your payment was applied. Be sure to do this so that your books match up with those of the financial institutions.

One final step you should do to ensure that the business loans and lines of credit on your books match your statements is to reconcile these accounts on a monthly basis. The steps to reconcile business loans and lines of credit are identical to reconciling your bank accounts. Refer to *Chapter 10, Reconciling Downloaded Bank and Credit Card Transactions*, for step-by-step instructions on reconciling.

Remember, it's important for your financial statements to be as accurate as possible. This means including all of the money that is owed to creditors, such as loans and lines of credit. In addition, in order to deduct the interest expense, you need to keep track of it in QuickBooks.

If you tend to pay cash for small incidentals for the office, such as a Starbucks run for the office or stamps, you need to set up a petty cash fund to keep track of these types of expenses. We will show you how to manage petty cash in QuickBooks next.

Managing petty cash

Petty cash is a small amount of money that's used to cover incidentals such as postage, lunch for the office, or other items. Petty cash is generally no more than $500 and is kept under lock and key and managed by the business owner or someone designated by the owner. Like all business expenses, you need to keep track of all your receipts so that you can record the expenses in QuickBooks.

In this section, we will discuss how to track petty cash, record petty cash expenses, and reconcile the petty cash account. Let's get started by creating a petty cash account.

Adding a petty cash account in QuickBooks

In order to track petty cash in QuickBooks, we need to add a petty cash account to the chart of accounts.

Follow these steps to add a petty cash account:

1. Navigate to the **Accounting** section, as shown in *Figure 18.16*:

Figure 18.16: Navigating to Accounting

2. Select the **Chart of Accounts** and then click the **New** button, as shown in *Figure 18.17*:

Figure 18.17: Clicking the New button

3. Fill in the new account setup window, as shown in *Figure 18.18*:

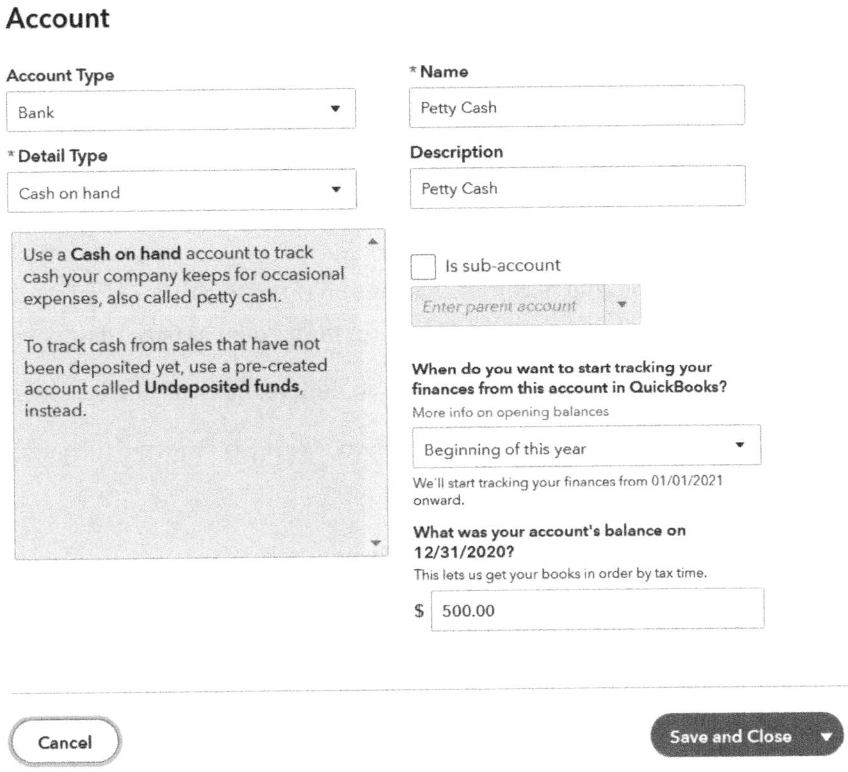

Account

Account Type

Bank ▼

* Detail Type

Cash on hand ▼

Use a **Cash on hand** account to track cash your company keeps for occasional expenses, also called petty cash.

To track cash from sales that have not been deposited yet, use a pre-created account called **Undeposited funds**, instead.

* Name

Petty Cash

Description

Petty Cash

☐ Is sub-account

Enter parent account ▼

When do you want to start tracking your finances from this account in QuickBooks?
More info on opening balances

Beginning of this year ▼

We'll start tracking your finances from 01/01/2021 onward.

What was your account's balance on 12/31/2020?
This lets us get your books in order by tax time.

$ 500.00

Cancel   Save and Close ▼

Figure 18.18: Completing the fields to add a new petty cash account

The following is a brief explanation of the information you will need to fill in:

- **Account Type**: From the drop-down menu, select **Bank** as the account type. All petty cash accounts should be categorized as bank accounts and treated as such.

- **Detail Type**: From the drop-down menu, select **Cash on hand** as the detail type. All petty cash accounts should be categorized as cash on hand.

- **Name**: In this field, you can put **Petty Cash** as the name of the account and any additional details required.

- **Description**: If there is additional information that will help you to identify this account, you can include it in this field.

- **When do you want to start tracking your finances from this account in Quick-Books?**: From the drop-down, select the date you will begin entering transactions for this account.

> **Pro Tip**: Instead of entering a starting balance in this account, you can record a transfer from a business checking account to the petty cash account in QuickBooks. In general, this is the most likely place that the cash will originate from.

- **What was your account's balance on 12/31/2020?**: Based on the date chosen in the field above, enter the balance in the account as of the date chosen.

4. Save your changes to add the petty cash account to the chart of accounts list.

Now that you have created a petty cash account, you are ready to record the purchases that are made using petty cash.

Recording petty cash transactions

Receipts for petty cash expenditures should be kept in the same place the petty cash is kept: under lock and key. If possible, you should enter the petty cash receipts into QuickBooks on a weekly basis. If petty cash is not used that often, monthly should be sufficient.

Follow these steps to record petty cash transactions:

1. Navigate to the chart of accounts, as we did in the previous section.

2. Click on the **View register** link to the right of **Petty Cash**, as shown in *Figure 18.19*:

Figure 18.19: Clicking on the View register link

3. Click on the arrow next to **Add check** and select **Expense**, as shown in *Figure 18.20*:

Figure 18.20: Clicking the drop-down arrow next to Add check and selecting Expense

4. Fill in the remaining fields, as shown in *Figure 18.21*:

Figure 18.21: Completing the fields to record the expense

Explanations of the fields to fill in are as follows:

- **DATE**: Enter the date of purchase in this field.

- **REF NO.**: If you have a reference number such as an invoice number or account number, enter it in this field.

- **PAYEE**: Select the payee from the drop-down menu. If the payee has not been set up in QuickBooks, begin typing the name of the payee. You will see an option to add the payee to QuickBooks.

- **ACCOUNT**: Select the account the expense should be charged to from the chart of accounts drop-down menu.

- **MEMO**: Type a brief description of what was purchased in this field.

- **PAYMENT**: Enter the amount of the purchase in this field.

5. Be sure to click the **Save** button to record the transaction.

Repeat the preceding steps to record each petty cash receipt in QuickBooks.

Replenishing petty cash

Eventually, you will get to a point where you've run out of petty cash or you don't have enough to pay for an item. Before replenishing petty cash, make sure you have entered all of the receipts for petty cash purchases that have been made thus far. Similar to a bank account, you can record a transfer in QuickBooks so that you can transfer money from a checking account to a petty cash account. Of course, to get the actual cash, you will need to make a withdrawal from your business checking account to replenish the actual funds.

To record a transfer from the business checking account to petty cash, follow these steps:

1. Navigate to the petty cash register by going to the chart of accounts and clicking **View register** to the right of **Petty Cash**, as you did in the previous section.

2. Click on the drop-down arrow next to **Add transfer** and select **Transfer**, as shown in *Figure 18.22*:

Figure 18.22: Clicking on Add transfer and selecting Transfer

3. Fill in the fields shown in the following screenshot to record the transfer:

DATE ▾	REF NO.	PAYEE	MEMO	PAYMENT	DEPOSIT
	TYPE	ACCOUNT			
Add transfer ▾					
12/05/2021	Ref No.	Payee	Replenish Petty Cash Fund	Payment	50.00
	Transfer	Business Checking			

Figure 18.23: Completing the fields to record the transfer

Brief explanations of the fields you need to fill in to complete the transfer are as follows:

- **DATE:** The date the funds will be deposited into the petty cash account.

- **PAYEE:** Since you are the payee, you can leave this field blank.

- **ACCOUNT:** Select the bank account where the funds will be drawn from. In our example, it is the business checking account.

- **MEMO:** Include a brief description, such as **Replenish Petty Cash Fund**.

 If you have recorded all the money that you have paid out of petty cash, this transaction will increase the balance back to the cash on hand in your petty cash box.

- **DEPOSIT:** Enter the amount that is being transferred to the petty cash account.

4. Once you have completed all of these fields, click the **Save** button to complete the transfer.

Now that you know how to add the petty cash account to the chart of accounts, record petty cash expenses, and replenish the petty cash fund, you need to know how to ensure that it stays in balance. Like most bank accounts, this will require you to reconcile the petty cash account.

Reconciling petty cash

As we mentioned previously, petty cash is similar to bank and credit card accounts you track in QuickBooks. You need to ensure these accounts remain in balance. To do that, you must reconcile them. In *Chapter 10, Reconciling Downloaded Bank and Credit Card Transactions*, we showed you how to reconcile these accounts in QuickBooks. Refer to that chapter for step-by-step instructions on how to reconcile your petty cash account. I recommend that you reconcile your petty cash account *before* you replenish it. This will ensure that you have accounted for all the expenses that have been paid for using petty cash and that you have all the receipts to support these purchases.

While you will hope to avoid such a situation, there may come a time when a customer cannot afford to pay their outstanding balance. If this happens, you will need to write off the receivable as bad debt. We will discuss how to record bad debt expense next.

Recording bad debt expense

If you're in business long enough, there will come a time when a customer is unable or unwilling to pay you. If you use cash basis accounting, you don't need to record bad debt expense because you don't have accounts receivable. However, if you do extend credit to your customers and, after attempting to collect the payment, you become aware that you will not be able to collect payment, you should write off the bad debt. This will ensure that your financial statements remain accurate and that revenue is not overstated.

There are three steps you need to follow in order to write off bad debt: first, you need to add a bad debt item to the products and services list; next, you need to create a credit memo; and finally, you need to apply the credit memo to the unpaid customer invoice. We will walk you through these steps in this section.

Creating a bad debt item

The first step of recording bad debt expense is to add an item to the products and services list for tracking.

Follow these steps to create a bad debt item:

1. Click on the gear icon and select **Products and Services**, as shown in *Figure 18.24*:

Figure 18.24: Navigating to the Products and Services list

2. Select the item type, as shown in *Figure 18.25*:

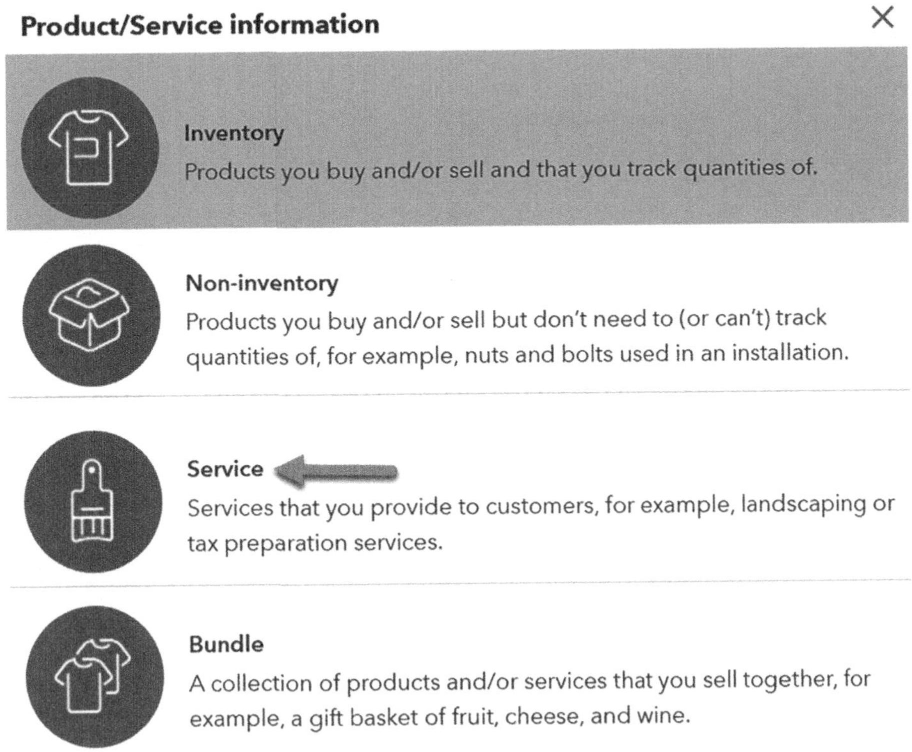

Product/Service information

 Inventory
Products you buy and/or sell and that you track quantities of.

 Non-inventory
Products you buy and/or sell but don't need to (or can't) track quantities of, for example, nuts and bolts used in an installation.

 Service
Services that you provide to customers, for example, landscaping or tax preparation services.

 Bundle
A collection of products and/or services that you sell together, for example, a gift basket of fruit, cheese, and wine.

Figure 18.25: Selecting Service as the item type

As you can see, there are four item types to choose from. **Service** is the item type we will use for bad debt expense.

3. Fill in the following fields to add bad debt to the items list:

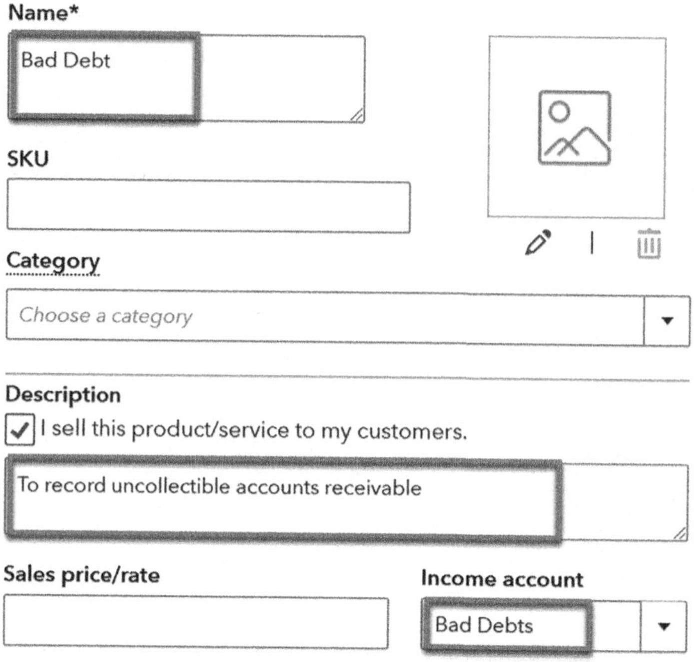

Figure 18.26: Completing the fields to add Bad Debt to the products/services list

Brief descriptions of the fields to fill in are as follows:

*   **Name:** Enter Bad Debt or Bad Debt Expense in the item name field.
*   **Description:** Enter a brief description of the types of transactions that will be recorded using this item.
*   **Income account:** From the dropdown, select **Bad Debts**. This should be an expense account on the chart of accounts list. If you did not create this account, click on the drop-down arrow, scroll up, and select **Add new** to create the bad debt expense account.

Now that you've set up the new bad debt expense item, you can use this item to record the bad debt on a credit memo form.

Creating a credit memo

A credit memo is generally used to refund a customer for items purchased that were returned or services that were not rendered in full. After creating the credit memo, we can apply it to the unpaid customer invoice.

Follow these steps to create a credit memo:

1. Click on the **+ New** button and select **Credit Memo**, as shown in *Figure 18.27*:

Figure 18.27: Navigating to Credit Memo

2. Fill in the following fields, as shown in *Figure 18.28*:

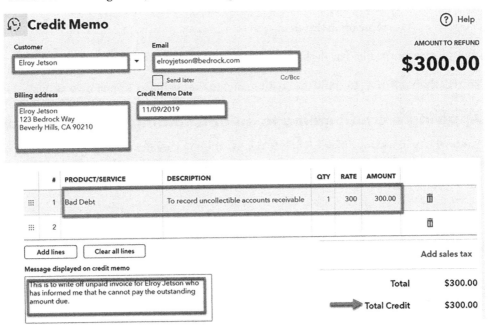

Figure 18.28: Completing the fields in the Credit Memo form

Brief explanations of the fields to fill in to complete the credit memo are as follows:

- **Customer**: Select the customer from the drop-down menu.

- **Email**: The email address that you have on file will automatically populate this field. If you don't have an email address on file, you can type one in directly.

- **Billing address**: The billing address you have on file will automatically populate this field. If you don't have a billing address on file, you can enter one in this field.

- **Credit Memo Date**: Select the date you would like to record this credit memo for.

- **PRODUCT/SERVICE**: Select the bad debt item you created in the previous section from the drop-down menu.

- **DESCRIPTION**: The description field should automatically be populated with the description of the bad debt item.

- **QTY**: Select **1**.

- **RATE**: Enter the amount of the invoice that you want to write off in this field.

- **AMOUNT**: This field will automatically be populated with the amount you entered into the rate field.

- **Message displayed on credit memo**: Provide a brief explanation for the bad debt to write off in this field.

3. Once you've filled in all the fields in the credit memo, save it.

We will show you how to apply the credit memo to the customer's open invoice next.

Applying a credit memo to an outstanding customer invoice

The final step in writing off bad debt is to remove the open invoice from accounts receivable. This is accomplished by applying the credit memo you created in the previous section to the open customer invoice.

Follow these steps to apply a credit memo to an outstanding customer invoice:

1. Click the **+ New** button and select **Receive payment**, as shown in *Figure 18.29*:

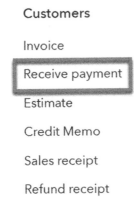

Figure 18.29: Navigating to Receive payment

2. On the next screen, a list of unpaid invoices and open credit memos will be displayed for the selected customer:

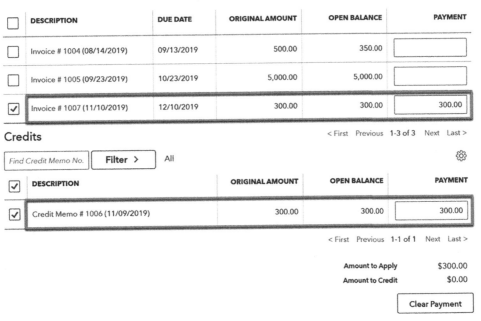

Figure 18.30: Selecting the invoices and/or credit memos to process

In the preceding screenshot, we have selected the invoice that needs to be written off (**Invoice # 1007**) and below that, we have selected the credit memo to apply (**Credit Memo # 1006**). Save your changes to record the bad debt as being written off.

3.   After saving your changes, go back to the invoice dashboard, as shown in *Figure 18.31*:

Figure 18.31: Invoice dashboard showing invoice status as Paid

As we can see, invoice #1007 now shows the status of **Paid**. This **Paid** status reduces the accounts receivable balance and increases the bad debt expense so that the financial statements reflect the correct balances for these accounts.

To summarize, it's important that you write off accounts as soon as they become uncollectible. This will ensure that the accounts receivable balance is not overstated. If you are an accrual basis taxpayer, you will not want to pay tax on income that you will never receive.

If you provide ongoing services to customers on a weekly or bi-weekly basis but you don't want to invoice customers that often, you should consider using delayed charges. Delayed charges allow you to accumulate charges in QuickBooks (without affecting the financial statements). Once you are ready to bill a customer, you can easily transfer the delayed charges to an invoice. We will discuss delayed charges and credits in detail next.

Tracking delayed charges and credits

Delayed charges and credits are used to keep track of services that are provided to customers so you can bill them sometime in the future. For example, if someone provides weekly pool maintenance to customers but does not want to bill them until the end of the month, delayed charges are ideal for keeping track of the services that are provided each week. These weekly services can easily be added to an invoice when it's time to bill the customer.

Follow these steps to record delayed charges:

1. Click on the **+ New** button and select **Delayed charge**, as shown in *Figure 18.32*:

Figure 18.32: Navigating to Delayed charge

2. Fill in the necessary fields to record the delayed charge, as shown in *Figure 18.33*:

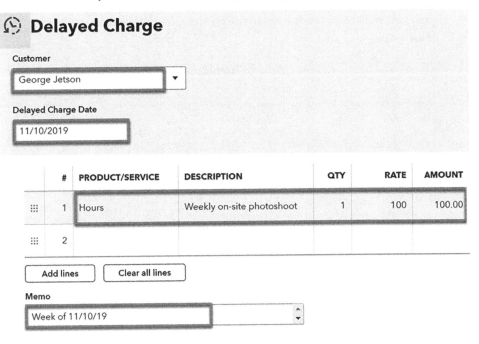

Figure 18.33: Completing the Delayed Charge form

Brief descriptions of the fields to fill in are as follows:

- **Customer**: Select the customer from the drop-down menu.
- **Delayed Charge Date**: Select the date the services were provided.
- **PRODUCT/SERVICE**: Select the type of service that will be provided from the drop-down menu.
- **DESCRIPTION**: This field should automatically be populated with the description that was used to set up the product/service. However, you can also enter a description directly in this field.
- **QTY**: Type a quantity into this field, if applicable.
- **RATE**: Enter the total amount or the hourly rate for the service.
- **AMOUNT**: This field is automatically calculated by taking the quantity and multiplying it by the rate.
- **Memo**: Enter a brief description in this field.

When you save a delayed charge, it is a non-posting transaction, which means it doesn't affect the financial statements. Next, we will show you how to add delayed charges to an invoice.

1. From the Quick Create menu, select **Invoice**. Select a customer from the drop-down menu and you will see a drawer open to the far right, listing the delayed charges that haven't been billed:

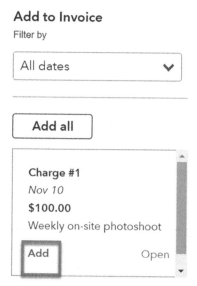

Figure 18.34: Selecting the delayed charges to bill the customer for

2. On this screen, click the **Add** button to add the charges to an invoice.
3. Save the invoice to record an increase to accounts receivable and income.

If you would like to review a list of unbilled charges before creating an invoice, you can do so by running an unbilled charges report. We will show you how to generate this report next:

1. Click on **Reports**, scroll to the **Who owes you** section, and select **Unbilled charges**, as shown in *Figure 18.35*:

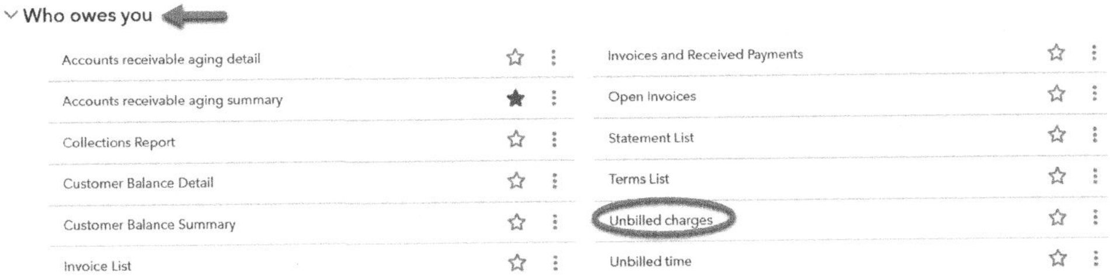

Figure 18.35: Navigating to the unbilled charges report

2. The unbilled charges report will appear:

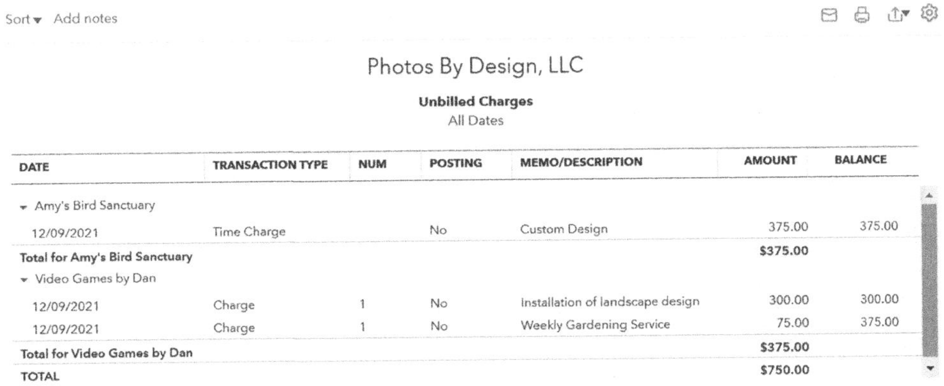
Sort Add notes

Photos By Design, LLC

Unbilled Charges

All Dates

DATE	TRANSACTION TYPE	NUM	POSTING	MEMO/DESCRIPTION	AMOUNT	BALANCE
Amy's Bird Sanctuary						
12/09/2021	Time Charge		No	Custom Design	375.00	375.00
Total for Amy's Bird Sanctuary					**$375.00**	
Video Games by Dan						
12/09/2021	Charge	1	No	Installation of landscape design	300.00	300.00
12/09/2021	Charge	1	No	Weekly Gardening Service	75.00	375.00
Total for Video Games by Dan					**$375.00**	
TOTAL					**$750.00**	

Figure 18.36: Sample unbilled charges report

That's how delayed charges work. One last thing you need to know is that if you need to reverse a delayed charge, you can do so by recording a delayed credit. Similar to delayed charges, navigate to the Quick Create menu and select **Delayed credit**. Follow the onscreen instructions to record the delayed credit. Delayed charges are used a lot in landscaping and maintenance industries for routine services that are billed monthly.

Summary

In this chapter, you have learned how to handle many special transactions in QuickBooks Online. You may be able to take advantage of a few of these now or keep them in your back pocket for later on when you need them. To recap, you now know how to locate apps in the QuickBooks app store and add them to QuickBooks. We have shown you how to manage credit card payments from customers and how to customize sales templates such as invoices to fit your business style and brand. For those expenses that occur often, you know how to add them to QuickBooks as recurring transactions and use them when needed. If you obtain a business loan or line of credit, you know how to set these up in QuickBooks and track payments. For those incidental purchases, you can create a petty cash account, track purchases, and reconcile the account, just like bank accounts. We also discussed the importance of recording bad debt expenses, which you now know how to record in QuickBooks to ensure that your financials are accurate. Finally, you learned how to record delayed charges and credits to track services that are provided to customers that will be billed sometime in the future.

Be sure to check out the *Appendix* section of this book for additional resources and materials.

Join our book's Discord space

Join the book's Discord workspace for a monthly *Ask me Anything* session with the author: `https://packt.link/QuickBooks`

Appendix

Shortcuts and Test Drive

QuickBooks Online keyboard shortcuts

Keyboard shortcuts help speed up navigation, which will save you time when you're using **Quick-Books Online (QBO)**.

The following screenshot shows a list of the QBO keyboard shortcuts. To access them directly in your QBO file, press the *Ctrl + Alt + ?* keys simultaneously:

Keyboard Shortcuts

To use a shortcut, press and hold **ctrl/control** and **alt/option** at the same time. Then press one of the keys below.

On main pages, like the dashboard or customers

SHORTCUT KEY	ACTION
i	Invoice
w	Check
e	Estimate
x	Expense
r	Receive payment
c	Customers
v	Vendors
a	Chart of accounts
l	Lists
h	Help
f	Global search
d	Focus the left menu
? or /	This dialog

On transactions, like an invoice or expense

SHORTCUT KEY	ACTION
x	Exit transaction view
c	Cancel out
s	Save and new
d	Save and close
m	Save and send
p	Print
? or /	This dialog

Figure A.1: Keyboard shortcuts

QuickBooks Online test drive

Before signing up for a QBO subscription, you can check out the QBO test drive, which we introduced in *Chapter 2, QuickBooks Online Advanced*. The test drive account contains sample data for a fictitious company.

Here, you can enter test transactions before you put them in your actual QBO file. For example, you can enter a credit memo or a journal entry to see how it affects the books before entering the transaction in your QBO file. Just click on the following link (depending on your region) and follow the onscreen instructions:

- United States: `https://qbo.intuit.com/redir/testdrive`.
- United States QuickBooks Online Advanced: `https://qbo.intuit.com/redir/testdrive_us_advanced`.

The US edition of QBO was used to create this book. If you are using a version that is outside of the United States, results may differ.

Discount on a QuickBooks Online account

You can use my referral link to save money when you sign up for a new QBO account: `https://quickbooks.grsm.io/crystalynnshelton4264`.

Join our book's Discord space

Join the book's Discord workspace for a monthly *Ask me Anything* session with the author: `https://packt.link/QuickBooks`

QuickBooks Certified User Exam Objectives

The Intuit QuickBooks Certified User certification is a credential that is recognized in the industry as a way for bookkeepers and accountants to demonstrate their proficiency in the Intuit QuickBooks accounting software. Once you have achieved this certification, you will receive access to a digital badge that you can put on your resume, social media profiles, and your website. This certification will automatically set you apart from other candidates looking to obtain employment as a bookkeeper or accountant.

In this chapter, we have included a list of the objectives that are covered on the exam. In addition, we have provided the corresponding chapter where you can find the information on each topic in our book, *Mastering QuickBooks 2022*.

 For more information on how to take the exam, visit the Certiport website:
https://certiport.pearsonvue.com/Certifications/Intuit/
Certifications/Certify/QuickBooks-Certified-User

	Objective	Chapter
1	**QuickBooks Online Administration**	
1.1	**Set up QuickBooks Online**	
1.1.1	Recognize features and benefits of QuickBooks Online Plus	1, 18
1.1.2	Describe licensing requirements for setting up an entity in QuickBooks Online	1
1.1.3	Describe the process of migrating a company to QuickBooks Online	4
1.1.4	Describe the access of each default user role	5
1.2	**Manage QuickBooks Online settings for a company**	
1.2.1	Identify the company information that you can and can't edit	3
1.2.2	Recognize the benefits of the Close the Books feature	17
1.2.3	Compare and contrast the cash and accrual accounting methods	1

1.2.4	Identify the purpose of project tracking, class tracking, and locations	3
1.2.5	Describe how to activate project tracking, class tracking, and locations	3
1.2.6	Identify the tasks performed by automation	2
1.3	**Manage lists**	
1.3.1	Identify the lists that you can import	5, 6
1.3.2	Identify the content of various lists	5, 6
1.3.3	Identify the appropriate lists for different purposes	5, 6
1.3.4	Identify when and how to add, edit, delete, and merge list items	5, 6
1.3.5	Manage the Chart of Accounts	5
1.4	**Manage recurring transactions**	
1.4.1	Describe reasons for making transactions recurring	9
1.4.2	Define types of recurrence	9
1.4.3	Describe how to implement recurring transactions	9
1.5	**Manage journal entries**	
1.5.1	Identify the information required for journal entries	17
1.5.2	Describe how to implement journal entries	17
1.6	**Connect QuickBooks Online to apps**	
1.6.1	Identify the purpose of apps	18
1.6.2	Identify where to get apps	18
1.6.3	Identify the risks and benefits of extending functionality through apps	18

2	**Sales and Money In**	
2.1	**Set up customers**	
2.1.1	Identify the importance of the Display Name field	6
2.1.2	Differentiate between billing and shipping addresses	6
2.1.3	Define and describe the use of customer payment terms	6
2.1.4	Identify taxable and non-taxable customers	6
2.1.5	Define and describe the correct use of sub-customers	6
2.2	**Set up products and services**	
2.2.1	Describe and differentiate between products and services	6
2.2.2	Identify the information required to set up products or services	6

2.2.3	Describe reasons for setting up products or services	6
2.2.4	Contrast inventory products and non-inventory products	6
2.3	**Manage sales settings**	
2.3.1	Customize sales forms	18
2.3.2	Customize email message forms	3
2.3.3	Describe the purpose of activating customer discounts	3
2.3.4	Describe the QuickBooks Payments feature and how it differs from traditional payments	3, 18
2.4	**Record basic money-in transactions**	
2.4.1	Describe the money-in transaction workflow	8
2.4.2	Record and manage invoices and sales receipts	8
2.4.3	Receive, record, and manage payments, undeposited funds, and deposits	8
2.4.4	Record credit memos and refund receipts	8

3	**Vendors and Money Out**	
3.1	**Manage vendor records**	
3.1.1	Describe how to identify existing customers as vendors	6
3.1.2	Describe when and how to merge vendor accounts	6
3.1.3	Describe how to add or change vendor payment terms	6
3.1.4	Describe how and why to identify vendors as 1099 contractors	6, 16
3.2	**Manage expense settings**	
3.2.1	Describe how and why to activate expense tracking by customer	3
3.2.2	Describe when and how to make expenses and items billable	3
3.2.3	Describe how to identify unbilled billable expenses	3
3.3	**Record and manage basic money-out transactions**	
3.3.1	Describe the money-out transaction workflow	9
3.3.2	Identify types of money-out transactions	9
3.3.3	Compare and describe the appropriate use of checks and bill payments	9
3.3.4	Describe the effects of recording bills, checks, and credit card transactions	9
3.3.5	Differentiate between expense transactions and bank feed transactions	9

3.3.6	Describe how to record check, credit card, and debit card expense transactions	9
3.3.7	Describe the use and effects of vendor credits and refunds	9
3.3.8	Describe why and how to void, delete, and edit money-out transactions and the impact thereof	9

4	**Bank Accounts, Transaction Rules, and Receipts**	
4.1	**Implement financial account connections**	
4.1.1	Identify the types of financial accounts QuickBooks Online can connect to	5
4.1.2	Describe the benefits of connecting QuickBooks Online to accounts	5
4.2	**Manage bank feeds**	
4.2.1	Process bank feed transactions	10
4.2.2	Define and describe the use of bank rules	10
4.3	**Manage receipts**	
4.3.1	Identify methods of uploading receipts	9
4.3.2	Describe how to record transactions from uploaded receipts	9

5	**Basic Reports and Views**	
5.1	**Describe the content and purpose of reports**	
5.1.1	Describe the content and purpose of financial reports	7, 11, 12
5.1.2	Describe the content and purpose of money-in reports	13
5.1.3	Describe the content and purpose of money-out reports	14
5.2	**Customize and deliver standard reports**	
5.2.1	Customize standard reports	11
5.2.2	Identify report delivery formats	11
5.3	**Access other reports and views**	
5.3.1	Describe the content of the Audit Log	12
5.3.2	Describe the content and functionality of the dashboards	1

Join our book's Discord space

Join the book's Discord workspace for a monthly *Ask me Anything* session with the author:

`https://packt.link/QuickBooks`

Packt>

Subscribe to our online digital library for full access to over 7,000 books and videos, as well as industry leading tools to help you plan your personal development and advance your career. For more information, please visit our website.

Why subscribe?

- Spend less time learning and more time coding with practical eBooks and Videos from over 4,000 industry professionals
- Improve your learning with Skill Plans built especially for you
- Get a free eBook or video every month
- Fully searchable for easy access to vital information
- Copy and paste, print, and bookmark content

At www.packt.com, you can also read a collection of free technical articles, sign up for a range of free newsletters, and receive exclusive discounts and offers on Packt books and eBooks.

Other Books
You May Enjoy

If you enjoyed this book, you may be interested in these other books by Packt:

Data Analytics Made Easy

Andrea De Mauro

ISBN: 9781801074155

- Understand the potential of data and its impact on any business
- Influence business decisions with effective data storytelling when delivering insights
- Import, clean, transform, combine data feeds, and automate your processes
- Learn the basics of machine learning to add value to your organization
- Create professional-looking and business-centric visuals and dashboards

Hands-On Microsoft Teams, Second Edition

João Ferreira

ISBN: 9781801075275

- Perform scheduling and manage meetings, live events, and webinars
- Create and manage Microsoft Teams templates to streamline company processes
- Deal with permissions and security issues in managing private and public teams and channels
- Extend Microsoft Teams using custom apps, Microsoft 365, and PowerShell automation
- Build your own Teams app with The Developer Portal without writing any code
- Deploy helpful chatbots using QnA Maker and Power Virtual Agents
- Explore Teams use cases for education, frontline work, and personal life
- Bring together knowledge, learning, resources, and insights with the new employee experience platform, Microsoft Viva

Packt is searching for authors like you

If you're interested in becoming an author for Packt, please visit authors.packtpub.com and apply today. We have worked with thousands of developers and tech professionals, just like you, to help them share their insight with the global tech community. You can make a general application, apply for a specific hot topic that we are recruiting an author for, or submit your own idea.

Share your thoughts

Now you've finished Mastering QuickBooks® 2022, Third Edition, we'd love to hear your thoughts! Scan the QR code below to go straight to the Amazon review page for this book and share your feedback or leave a review on the site that you purchased it from.

https://packt.link/r/1803244283

Your review is important to us and the tech community and will help us make sure we're delivering excellent quality content.

Index

C

Made in the USA
Middletown, DE
12 July 2022

69144545R00265